There's a baby in my bed!

Learning to live happily with the Adult Baby in your relationship.

First Edition

Rosalie Bent

ISBN: 978-1-61098-306-8
Ebook ISBN: 978-1-61098-307-5

Published by

The Nazca Plains Corporation ®
4640 Paradise Rd, Suite 141
Las Vegas NV 89109-8000

Cover Images,
Blocks - Suzana Opacak
Baby Items - Tara Flake

Art Director,
Blake Stephens

There's a baby in my bed!

Learning to live happily with the Adult Baby in your relationship.

First Edition

Published by The Nazca Plains Corporation
Las Vegas, Nevada
2012

"'Littles' are up against a cultural bias. This bias is so ingrained that it has become invisible. Square pegs won't fit in round holes, but why do we presume that this is the peg's fault? Why is it the peg's fault for being square, and not the hole's fault for being round?" – by BitterGrey

DEDICATION

To my life-long partner, my soul-mate.
The one who has made it all possible.

CONTENTS

FOREWORD

Long ago, back in the Dark Ages of information – prior to the Internet – Adult Babies were very much alone. Indeed, most of them, be they Adult Babies, Teen Babies, Diaper Lovers, Little Ones or Regressives believed that they were *literally* alone; the only person on the entire planet with feelings and desires like theirs. They were isolated, secretive and hidden from public view and cut off from sharing their inner selves with others, but the early 1990s and the advent of that most ubiquitous of communication mediums, changed all of that in dramatic fashion. Suddenly, Adult Babies found other Adult Babies. Websites sprung up to connect long disenfranchised individuals with whole communities just like themselves.

Now of course, we know that the Adult Baby and associated groups are not alone at all, numbering in the tens of millions world-wide, but in the middle of all of this new-found connection and openness, there has remained one stubbornly deficient area: *relationships*.

The relationships of Adult Babies with their families, friends and life partners has remained pretty much just as it was in those long ago Dark Ages – poor to non-existent.

This book aims to help resolve some of those relationship problems. It is not primarily for the Adult Baby himself, but rather for his partner and even possibly for family and friends. For most people, the Adult Baby lifestyle and experience is quite literally incomprehensible. From that almost total lack of understanding and empathy, comes anything from dysfunctionality to total relationship failure.

Just as the world has millions of Adult Babies, it also has millions of people who are in a relationship with them and who want to make that relationship work. Many people find that task to be hard, bordering on the impossible. This is not so much from a lack of love or commitment, but rather from a lack of any idea of *how* to make it work. And Adult Babies themselves are really no better.

There has to be a way to have an working adult relationship with an Adult Baby! And now there is.

If you are ready for a wild ride and come with an open mind and an accepting heart, it *can* work. It will be odd, frustrating, eye-opening and yet strangely rewarding and you never know, you may even find that you *enjoy* it!

Here's to the great journey of discovering the inner world of *your* Adult Baby...

SECTION ONE – INTRODUCTION

About this Book

This book is designed specifically for the partner of a regressive Adult Baby or similar Little One. In these pages are the clues, concepts and skills that you will need to forge a good relationship with the person you love, but don't really understand that well. It is a struggle for most partners to come to grips with a behaviour that seemingly *makes no sense*. This book not only attempts to make sense out of it, but to also find a way that will make it easier for you, the parent to deal with and perhaps even be pleasurable to you both.

The book is divided into seven sections:

1. **Introduction** – why we are here and what we hope to accomplish.

2. **Information** – finding out as much as you can about what regression actually is, who Adult Babies are and how it all came about.

3. **Identification** – how to work out who your Little One is and how to describe his various aspects and needs.

4. **Communication** – how to talk to and communicate with your partner, no matter if they are regressed or not and what to expect.

5. **Interaction** – how to work and play with your Little One and how to safely and effectively integrate regression into real life.

6. **Modification** – how to help your Little One behave better and more appropriately and for you both to gain more enjoyment and satisfaction from regression.

7. **Summary** – how to put it all together and achieve a functioning and enjoyable Parent/ Child relationship.

You may find this book confusing at times and difficult to comprehend, as you have a whole lot of probably new concepts thrown at you. Stay with it! The good part is at the end, when we put all the information and concepts together, and try to build a long-lasting and effective relationship out of the regressive behaviours that frustrate you now.

The best way to approach this book is to read it right through once and then start all over again. It will make much more sense the second-time through. A good idea is to use a notebook to make comments on the parts you find important and those ones which you want to work on or refer to later.

———————————

Not everything here will apply to you and your particular situation. The one thing you will learn very quickly is that all Littles are different. They are individuals – as are you. So don't be surprised to come across material that has no relevance to your circumstances whatsoever.

———————————

NOTES ON TERMINOLOGY: This book is *entirely* about adults and is in no way meant to infer any involvement of biological children either in participation or as observers. In every case in this book, any reference to 'child', 'infant' or 'toddler' is referring to an ADULT version of this age-group through regression or age-play. Any reference to *actual* children will always be prefaced by the word 'biological', as in 'biological child'. Do not misinterpret anything being written as to apply to underage children in any way.

NOTES ON GENDER: throughout this book, I will refer to the Little One as 'male' using pronouns such as 'him' and 'his' etcetera. This does not imply that all Little Ones are male, as they aren't. I do so simply for consistency. If your Little is female then just replace the pronoun in your head as you read and if your Little is an adult male, but a Little female then it's up to you!

NOTES TO BIOLOGICAL PARENTS: You may have picked up this book because you have, or suspect that you have, a child who is regressive or is perhaps a Teen Baby. While this book is not really suited to your situation, you may gain some insight into what your child is thinking and doing in the early chapters and this could be of enormous value. Please be aware however, that none of the practical suggestions given in this book apply to your situation. They are written exclusively for the adult couple. The very best you can do for your child is to love and accept them and to understand, that at the very core of this, is a desire to be true to themselves.

NOTES TO COUPLES: This book uses the traditional male-female couple for its examples with the male as the Little and the female as the Parent. This is for convenience only, although it represents the majority of real-world Parent/Child relationships. There are many non-traditional couples, including gay and even polyamorous couplings and there are certainly many variations on the theme. You will need to make the transition from the text's examples dependant on your own circumstances.

The Journey

Many thousands of years ago, an ancient race found themselves in a terrible situation that was not of their own making. The land they were living in no longer accepted them and indeed, treated them as slaves. They had to leave their previously safe home, because they now had no choice. Everything had changed around them.

The solution was to take their rag-tag community and forge a whole new life for themselves in a foreign land a long way away. But to get there, they had to cross an enormous desert with few skills, few provisions and a multitude of enemies in their path. It took them a long time to cross that desert and in the process, they had to learn a lot of very hard and difficult lessons. Forty years later, that rag-tag community had become a cohesive and powerful nation that marched out of the desert and into their 'Promised Land'.

The journey you have ahead of you is similar in many ways. The partner you married or live with, seems to have changed. In a situation 'not of your own making', you have a dilemma in how to relate to, and deal with, your Little One. You may even be unsure if your partner is a Little One or not. Or he may be a Little One that you know about, yet don't understand or know how to relate to. This is all part of your journey.

It may be that both of you may want to move to some kind of Promised Land where you feel safe and secure; where you understand each other and can easily navigate the unusual dynamic of a partner who is both an adult and a child.

The Promised Land you are seeking does not flow with milk and honey. Instead, it flows with love and commitment, adorned with satisfaction and ultimately lined with care and understanding.

It is called 'The Parent/Child Relationship' and it is the Promised Land that you are both seeking after.

To get there however, you need to traverse a desert of learning and struggle, but, trust me when I tell you that your desert experience won't take you forty years!

The Parent/Child Relationship:

There is a very special kind of relationship that can exist between a loving couple, where one of them is a regressive Adult Baby, or what I call Little One. Rather than something to be feared, it is in fact an aspect that can greatly enhance and build the relationship.

It is what I call the <u>Parent/Child Relationship</u> and it is where you have a deep, meaningful and substantive relationship, not just with your adult partner, but also with their Inner Child as well.

I understand that at this stage, this may all sound confusing and scary, but the truth is, that by relating to the Inner Child as you currently do to the adult, you will build up and strengthen your relationship significantly. On its own, the regression can harm and even destroy relationships, and I am sure most readers of this book will have experienced at least some measure of that. By developing a *genuine* relationship with the Inner Child or Little One, you not only disarm this destructive force, but you also co-opt it into building your own relationship into something even stronger.

The Parent/Child relationship operates at two basic levels. In the primary level, you will relate to your partner as adult to adult, just as you do right now. The secondary level is where you relate to the Little One as a child, with you as their parent. This sounds intimidating and scary and perhaps it is both, but the outworking of this is that it will remove the stress in your partner and in your relationship that you are currently experiencing and in its place, build a strength and security which is not easily broken. This entire book is about helping partners discover this relationship and to then enhance it for their mutual benefit.

The Desert Experience:

It is unfortunately a truism, that life's big challenges and successes are all prefaced by some period of time in the metaphorical desert: a time of lack, stress and seeming failure. But what the desert experience teaches us is skills, self-belief and a determination that can be learned nowhere else. Success is always preceded by time in the desert. Are you ready for your own desert experience?

There is no sand, sun or flies in this desert and you won't need to use a camel, but there will be times when you will wonder just what you are doing there! The true pinnacle of human experience is not standing on Mt Everest or landing on the Moon or other such dramatic and exciting events. Rather, it is the experience of a relationship with another person which grows and develops to such an extent that 'two have become one'. In a world that is intent on personal rights and personal experiences, the notion of the 'soul mate' is bandied about often, yet never really understood. Your partner is different. How different is something you may or may not yet know. He is regressive. He is an Adult Baby or a Little Kid, but more importantly, he is your *partner*.

Very few couples ever really achieve this 'soul mate' status and that is in part, because they don't really know each other as intimately as they wish. If there is one aspect of the Parent/Child relationship that is truly unique, it is the depth of interaction that can eventuate from it. Within a functioning Parent/Child relationship, there can be a level of communication between two souls that can be truly unique and exquisite.

A physically young child looks upon his parents as omnipotent and omniscient. He adores them and wants to do everything he possibly can for them. The biological parent views their child as a gift from God – a truly remarkable creation they have been given to mould and develop, and to whom they can give their unswerving love and affection.

You and your partner have the opportunity to have all of that, as well as the power and commitment of a wonderful adult loving relationship. Rather than treat regression as a curse, it should be treated as an opportunity to have a relationship that combines the very best of both worlds, something that very few will ever get to experience.

If you are ready to work through the trials, the lessons, the successes and the failures, you will find your desert experience a hard, yet delightful time. Are you ready for some trudging in the sand with me?

Keeping a Journal or Diary:

It is of enormous value for you, as a new or prospective Parent of a Little One, to be keeping a regular journal of the journey you are taking with him. It should be totally private and confidential, and thus allow you to be brutally honest about the progress that you are making, or lack thereof. It is your private vent space, your private zone of reflection. As the months and then years go by, you will look back and see the progress you have both made and measure the increased enjoyment you are now getting.

Like any journal, it should record what you did, what you learned, how you felt and what you plan to do in the near future. By being absolutely confidential, it allows you the space to be angry, frustrated, pleased and confused.

Let it be your own space and start it today – <u>before</u> you read this book.

The Journey ahead:

Let's start by celebrating the journey! It's a great place to be and it's a good attitude to have, especially when for many, there may be no other viable choice than to go on the journey!

First of all, let me explain the term 'Little One', which I use extensively in this book. It covers all of the various names for adults who regress to any age, from infant to pre-pubescents. I talk about the various subcategories later on, but for now, 'Little One' works well as a general term.

Let me outline the big stages in our journey together:

1. **Information:** the first key to being a better parent is information: 'just what is this?'. This section explains regression, infantilism and other questions you may have in simple, yet expansive terms, so that at the end of this section, you will know a great deal more about what regression is and more importantly, isn't.

2. **Identification:** You *must* know your Little One intimately. You need to identify exactly <u>who</u> he is, how <u>old</u> he is and his <u>name</u>(s). You *must* accept that he exists and treat him as an individual. You also need to know what *kind* of Little One he is. What does he like or dislike? What can he do and what can't he? What are his fears and hopes? If you don't or won't identify him correctly as a Little One, apart from the

adult, then you will probably fail at obtaining and maintaining a good Parent/Child relationship with him.

3. **Communication:** It is true of all relationships that communication is the oil which keeps the engine turning over without seizing up. You obviously *must* talk with your adult partner, but you must also talk with your Little One. You must talk regularly, both at the trivial level as well as at the deep level. You need to discuss deep needs with your Little One, but also discuss boring day-to-day things. You need to communicate with him at his 'age level' even if this means by playtime and drawing. If you refuse to communicate with the Little One in a substantial and regular manner, you will doom the Parent/Child relationship to wither and die before you even commence.

4. **Interaction:** When you interact with your Little One, you both acknowledge his existence and automatically communicate to him that you care. When you play with him at his level, you show that you love him in a very practical way. When you comment on his clothes or change his diaper or give him a bottle, these interactions speak far louder than words. Interaction is at the core of a functional Parent/Child relationship. If you treat the Little One as a piece of furniture or look right through him, you tell him that he doesn't really mean anything to you. Words are one thing; actions another. Only by your interaction do you *truly* prove to him that he is valued and that you care enough to help him along one of the most difficult journeys he will ever face: regression.

5. **Modification:** No behaviour remains the same forever. No behaviour is intrinsically good or bad. As part of a decent Parent/Child relationship, we enhance and expand the good and we try to modify the bad. We discuss how to encourage some things, discourage others and allow yet other behaviours to appear and to flourish.

6. **Putting it all together**: Now that you have the knowledge and the keys to making it work, we look at how to put it together to forge a Parent/Child relationship that is positive for everyone. We will be seeking to find a sense of *balance* in your Little One's life and by extension, in your adult relationship as well. Balance is and will remain our ultimate goal.

In Summary:

You didn't ask for this, but then again, neither did your Little One. A true measure of the character and strength of a person, is in their ability to deal with adverse circumstances. Your Little One may be an 'adverse circumstance'. The world will never accept him as a regressive. The world will mainly identify him as a degenerate, a loner or think of him as mentally defective. After not many years, your Little One will feel the same way about himself, unless you help to change his self-image.

You may feel as if you are the one doing all of the changing and making all of the concessions and in the early days, that will be true. As the parent, you will be giving more and compromising more than your Little One will, but you will *both* be putting in the effort. Think of it like having a real baby. In the first couple of years, you give and give and then give some more, but as they get older, the balance slowly shifts and they begin to give back and contribute something to the family. It is the same thing here. Persevere with the process and keep on giving, until you see your Little One able to give back. It won't happen overnight, but it *will* happen.

———————

You alone hold the keys to helping your Little One find solace and satisfaction in the hand that has been dealt to him. I hope you have the courage and character to love and help the Little One that has been gifted to you. It will be better than you dared hope, harder than you can imagine and more rewarding than you can possibly believe. All it really takes is love and commitment and a handful of special skills.

———————

SECTION TWO – INFORMATION

Whenever confronting a complex or difficult problem, the first task at hand is always to try and obtain as much information as possible about the problem and then to sift through it all, to try to work out how it applies to your particular situation. The same is just as true here. The level of understanding regarding regression, Little Ones and Adult Babies in the general community is very poor. Even mental health professionals don't understand it very well at all and they are supposed to be the experts!

Before launching into a Parent/Child relationship, it is incumbent upon you to understand exactly what makes your Little One 'tick', or at least have some idea what is going on inside his head. And to a Little One reading this, you also need to be better informed of the facts about yourself. While you almost certainly know a great deal about the topic as it relates to you personally, it is also almost certain that you don't have the perspective or wide vision to see the needs of other Littles or Bigs. Keep on reading and see how much of this you can learn.

This can be a daunting section. A lot of the material may seem incomprehensible and overwhelming at first, but keep on going. It only *seems* daunting, because most people are coming from a very low knowledge base When you re-read this in a year's time, most of it will be far more understandable and familiar.

It might be worth reading this section twice before moving on, unless you understand it clearly the first time.

What is Infantilism?

This is a huge topic, so bear with me here. 'Infantilism', is the commonly-used generic terminology for the desire that drives the behaviour of Adult Babies, Teen Babies, Adult Little Girls, Diaper Lovers and the various subsets of each of these groups. It is not a particularly helpful term, but unfortunately like so many other mental health terms, it is both accurate, while being hopelessly uninformative and unhelpful. However, it is the term that is commonly used, so let's start by defining it.

Historically, Infantilism used to be known as 'Psychosexual Infantilism', which was a term coined by Freud in his theory of psychosexual development to refer to individuals who had not matured enough into heterosexuality. Clearly, this is a woefully inadequate definition and is no longer commonly used. It also manifestly ignores the fact that infantilism often has totally *non-sexual* beginnings in preschool or preteen children.

The Psychiatrists Bible – the *Diagnostic and Statistical Manual of Mental Disorders (DSM)* – now describes it as 'Paraphilic Infantilism' (or autonepiophilia). While this is an improvement, it continues to display the mental health profession's almost total lack of understanding of Infantilism and its many flavours and variations. So what exactly is a 'paraphilia'?

The classic definition of paraphilia from the latest DSM is: *"recurrent and intense sexual urges or sexually arousing fantasy generally involving either objects, suffering or humiliation, children, or other non-consenting partners."*

You can quickly see why this definition is so hopelessly inaccurate and highly offensive. Pseudo-defining infantilists as masochists, paedophiles or rapists is hardly going to be a constructive starting point for discussion. It is a major part of the reason why therapy for infantilism is so rarely sought out and even less successful. Just to re-assure the reader, let me make the forceful reminder that infantilists are no more likely to be paedophiles or rapists than any other segment of the community.

Fortunately, not all professionals agree with this narrow and ludicrous definition of infantilism. Psychologists D. Richard Laws and William O'Donohue state that:

"Although infantilism is classified as a sexual masochism in the DSM-IV and DSM-IV-TR, it is questionable whether the criteria for sexual masochism are always met. For example, if the infantile role playing does not involve feelings of humiliation and suffering, then the diagnosis of sexual masochism would not be appropriate and a diagnosis of infantilism as a paraphilia [not otherwise specified] is [not] warranted."

[D.Richard laws: Sexual Deviance: Theory, assessment and treatment P402]

Infantilists are also sometimes referred to as AB/DLs (Adult Baby/Diaper Lovers). This terminology is convenient and very common, but it seeks to include diaper fetishists with infantilists, despite the fact that the only common element is the use of a diaper. They are two very separate behaviours with very different needs and desires and I discuss this in more detail later on.

"Infantilism is best described as the behaviour of a post-pubescent person seeking the emotional experience of returning to childhood or infancy using regression and/or other props, such as diapers, to build an authentic experience. Infantilists don't want to involve children; they want to be a child."

This definition seems a bit cold and inadequate however, but at least it is accurate, if a bit thin on the details. The term 'infantilism', is old-fashioned and tends to be misleading for the general community. While some want to regress to actual *infancy*, the vast majority actual play being toddlers. Despite the term Adult Baby being in common use, Adult Toddler would be far more accurate.

I far prefer the term 'Little Ones' and is the terminology I will use throughout this book. This term implies that they like to be 'little', but without specifying a target age or gender. Nor does it imply a sexual drive or any dysfunctional aspects. Adults in the regressive scenario are commonly referred to as 'Bigs' or perhaps 'Mummy' or 'Daddy'.

Littles are everywhere and while labels can be helpful at times, they can also be highly destructive if applied too narrowly. Defining your Little One (or yourself) as either a *psychosexual infantilist* or as *a paraphilic infantilist* is not particularly helpful. Little Ones often have a very poor self-image at the best of times. Pinning these narrow definitions onto them just makes matters worse. Let's see if we can expand these definitions a little and perhaps make them more attractive.

What is a 'Little One'?

A Little One encompasses all of the following terms:

- Adult Baby.

- Teen Baby.

- Adult Infant.

- Adult Toddler.

- Adult Preschooler.

- Adult Kid.

- Adult Little Girl.

- Adult Little Boy.

The following diagram (Fig 1.) shows how these definitions work together:

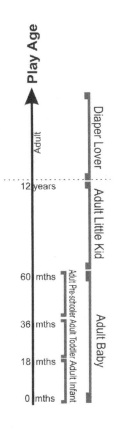

Figure 1

The generic term 'Adult Baby' (AB), comprises Adult Infants, Adult Toddlers and Adult Preschoolers and applies to Little Ones who identify as ages newborn to five years. Note that these ages are at best approximate. A Little might say they are six years old, yet still refer to themselves as an Adult Baby or Adult Pre-schooler. These ages and definitions are deliberately flexible, to meet the rather flexible self-image of the average Little One.

For ages five to twelve years, Littles are often known as 'Adult Kids', who are made up of Adult Little Girls or Adult Little Boys. In this age range however, Adult Little Girls (or Adult Little Sissies) form the vast majority and the term Adult Kid can also be used synonymously with Adult Little Girls.

You may have noticed that Diaper Lovers (DL) are included on the chart above the dotted line in the 'adult' age range. **This is because Diaper Lovers are not actually age-players or regressives at all.** They are only included here because most people incorrectly combine them with Little Ones. I will mention Diaper Lovers occasionally during the book, but usually to draw a clear distinction between them and Little Ones.

Also note that there is no functional difference between a Teen baby (TB) and an Adult Baby (AB). The only difference is the age of the person who has these behaviours.

If you are the biological parent of a Teen Baby and are reading this book, then please take note that the primary focus of the information here is on <u>adult-adult</u> relationships that have a Parent/Child aspect and <u>not</u> on biological parent/child relationships. You are encouraged to read the entire book, but be advised that the practical tips and suggestions do not generally apply to your situation.

Little Ones are not dysfunctional by definition. They do however, have a sometimes over-powering drive and need which *can* cause them problems. But then again, who doesn't have a drive or need deep inside that causes them occasional problems? Where the dysfunction generally comes in, is when these needs and drives overwhelm or consume to such an extent, that life itself and its relationships are compromised. This is where this book comes in.

Many Little Ones are actually highly intelligent, very effective (and sometimes very well known) people, who conduct businesses and relationships with a high degree of success. Yet at night, these same people may wet the bed or wear diapers, and in their closets may hang baby clothes and other assorted items. They are clearly *not* dysfunctional. They are however, very different.

Society has a common and disturbing habit of expecting everyone to conform to a common set of ideals and behaviours, while still proclaiming the right to individuality. In a general sense, this is a good thing, as it brings a unity of purpose and a cohesive society. However, if conformity is taken too far, individuality suffers and those who don't fit neatly into society's pre-formed little boxes begin to suffer. Little Ones very clearly do not fit into society's pre-cut definitions of *normal*. The 21st century has seen a lot of previously marginalized groups integrated into society as a whole. Adult Babies and Little Ones are however, not among them. Society is still in the process of discovering that they even exist.

While most Little Ones are not dysfunctional, others however, may struggle with the impact of regression and the deep need to wear a diaper and to be a child. At times, it stands in the way of life's natural progress. For some, being Little holds them back from better life outcomes and from good relationships. There is no point in denying this if it applies to you or your partner.

Part of the true value of the effective Parent/Child relationship is that it has the power to reduce or eliminate the negative aspects of regression, and can in fact, enhance the creativity of the average Little One to greater effect. In short, you can turn the disadvantage of regression into an advantage.

Just don't lie to yourself or pretend it is something it is not. It is in facing the *truth* of regression that we find solutions and compromise.

Regression versus Age-Play:

One of the most important and least understood differences between the various types of Little Ones can be best defined by *when the behaviours and desires first started.* This is probably the most important distinction which can be made. Make sure you understand this distinction, as it is crucial. It is of enormous importance to understand when the Little One first 'appeared' – before or after puberty.

An outside observer watching a group of Little Ones playing at their preferred age, might see no differences between those that began this behaviour as children and those that started as teens or adults. However the differences are huge *internally.*

A person who started to want infantile and childish behaviours and objects prior to puberty is known as a Regressive Little One. Someone who began these behaviours after puberty, primarily as a response to the sex drive, is a Fetishist Little One or Age-Player.

The following graph (Fig. 2) shows how 'Age of Onset' and the 'Play Age' correlate, using puberty as the all-important change-point.

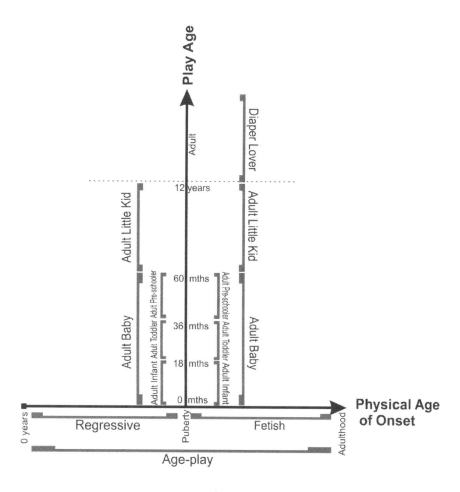

Figure 2

The first thing you may have noticed, is that the Regressive Age-Play side exactly mirrors the Fetish Age-play side. This is deliberate and is done to underscore the fact that while the behaviours *look* alike, the inner experience and motivations are quite different. Looks can be deceiving, and in this case, very much so. You can usually tell the difference between fetish and regressive age-play once you get more exposure to the behaviour. Regressives tend to be more interested in *authentic* experiences, while fetishists are more directed towards sexual experience and fulfilment. But if you just watch them at play, they are very similar.

At the bottom of the graph, I use the all-encompassing term 'Age Play'. While accurate, it can be confusing in this context, since this book is targeted specifically at *regressive* Little Ones.

From here on, the following definitions will apply:

Age-Play: fetish-driven age play

Little Ones/Regressives: Regressive age-players

While these definitions are not strictly correct, it saves having to write the qualified term 'regressive Little One', every time I use it from here on.

Let's take a look at some of the differences between regressive and fetish Age Play.

- **One of the big differences is one of *choice*.** Fetish Age-Play (Age-play for short), is essentially the *choice* of the person to engage in. Like most fetishists, the desire is under the person's conscious control. They might not like being denied their fetish and it might create some problems, but it can be controlled. Regressive Little Ones however, find that their needs are almost insatiable and will not be easily denied. One of the biggest problems that Little Ones face, is that their need to be Little often flies in the face of their relationship or other aspects of their lives. The purpose of this book is, in fact, built upon this premise: that **Little Ones cannot go on without this need being met.** Your relationship with your Little One has to build some of this need into it, otherwise it risks failure or diminishment. We spend a lot of time in this book discussing this issue and also giving clues on how to deal with it.

- **Regression rather than role-play.** A Fetish Age-Player *acts* like a child or infant, using typically stylised behaviours and various props. A regressive Little One however, actually *regresses* to a state where they feel that they *are* a child in everything except physical age. It is not a psychotic delusion, but rather a self-image alteration to allow them to think and feel that they are a child. *(Refer to the topic 'Regression in the Little One' for more detail on the inner workings of regression).*

- **Regressive Little Ones tend to mirror child-like behaviours** and speech more accurately and in more ways, than Fetish Age-Players. Age Players generally are not after authenticity, but rather an experience that is as approximate or as close as they want. For most Little Ones however, authenticity is a huge goal, just as is seeking to be *identified* as a child. *(Refer to Attachment Objects for more information on Identification)* Typically, a regressive Little One will have more childish behaviours as part of their behaviour than fetishists – not because they need or want them, but because they are unlocking their inner child, rather than seeking to merely imitate one.

- **Sexuality is optionally *added* to the behaviour,** rather than being the central role. Fetishes are by definition sexual, both in origin and in behavioural goals. They are part and parcel of many a post-pubescent's experience. Little Ones however, are not *primarily* sexual, as the regressive need did not typically originate from sexual needs or desires and began well before the sexual nature was developed. However, at puberty, most Little Ones develop strong sexual desires – just like all of us – and this aspect of their life is usually *overlaid* on top of their Little nature. Little Ones can be both non-sexual and highly sexual in their play, as they are still hormonally adults, however the primary gratification of a Little One is not sexual, but rather emotional and experiential. This is why orgasm may temporarily end a regressive need, only for it to reappear shortly after, because the need itself is *not* being met. Fetishists *always* seek sexual gratification. Regressives however, seek the *experience* of being a child and sex can be an added, but optional, bonus.

- **Leakage of behaviours from child to the adult**. 'Leakage' refers to regressed behaviours that appear in the adult. *(refer to 'Behavioural Leakage')*. Age-players rarely have problem with their age-related behaviours leaking into normal everyday life, but Little Ones can sometimes struggle with this, particularly if they have no relationship in which to place their Little self.

- **Internal placement of the self into different relational structures** e.g. genuine parenting. This rather confusing sentence simply means that a Little One will usually seek to not simply regress, but to place themselves into a relationship where they do not simply act out being a child, but take the *literal* place of a child, as much as possible. One of the strongest needs and desires of a Little One is to form a Parent/ Child or similar familial relationship that extends beyond just the times of regression. Age-players of course do not seek that. They seek age-play, sexual satisfaction and then back to their normal lives. This is the first time I have referred to a Little One's needs outside of a period of regression. I will refer to this in more detail later.

Dysfunctional Little Ones:

There are those that maintain that as a Little One, they can do anything they like. This is a very typical childish thinking pattern, which we are all disavowed of very early on. I discuss behavioural boundaries later on, but for now, I want to just bring up the concept of the 'coercive and non-coercive paraphilia'.

To quote the idiaper.me website…

"…infantilism [or regression] is a non-coercive paraphilia. In the grand spectrum of sexual disorders, the paraphilias that cause the most distress and feelings of guilt or remorse are coercive in nature. This is because in order for someone with a coercive paraphilia (CP) to become aroused, they must involve unwilling participants. Some obvious examples of coercive paraphilias include: sex with younglings (pedophilia), sex with dead people (necrophilia), flashers (exhibitionism), and sex with animals (zoophilia)… Other CPs include: voyeurism (watching someone have sex or undress without their permission) and frotteurism (rubbing up against someone in public).

In all of these cases, the sexual activities involved in achieving arousal are illegal because the object of arousal has not given their consent."

The nature of a coercive behaviour is one that 'coerces' another into the behaviour without their explicit consent. For example, wearing Adult Baby clothing in public is coercive, as it brings others into the orbit of their behaviour without their permission. If a biological child is involved, then it is usually considered *highly* coercive. Overt infantile behaviours such as loud baby talk, crawling or other such actions are also coercive, if done publically. Some Littles will argue that it is *only clothing,* but it is far more than that. I discuss later the *identification aspect* of baby clothes, but in short, wearing such clothing *clearly and obtrusively* defines the wearer as a baby/toddler to the other non-consenting person, or could even define them as a deviant and a danger.

While inviting a stranger to change an adult's diaper is obviously highly coercive (and stupid), many Little Ones do not understand that exposing a stranger to *any* of their lifestyle without their consent, is intrinsically wrong and coercive. Given that precisely none of his regressive behaviours fit into the general public arena, the Little One is simply *not* permitted to act in this fashion in public. Even using a pacifier in public is coercive, although it is mildly so.

The reason I bring up this topic, is to point out that while Little Ones are not intrinsically dysfunctional, some may still be so. It is just as unhelpful to think that all Little behaviours are good, as it is to believe that all of them are deviant.

In the Identification Section, I discuss a whole range of Little Behaviours, including the aberrant or dysfunctional, and in the Modification Section I discuss how some of these can be eliminated or reduced. It is important that the reader notes that I am not implicitly criticising a Little One's behaviours, but there are places and times for them. I am saying however, that a few Little Ones have trouble with *some* behaviours and may need help to bring them under control. Is that not one of the very essences of parenting?

How did it all begin?

This is *the* question all Little Ones ask, and sometimes with a great deal of emotional upset and distress. Being a strongly regressive Little can be limiting and debilitating and many would be glad to be rid of it – if that were indeed an option, which it generally isn't.

"How did this happen to me? Why can't I let it go?"

The short answer is, that for the vast majority of people, we don't really know. This book does not intend to go down the path of finding out why regression is part of the personality. It is a long and complex procedure that even if successful, rarely offers much in the way of resolution. This book's goal is to offer assistance to Little Ones and their partners on how to deal with it all, specifically in the area of relationships.

There are a number of potential causes of regression that have been promulgated and they may, or may not, be accurate. The truth is that there are a great number of triggers that can instil a regressive nature into a child. The obvious ones are severe trauma and physical and/or sexual abuse. Clear and obvious experiences like these always have a strong impact on the development of the child, but it is also true that the trauma may be a *perceived* one, as much as an actual occurrence.

A child that *perceives* he is not getting enough nurturing from a mother or father can sometimes feel traumatised. They can consequently, develop a strong need for regressive nurturing later on in life, even though the parenting may have been quite adequate. As any biological parent knows, all children are unique and even within the same family there can be wide differences in personality. Typically, the parent treats and nurtures each child in roughly the same manner, yet some sensitive children need far more attention than others and so, from their perception, they were not cared for enough. This is where I believe a lot of Little Ones came from – a place of *perceived* under-nurturing or under-recognition.

One researcher has hypothesised that being toilet trained too early can deny the infant the 'intimate experience and pleasure of being wet'. While obviously not true for many, it does explain children and teens who wet the bed either deliberately or who don't try to stop, as they find it comforting. It is an increasingly common problem that bedwetting, with or without diapers, is remaining present into late teens, without the child being overly concerned about it.

The other side of the bedwetting experience is that some claim their childhood history of extensive bedwetting initiated the regressive need. They comment that while they disliked the bedwetting, they also grew to attach deeply regressive feelings toward it. Eventually, it became a part of their own regression or escape back to childhood, despite finding it unpleasant and uncomfortable.

Triggers and objects in regression may not always be pleasant ones. Some may be harsh and unpleasant feelings and memories, yet they can still trigger regression. The thick cloth diaper may evoke painful or humiliating memories, yet still forms a large part of the regressive experience.

One regressive was often smacked harshly as a child and early teenager and hated it. However, the humiliation of the event always made him feel Little, as the discipline method was one normally used for much younger children. As an adult, when he regresses, he expects to be smacked by his partner. He does not enjoy the smacks, but unless he receives them, the regression is unsatisfactory. While not overly common, it reminds us that not everything about regression is necessarily comfortable and pleasant.

Regression is less about pleasure or pain, but rather about comfort and need.

Here is an example of one girl growing up and how the regression was affected by her mother's well-intentioned efforts to stop her.

"I've been an adult baby since I was a baby! Sound confusing? Well I first remember doing dress up in the attic when I was about six. Oh I did the mommy dress up, wearing her clothes and shoes, but I always gravitated to the box of my old diapers and baby things. As a young adult with hormones raging I was denying any interest in being little. Glad I got through all that madness and came to my senses when I started being a baby again. Sound familiar?

As soon as my parents told me that I couldn't act like a baby any more I knew they were wrong. Surely they thought I was potty trained and such, but I would spend hours in the attic doing dress up in more than just moms things. I loved putting on diapers and just being a baby.

At eleven years old my mom caught me. She was never one for being comfortable with things that weren't clearly defined by the protestant church. Her prepubescent daughter padding around in cloth diapers of the previous decade was not something her minister would have an answer for. It was immediately preached to me that I was not a baby any more, this was sick, not for me, and by the way I was grounded. It would have been so much nicer if she had just pulled my diapers down and spanked me. Of course I don't think she would have had any intention to pull them back up. The next day my world of baby things boxes in the attic were gone.

I admit I was frightened, angry, and confused. I sucked my thumb for another year or so. They couldn't take that away from me, although my blankie mysteriously kept getting smaller. I got even though. I was a raging hormone mad girl. It had to be the toughest three years of their raising me. No matter what, they were wrong, even when they were right.

I kept that longing of being a baby suppressed for a long, long time. I would be transfixed while reading about diaper fetishes, but never able to get past the ingrained guilt. It wasn't until fifteen years ago or so, that I actually allowed myself to try on a disposable. It was if someone had flipped a switch. I felt so calm, complacent, and comfortable. I started 'doing the research' to find an incredible AB/DL community, it was huge, who knew! I loved what I found. I wore diapers for thirty days straight. I kept denying that I was a baby, yet I would pick up toys, baby bottles, sippy cups and pacifiers when I was out shopping."

[FetLife 2012]

Growth and progression of the Regression:

One of the big questions that is often asked by Little Ones and their partners alike is, 'where will this lead to'? This is certainly a valid question. Most of us dislike the idea of starting a journey with no idea of the final destination. And when you realise that this journey is a *one-way* trip, the consternation level is even higher. Let's look at one opinion:

*"Paraphilias [such as infantilism] are usually <u>chronic and progressive</u> behaviors. This means that the longer you have a sexual desire that is not properly confronted, the more intense the desires become, and you'll probably always prefer kinky sex to vanilla sex. This **does not mean** that your sexual desires will control and haunt you for the rest of your life."*

[iDiaper.me 2010]

The truth of the matter is that the extent of the regression for a Little One *does* progress over time. The only real choice is *how* this progresses. I know it sounds a bit scary, but it is no different to anything else in our lives – it changes. We get older, weaker, wiser, need more sleep etcetera and yet we all survive it. Handling change in the regression of a Little One is an aspect that we have to deal with. Everything and everyone changes, but there is a real difference between the growth of an *unconfronted or secret* desire and the one that is openly lived out.

"That which grows in the dark does oft-times grow hideous."

[author unknown]

What we don't deal with and keep hidden continues to grow, but often this is where the behaviour veers off course and into dysfunction and other significant difficulties, including relational ones. Even if you decide to do nothing more about your partner's regression than to acknowledge and accept it, then you will already make a huge difference to your Little One and to his future. Letting regression grow and expand in the shadows is a recipe for disaster for both of you.

The real question however is: does it *expand* regardless of what you do? And the answer is a qualified *yes*.

The needs and behaviours of the Little are constantly evolving, even if sometimes quite slowly. Different circumstances develop different needs and wants. New experiences alter their feelings and perceptions. In short, like any biological child, your partner is changing. The difference is, that while a biological child *matures*, the Little One generally remains the same basic age. What does change however, is the *expression* of that age. He will add new behaviours, modify others and remove some altogether. He may add crawling to his behaviour, as he discovers a new facet of his regression, or he may discover that bottle feeds no longer meet his needs and he discards them.

You need to be ready for change and sometimes to help deliver it or modify it. Not all change is inherently good and a child cannot always be trusted to have good changes in behaviour. If you participate in his development as a Little, you can guide and interact with him to make it work out for the best, rather than witness the uncontrolled changes that most have.

The unstated question here is, 'will the regression overwhelm us'? In the vast majority of cases the answer is an unequivocal *no*. Most Little Ones are quite emotionally and mentally stable, but with a strong regressive aspect that they need to constantly deal with. However, if you have an obsessive compulsive (OCD) partner or one with other problems, then they could be overwhelmed by regression. In this case though, you are probably already more than aware of this tendency and hopefully helping him to seek treatment for it. In this circumstance, a Parent/Child relationship should be developed very carefully and probably with the assistance of a mental health professional.

There is no reason you cannot enjoy the growth and progression of your Little One along with him. It is change and excitement, whereas so much of our lives are static and predictable. Go on the ride with him as his child-like behaviours and feelings morph and change. By joining him on this journey, you can both help him and possibly enjoy the experience as well.

How many women are Little Ones?

Up until relatively recently, it was considered that almost all Adult Babies and Little Ones were male. We now know that this is a fundamental inaccuracy, typical of those who consider the internet a source of statistically correct information. While men still appear to be in the majority, it is approximately a 60/40 split, favouring men. One of the big changes in the world of Adult Babies in the last decade, has been the discovery that women can be just as regressive as men.

Women tend to be far more circumspect and hidden about their fetishes and inner regressive natures and so *seem* under-represented, but all of what I have written applies equally to both men and women.

Binge and Purge Cycle:

A common problem with hidden Little Ones and Adult Babies is the tendency to suddenly throw everything away that is related to their fetish or regression, go cold-turkey for a while, and then suddenly re-purchase large amounts all over again. This is known as the 'binge-purge cycle' and it usually happens many, many times to Little Ones.

This is a regular experience for Adult Babies and Little Ones who just want to 'give it all away', and so they impulsively throw out all their diapers and baby accessories. The problem is that they almost invariably soon regret it, and because their inner needs are still not being met, they now reacquire it all over again in a binge. A far better solution to the purge cycle, is to pack everything away and put it where it is not easily retrieved, even at a different physical address. Then, when the urge returns, there is at least no added expense. An even better idea (and the point of this book), is to come to grips with the inner life of the Little One and to develop a functioning and satisfactory lifestyle that does not want or need to purge in the first place.

Regression in the Little One

Mild regression is a relatively common experience for all adults at times, where we momentarily regress back to a semi-child-like state or adopt some childish behaviours in lieu of adult ones. This can be as simple as adopting an unnecessarily submissive posture in a conflict or an older teen still using a stuffed toy to sleep with. These are typically harmless behaviours and are just part of the fabric of life, but for the Little One, regression is far more substantial and a lot more detailed. Whereas adult regression is normally just a few aspects of childhood reappearing in the adult framework, such as thumb sucking or submission or irrational fears, Little One regression is more akin to attempting to replicate the entire child experience.

A Little One's regression is an attempt to recreate childhood or infancy in its totality and authenticity.

Clearly, such a goal is impossible to achieve in a literal sense, as a total child-like state is impossible outside of a total break with reality, which of course no one wants! However, regression can achieve an incredible degree of authenticity for the Little One and especially if it is accompanied by a full set of props and attachment objects (see later on for details), such as a nursery or play mat.

A regressed state is something most Little Ones enjoy and look forward to. The problem for most is that the absence of a partner or 'Parent' severely limits the degree of authentic child-like regression they can achieve. This is because practicality demands that the Little One limit some activities, and as any parent of biological children knows, *sharing* your child's experiences is half of the fun for them!

A primary desire for a Little One is an involved Parent.

Rather than being a limiting aspect in your relationship, regression can instead be a huge opportunity for you to *identify* your Little One in greater detail and to learn more about him than you can in almost any other way.

Meeting your Little One's true self:

The reality is that you have probably already seen your partner's inner Little One to some degree or other. When he sucks his thumb without realising it or behaves childishly or deliberately wets his pants or bed, you are probably seeing aspects of his inner child. Sometimes, the eyes can tell you when your wife or husband momentarily drifts away from you, to that *special place* inside.

The full-scale regressive experience however, is something altogether different. It is in this time, that the Little One is freed from the adult confines to a significant degree, and is able to experience a form of semi-autonomy, an ability to think, act and experience life as their regressed age, without the constraints of not only adult *behaviour*, but also adult *thinking*.

It would be simplistic to think of regression as either on or off. Few things in life are ever that simple and when dealing with the mind and human behaviour, it is *never* that simple. Simply put, regression can be anything from a mild behavioural change – such as quietness and submissiveness – all the way down to almost total child-like play and behaviours (including speech), that are virtually indistinguishable from that of a biological child. I discuss these ranges of regression in the next few pages.

A common aspect of deep regression is that the Little One *thinks* as a child. This is the defining difference between regression and role-play. It can lead to the whole array of childish behaviours, such as selfishness, timelessness, crawling, clinginess, crying and even tantrums. This can be quite disconcerting to a partner, but it is important to note the following:

During even the deepest regression, your Little One is still essentially an adult and has access to all of those adult abilities and emotions if needed. Choosing to sideline the adult side does not mean the adult disappears, only that it is in the <u>background</u> while the child plays in the <u>foreground</u>.

The obvious corollary of this, is that in non-regressed times, the child is there in the background, while the adult is in the foreground. The startling news for you is that the child is *always there*. This can be staggering information to most partners who never really considered the possibility. Let's think about this for a minute so we can understand it a little better.

The 'inner child' concept that is so in vogue in pop culture is actually no such thing at all. That description is no more than simply remembering how to enjoy the simple things of life, to recall the wide-eyed wonder of our childhood days and then to embrace some of it in our adult experiences. In the case of your Little One however, there is a very real inner child that is well-formed and accessible via deep regression.

This sounds scary and perhaps that is justified, but again it is important to realise that nothing has actually changed for you. Your Little One is still the same person before you knew any of this. You are just now more informed, but don't assume that your Little One is all that aware of this either.

Unless he has had opportunity to explore his regressive nature, he may also be unaware of the true extent of his Little One. All he feels is the stress and tension of holding back his Little One inside.

Regression is not intrinsically bad or dangerous, but like so many other aspects of life, regression must be handled responsibly. Your Little One has regressive *needs*. If these needs are not met, then it leads to frustration, anger and other negative experiences. On the other hand, giving carte blanche to these needs on a regular basis, risks taking too much time away from the essential adult experiences of life and thereby diminishing the *whole* of the person. Once again, *balance* is the goal, not elimination. I will refer often to the goal of achieving balance between the adult and Little selves. It is the primary goal of the Parent/Child relationship.

What happens when the Little One regresses?

If your Little One regresses deeply, it can be a little scary at first, so let's take a good look at what is happening inside. Let's start with one very big, very important observation that you must understand and understand well.

---

*There is no actual inner separate personality. Your Little One is **not** a multiple personality. What is actually happening is that your partner has deep un-met needs and therefore constructs a pseudo-personality that can help meet these needs. The power of an intelligent and creative mind takes a set of behaviours and thinking patterns that are deeply separated from the usual adult patterns and then builds an age, name and a pseudo-personality around these needs and behaviours. Thus a Little One is 'born'.*

IMPORTANT: To an untrained observer looking on, very deep regression can appear like multiple personality, but the two are vastly different. Multiple Personality – properly known as Dissociative Identity Disorder – is a rare and very serious and debilitating mental disorder, which should be treated professionally. This is *not* what is happening here.

Let's take a look at what is taking place internally when regression occurs. The psychological mechanics of a Little One's regression is as follows:

1. A stressor or trigger occurs to begin the process. This may be an event, a sight, a memory or a sudden emotion. It can also be a smell or the presence of a specific object that can trigger regression. It may also take some time to occur. Most adults are aware of the need to regress, but also of their circumstances, which will dictate when and where they can regress. Sometimes however, the inner pressure can build up so strongly that regression can occur very quickly and even spontaneously.

Regression rarely happens just on its own, but rather is the sum of many incidents or stresses building up, until the adult feels overwhelmed and seeks the *known release* of regression. Because the adult knows that regression eases the tension, he will often seek an opportunity to regress, such as is allowed by his lifestyle and circumstances. Allowing the pressure to build inside can lead to outbursts of anger and sometimes, uncontrolled regression.

2. Regression is almost always a conscious choice, but it is not always that simple. When this choice is made, the adult self moves to the conscious *background* and remains aware of what is happening and has control still available to him. It sounds complex to most people, but it is less of a conscious decision to regress, than it is just *letting go* and allowing the child to move naturally forward and for the stressed, tired and upset adult to peacefully drop into the background.

3. The inner child then takes the *foreground* and the child's behaviours and needs become primary. The person then adopts the childish pseudo-personality and emotions which may (or may not) differ significantly from the adult. Again, this is not a separate personality, but rather an artificial construct built from the intelligence and creativity of the adult. The emotions and behaviours are still essentially the adult's, but unable to be easily expressed in the adult world.

4. When the inner need has been met, the child will usually naturally return to the background and the adult automatically comes forward. This can also happen abruptly in case of need or emergency, but it normally happens in a slower, controlled fashion. It is worth noting though, that just because the deep need is met, it is not always enough for the regression to immediately end. You must understand that your Little One *enjoys* being little and feels no rush to end the experience. The need may be met, but there is still enjoyment and fun to be had out of being Little. Do not be concerned if your Little One is in no rush to end the regression. It is natural and safe. Would you want to leave a place you were happy in, just because you were no longer sad?

5. It is worth noting that there is never a total separation of the two personalities. Even as an adult, the child still exerts some influence over behaviours, e.g. bedwetting, groin-rubbing etcetera. Likewise, the child is still affected by the adult, e.g. walking, sexual arousal, ability to read etcetera. The degree of crossover from child to adult (behavioural leakage) can be embarrassing and one of the goals of the Parent/Child relationship is to mitigate those effects to make life a bit simpler and easier.

I explain the various Levels of Regression in the next section. Regression can be anything from very shallow and brief, to very deep and long-lasting. You need to know the difference and to learn to recognise the signs.

Your adult partner is probably acutely aware of his inner Little One most of the time – some more than others. Even in adult mode, they may see a child's toy and instantly feel the desire for it from their Little One. They may see a child's outfit and suddenly wonder what it would look like on them. This is their *regular experience*. Keep that in mind and be understanding of some of the odd comments they can make at times! The separation between adult and Little One is not absolute and for many, seems almost non-existent. One of our goals – and one that should be yours as well – is to help bring some degree of functional separation between the two, by properly meeting the needs of the Little One. A major key in living with a regressive Little One is being able to keep the Little and Big selves apart and under control. We deal with how to seek this balance later on.

Levels of Regression:

Like everything else in behaviour, there are various levels of regression. You will soon learn to identify them. They are not something to be afraid of, as they are integral to the regressive nature of the Little One, nor is there just one level of regression. It is not an on/off switch. The traumas and triggers that move your child to regress will be different and they may lead to different levels. Each level has its pros and cons, except level five which is entirely negative.

A Little One who is living in balance may experience mainly levels one and two, with occasional time in levels three and four. An out of balance Little One will be all over the place, including possibly, the highly dysfunctional level five.

Age-play, role-play and other non-regressive behaviours do not apply to this scale. This is solely for Little Ones who literally regress to a lower age, not those who role-play this situation.

The Regression Scale is as follows:

- **LEVEL ZERO**: At this level, the adult is fully in charge, as there is no subsuming of the adult personality in any way. The Little One is still in existence and the adult is aware of him, but has no impact whatsoever on behaviour. In some cases, people consider the Little One to be *asleep* and therefore exerts no influence. This is a very safe level with no adverse consequences. A majority of Little Ones spend much of their time at this level, but this should not be assumed. A number also spend large slabs of time at level one and just cope with the conflicts that result. It is ideal that the adult spends most of their time at level zero if possible. A well balanced Little will find that a lot easier.

- **LEVEL ONE**: At this level, the adult steps back from the front and *shares* the limelight with the child. This level is a good one for Parent/Child communication and learning, as the child is there, but is also able to communicate using adult skills and behaviours. It is the level that many inexperienced parents confuse with level zero or may even think that their partner is lying to them or 'faking it'. It is a very safe level, but it does little to meet the deep needs of the child or to communicate them to the parent. Some Little Ones spend large amounts of the day and night at this level. It doesn't restrict their adult abilities significantly and yet they feel comforted that their inner child is there.

- **LEVEL TWO**: The child moves to the front and the adult behaviours are partly removed and replaced with some childish ones. For example, language may become simpler and softer, yet still remain quite adequate. The child may alternatively withdraw from conversation or interaction, as they feel unable to fully communicate as either child or adult. It is an easy level for a Little One to exist in and one of the more common levels for living for extended periods, including days at a time, if that is a planned activity. It lacks much of the internal conflict of higher levels, as the adult is still there and easily accessible if needed. It is a good level for the Parent/Child to communicate and discuss some of the more meaningful aspects of regression. If the Little One is a deeply troubled or traumatised child, this level gives little to no information as to the cause. Communication yes, but deep information, no.

- **LEVEL THREE**: This is the first of the two deeper levels. The adult is now some distance away from the child and the child *is primarily responsible for most of the behaviours*. The adult remains accessible, but is rarely used for much beyond speech and walking and sometimes sexual or sexualised behaviour. This is the level where the parent begins to see a marked difference in adult and child behaviours. The language is closer to the regressed age and it is the beginning of significant crawling for the younger ones, who do not normally crawl at lower levels.

  A child at this level may have marked differences in preferences, e.g. at levels zero to two a child may not like or accept a formula bottle, but at level three or higher will drink it happily. A level zero to two child may have limited enjoyment of children's TV shows and books, but at three and higher will become engrossed and even respond to the characters at the correct age level. At level three and higher, *genuine* fears may appear from things like darkness, absence of the parent or scary Television shows.

  This is the level where the parent learns the most about their child, but it can be hard work at times, as you are communicating with a predominantly regressed child. It is the highest level that is considered healthy and functional for extended experiences (multiple days). It is a level to be treated seriously, not feared. You can learn much from your Little One here and the regression will also ease much of his internal pressures.

- **LEVEL FOUR** is like Level Three, except that there is *little influence from the adult*. This is where you can see a Little One with total refusal (or inability) to walk or talk, poor motor skills or at least, skills more in keeping with the regressed age. Behaviour begins to mirror the self-identified age far more closely. To an onlooker, such as a parent, there doesn't appear to be much of a significant adult presence. Whilst not true, it can be initially scary for some parents. It is not considered a healthy level to spend too much time at, although almost all Little Ones do go here from time to time. If it is irregular and is supervised then it is fine, but if visited too often, the Little One could develop some problems existing in the adult realm competently. However, this would indicate deep-seated traumas, which would need professional help anyhow. The deeper Little One issues are on display here, but communication may not be very good or accurate. The more advanced, as well as the dysfunctional behaviours, such as faecal play (including oral) and other potentially harmful activities, could also manifest themselves here if they are part of their behavioural profile (discussed later on).

- **LEVEL FIVE:** The regressive child and his behaviour *almost* totally overwhelms the adult. While the adult remains technically capable of control, that control is difficult to exert. The child may refuse to revert to adulthood and the inner adult may have trouble coming forward without external help and assistance. Typically, the Little One sees no reason to leave and wishes to remain at their regressed age. <u>This is a potentially dangerous situation and is always unhealthy.</u> It does happen occasionally and briefly with Littles that have experienced deep trauma or distress. Continued existence at this level however, is damaging. It risks the subsuming of the adult self and relegating it to a place where the Little One won't easily find it. Do not attempt to learn at this level. Move them up, forcefully if necessary. It is a rare place however, and there is little likelihood that you will ever see this level.

Some Little Ones retain a full or nearly full command of language, even at the higher levels, but only when done through writing, drawing or typing. This phenomenon is not available in every Little One, but if it is, then it is a gold-mine of opportunity for the parent to communicate with their Little One in detail, even at deeper levels. Your child may be at level four, yet through a keyboard, he can communicate with you competently, without altering the essentially firmly regressed state. Handwriting may also be childish in style – like using crayons – but the message will be adult. It is as if some part of the adult personality remains in total contact, but only through one limited mechanism. If your child can communicate this way, then use it to learn.

Each Little One is different. They might go through the lower levels so fast, you don't even see them go by! Levels one and two are great safe places for your Little One to spend extended time; hours or even days, if you are able. It is not terribly exhausting and can give a lot of satisfaction and happiness. Levels three and four are more demanding, but sometimes the emotional distress is such that only a higher level will suffice.

You need to find and discover your own level descriptions. I have given my descriptions, but it can be helpful if you tailor them to your own circumstances. The best thing to do is to use a notebook and write down the various different behaviours you observe. In time, you will see identifying behaviours that will help you to know which level they are at. At level one, the child might want their pacifier, but is not that upset if it is not available, whereas at level four they could cry or have a tantrum if not available. A level one infant may be fully continent, but at level four wets and messes without any apparent control.

The two activities that are the most consistent identifiers of level and age are drawing/colouring and speech. Your three year old Little may decide to draw neatly, more like that of a ten year old in levels one and two by virtue of the strong adult influence. By level three, it has deteriorated noticeably and by level four it will be a three year old's drawing without exception. This is not the deterioration of *age*, but rather the reduction of the *adult influence*. By level four, the Little One speaks and draws at the correct age, with little to no adult dilution of this effect.

Sexual activity may be totally absent from some Little Ones, but in most cases it will exist and generally occur in levels three or four. This may be masturbation to orgasm or sexual interplay with the parent. *(Refer to 'Sexual Intimacy and the Little One' further on).* In the case of a Little One with multiple ages, just one or two will be sexually interested and capable, while the others are not. You need to work these things out and record it as part of the Behavioural Profile, as discussed further on.

Behavioural Leakage

The regressive Little One and the adult do not live in neat, self-contained boxes with no influence or effect on each other. Even if that were possible, it would not be healthy. This is one of the symptoms of Dissociative Identity Disorder, where individual identities are totally unaware of, and do not exert an internal influence on, each other. As I have said several times before, Little Ones are *not* dissociative.

All Littles will have leakage of behaviours and emotions from the adult to the Little and vice-versa. A simple example is speech. Even though the Little may be regressed to the level of a one or two year old, they often still have speech well above that age level. In fact, it is rare for a Little to lose this ability totally, as it is intrinsic to each of us. The Little One may use a stylised form of baby-talk, which is an approximation of genuine age-appropriate speech, but they still retain speech functionality, which is an adult attribute.

Walking is another such example of leakage from the adult to the child. Even a Little One that crawls a lot, still retains the ability to walk, even if they don't use that skill much. Even at the very highest levels of regression, there is a great deal of adult behaviour and thinking that is evident within the child. It can come as a shock for many Little Ones to realise that their behaviour is not really authentic, but is more of a stylised approximation of genuine child behaviour, not that there is anything wrong with that at all. The needs are still being met, but it isn't necessarily *totally authentic* behaviour. What is important for the parent to realise is that the adult remains an influence in most of his behaviour, even if not obviously so.

Leakage from the child to the adult:

Leakage goes the other way as well – from the child to the adult – and in this case, it can sometimes be both problematic, as well as very positive. Behaviours such as thumb-sucking, young speech, wetting and the like, can sometimes leak from the child to the adult and this is where trouble can occur for normal living and relationships, where these things are not very desirable.

Leakage is not intrinsically bad. Some behaviours that we have in childhood such as 'a sense of wonder', creativity and imagination or unquestioning love and obedience don't always make it through to adulthood, and we are often the losers for it. How many of us know a person that lacks the essential spark of childhood in them and is an unhappy or unpleasant person as a result? Leakage isn't intrinsically wrong and in fact, the regressive Little One has an opportunity to draw from the child to enhance the adult far more than the rest of us. However, it is not always so simple or so positive.

Like what happens in the physical realm, an object leaks when it either has holes in it, or it is under so much pressure, that normally strong joints burst. The analogy has a lot of parallels for the situation of a regressive. A Little One under a great deal of internal pressure will exhibit – or leak – some of their basic behaviours into the adult world. Bed-wetting or pants wetting are very common examples of this. As one of the most basic regressed behaviours, it will leak out into the adult realm, in this case literally, if the regressive need becomes too powerful and the opportunity to express it, is non-existent. This is why I advise that regression needs to be managed, not prohibited. Prohibition will just send it underground, just like the alcohol prohibition in the United States. This means that you, as the parent, need to have a regression plan, where these needs are met in a regular and safe manner. I discuss this later on in the Interaction Section. Don't get too concerned about it at this stage. Most of these plans and profiles I describe are little more than common sense and observation.

Taking the analogy further, leakage occurs through 'holes'. The best parallel for this is a behavioural difficulty where it isn't *pressure* that is driving it, but rather a lack of control over it or a bad habit. Thumb-sucking in the adult world may have commenced due to pressure, but even with the pressure removed, the behaviour continues. The same may also apply to excessive masturbation or other such actions: simple bad habit. These aspects of leakage are dealt with through behavioural modification and often just plain discipline – internal or external – and again, I discuss this later on in the Modification Section.

However, some other behaviours leak because they have an impetus all of their own. Up until now, I have referred to regressive behaviours in fairly general terms. I have said that regressive behaviours may leak into the adult realm by virtue of the pressure on the Little in a *general* sense. There are however, some behaviours that have their own etiology (beginnings) and their own internal constructs. While they fit in with regression as a rule, they are behaviours *in their own right* and exist both inside and outside of regression. They are driven by their own separate needs and triggers.

In essence, these are very different from regular regressive behaviours because they are not really leaking from the child, but are part of the overall adult and child personality. Often these behaviours are the result of a trauma or abuse in the past or an event which has impacted strongly on the biological child and which now affects both Little and Adult. Depending on what the behaviour is, this can be either destructive or just moderately annoying. A destructive behaviour such as violence, criminal activity or anti-social activity, should be referred to a mental health professional for treatment. Most Littles do not have these kinds of behaviours, but I believe it is important for you to understand the difference. I mention this just in case your partner has a behaviour you do not like and wish to control or eliminate, yet may not really be part and parcel of his regression.

Summary:

Behavioural leakage is a fact of life for Little Ones and should be both enjoyed and monitored. Your Little One may be an excellent children's author, because the writing adult has full access to the emotions and actions of an almost literal child – their Little. He may be able to enjoy playtime in a way most adults never will and satisfy the inner child that we all have, but in a literal way.

Your Little can benefit from the responsibility and understanding of boundaries that the adult can bring to the regression. Sometimes, the discipline you impose on your Little One – timeouts, bedtimes etcetera – works best when you are teaching them to access their adult's understanding of behaviour.

Leakage is a fact of life so use it, observe it and enjoy it. You won't always be disciplining your child. The leakage will eventually come into a form of equilibrium. I talk more about modifying behaviour in the MODIFICATION section.

Attachment Objects

Early childcare theory talks about 'Transitional Objects' – objects that help the biological infant move to the next phase of their development.

In classical psychoanalysis the term 'transitional object' came into being in 1951 by Donald Winnicott as a designation for any material object (typically something soft – a piece of cloth, say, or part of a plush toy) to which an infant attributes a special value and by means of which the child is able to make the necessary shift from the earliest oral relationship with the mother to genuine object-relationships.

In his observation of infants, Winnicott noted that between the ages of four and twelve months children would often become attached to a particular object that they invested with a primordial significance. This object would be manipulated, sucked, or stroked, and often became an indispensable aid for falling asleep. [Clare Winnicott www. clarewinnicott.net]

Little Ones also have their own 'special objects' in their universe of play and behaviour – **Attachment Objects.**

An outsider (or new parent) looking on at many of the props and objects that Adult Babies and Little Ones use and collect, might make the mistake of taking them simply at their face value. Some of these objects appear to be inconsistent or inappropriate to the Little One's self-identified age or circumstances and others may just look plain ridiculous. But your Little One exhibits a very strong *attachment* to these objects. In many cases, the use of these objects is integral to his behaviour and without which he feels edgy or incomplete when regressing.

This confusion is a common one for many people, because a large number of the toys, clothes, accessories and furniture that Adult Babies and Little Ones use have a lot more hidden value than at first appears. Many of these objects are what are called Attachment Objects.

DEFINITION: Attachment Objects are items or objects that the Little One has and uses that have two or three special aspects to them in addition to the object's primary or natural function. These are Identification Aspect, Secondary Purpose Aspect and Initiation or Trigger Aspect. All Attachment Objects have an Identification and most have a Secondary Purpose aspect. Very few have an Initiation aspect.

Attachment Objects are similar to classic transitional objects in one aspect in that there is certainly a *transition* involved. However, in the case of the Little One, the direction of this transition is the reverse of infantile transition. The adult is seeking to transition **from** the predominantly adult state **into** the regressed state, albeit only temporarily.

IDENTIFICATION ASPECT:

Some objects, especially clothing, help the Little One to *identify* as their regressed age. For example, using a pacifier (dummy) is a very strong and obvious identifier to others that the user is a baby or toddler. When used, worn or played with, the object clearly identifies to the Little One that they are the child they feel they are inside. The Little One has a very strong hope and desire that others will see these identifiers and understand them in the same way as he does. It is important that the parent gets to understand the identification aspects of her child's attachment objects. Be aware that some of the identifiers are not as obvious as others.

One Adult Baby company has understood the identification aspect very well and sells its adult onesies and plastic pants with a 'Baby Pants' tag on it to *specifically* inform anyone that sees the tag, that the person is wearing *baby* items, not adult ones. Whilst probably done for marketing purposes, they have recognised that being *identified* as a baby is just as important as the intrinsic value of the garment.

SECONDARY PURPOSE ASPECT:

The Attachment Object has a clear primary purpose that is obvious to all. For example, a diaper's purpose is to keep the wearer dry and clean, but for the Little One, it can have additional *secondary purposes*. It can provide comfort, (sexual) pleasure, be a trigger for incontinence or have other aspects. Many of these secondary purposes are common to most, but some are relatively unique and meaningful to just a few. Again, it is important that the parent not be unaware of these aspects. You don't have to know them all, but you do need to be cognizant of most. The simple question to ask is, "how does he use this object beyond its intended application?"

INITIATION ASPECT:

This aspect of Attachment Objects is relatively rare. While Identification and Secondary Purpose aspects are almost always there, the Initiation Aspect is rarely present. This aspect describes some attribute about an object that can <u>trigger a regressive episode</u>. It is almost never a generic object, but rather something very specific that triggers a memory or emotion which in turn, triggers the regression. For example, it may be a soft toy, but not just any soft toy. It may be a Care Bear toy, but not just any one, but rather a pink one, of a specific size and style that clearly has a deeply-rooted memory attached to it. It could even be a classic Transitional Object that the Little has never properly disconnected from. If your Little One has an object like this, then you most definitely need to be aware of it.

Controlling and managing regression requires us to be aware of the various triggers. Most of these are smells, locations and a variety of other stressors and triggers. They are rarely objects in themselves, but occasionally they may be involved in the onset of a regressive episode. It certainly helps to know if a particular object has the ability to trigger a regressive episode.

So what does this mean in plain English?

Quite simply this: the items that your Little One has may mean a great deal to him and you probably have little idea why. Over time, you may understand what they mean or perhaps not, but you must never devalue or dismiss them, because they may be of huge importance to him.

Most Adult Babies have few objects (toys, clothes, diapers etcetera) due to the restraints of their lives and especially when they are hiding it from family and friends, but the objects they *do* choose are usually highly important ones. When a Little One *comes out* and is allowed to express themselves more fully, there will undoubtedly be a huge increase in the objects they collect. After all, children love to collect toys! Some of these objects will be Attachment Objects, which the Little One will hold in high regard and have a special place for. Other objects might be important, but be nothing more than what they outwardly appear to be. One example is baby powder. For some, it is an Attachment Object of some significance and it will be in open view, proudly visible to all, while to others, it is nothing more than an essential component of a diaper change.

Let's take a look at the objects that your Little One has or wants and what significance they may have.

Baby Bonnets:

A good example that can help explain these concepts is the traditional baby bonnet, which many Little Ones use. Its primary function of course, is to keep a baby's head warm and also possibly for some limited *baby-fashion* value. For a Little One, keeping the head warm is not really important, even if they are bald. It is however possible, that the Little One wears it from a fashion context such as a matching bonnet and dress. For some Little Ones, the bonnet is *just a bonnet*; a baby accessory like many others and the choice to wear one or not, is simply related to the primary purpose of matching outfits. However for some, a baby bonnet is an Attachment Object.

In this case, the purpose and value of the bonnet is far more than its obvious primary function. It has an **IDENTIFICATION ATTACHMENT**. In this situation, the bonnet symbolises and *identifies* the wearer as a *baby*. Not as a Little Girl or a preteen, but as an *infant or toddler*. The *presence* of a bonnet is far more important than fashion or that it matches the rest of the outfit. Its purpose is to *identify*, both to themselves and to anyone else, that they are an infant or toddler. If the Little One is not wearing a bonnet they may feel as if their self-image is inadequate. This is why you might see your Little One wearing a bonnet almost everywhere – day, night and even stressing if not wearing one. If your Little One has multiple self-identified ages (which are discussed later) then a bonnet also separately identifies the baby or toddler ages from the Little Girl ages.

The Bonnet also has **SECONDARY PURPOSE ATTACHMENT** as well. There can be more than one secondary purpose for an object and they can vary according to the individual. The bonnet can have the secondary purpose of *covering up the adult features*. A balding man may find his self-image is totally destroyed without a bonnet to cover up the majority of his adult facial features. With a large frilly bonnet on, the Little One feels that he is now viewed as a baby, rather than as an adult, because *he* sees it that way. Remember, it doesn't have to make perfect sense to you; only to the Little One.

Another secondary purpose is *safety and security*. To quote a Little One:

"When I wear a large bonnet which covers some of my face as well, I can lie down in bed and feel as if no one knows who I am. I feel safe and know that no one can hurt me. I feel safe from people who might stare at me if I don't have my bonnet on. I feel exposed and at risk without it." [from an internet blog]

If you have ever wondered why your Little One wears a bonnet so often and with seemingly scant regard for colour or style matching or any other aesthetics, then it is probably an Attachment Object. He may *prefer* a fashionable matching bonnet, but will take any bonnet at all, rather than none. If he only wears a matching bonnet or when it is age appropriate, then he is probably treating it as *just* a bonnet and nothing more. An exception to this rule is that regressed women tend to place significantly higher value on fashion than men and will usually only wear a *matching* bonnet. However, they may then stress if there is no matching bonnet to wear because it is still an Attachment Object to them. They *need* a bonnet, but are also constrained by the intrinsic feminine need for a fashionable matching one.

One common aspect of Attachment Objects is that the Little One may have far more of them than they need on a practical basis. A baby may have 15-20 bonnets, when clearly two or three would cover most of their needs, but each bonnet may have slightly different attachment properties. One might be very pretty and make *her* feel feminine and infantile and highly attractive. Another one might be oversized and cover a lot of the face and features, provide security and anonymity. Also, some Little Ones are just plain greedy and want more! Get used to that! Like any child, there is never enough of *anything*.

Diapers/Nappies:

Diapers (or nappies) are of course, the number one Attachment Object for Adult Babies and Little Ones. For a Little One, the diaper is usually the *primary identifier of infancy*. Many Little Ones report effective loss of bladder awareness and control when wearing diapers, even if they are continent at other times. The diaper tells them and anyone who sees them that *'I am a baby'*. Of course there are a variety of adult diapers that go out of their way to look as least babyish as possible. But never to be outdone, the adult community has also gone out of their way to design and manufacture diapers that are replicas of infant ones, except in adult sizes. They are patterned like baby diapers and even have the single tape on the side for added authenticity. And authenticity is hugely important in an attachment object!

Cloth diapers have not disappeared from the scene either. Adults can still buy traditional square diapers in a variety of materials, including flannel and towelling and in sizes large enough to fold the usual way for an authentic and bulky diaper. The bulk and size adds to the experience and enhances the identification attachment, by making it impossible to ignore. The array of adult plastic pants is also truly mind-boggling! Apart from the usual functional white plastic pants, there are clear ones and a large range of infant/toddler patterned plastic. Perhaps the most notable plastic pant is the frilly rhumba pant. Similar to infant pants, these are designed *specifically* to identify the wearer as an Adult Baby Girl or infant. The IDENTIFICATION ATTACHMENT of diapers is exceptionally high. Diapers have other purposes – the SECONDARY PURPOSE ATTACHMENT – as well as their obvious one. One is for a source of pleasure and masturbation. Almost all Little Ones report masturbating in their diapers and using the diaper as a pleasure object. Older biological children who are still in diapers become aware of the pleasure of a bulky item between their legs and this can sometimes lead to diaper fetishism (Diaper Lovers) later on in life, or even some regressive behaviour.

Diapers also provide *security* and I'm not talking about the obvious role that diapers have in providing literal security against leakage. For many Little Ones, diapers provide a form of emotional security and safety, even if the diaper isn't used to wet in. Some Little Ones wear a diaper for the sense of emotional security and stability that they give. Their anxieties and fears are effectively carried by, or transferred to, the diaper. It is a complex reaction internally, but to the Little One, all that matters is that it makes them feel better.

The diaper also provides *safety* – a safety that is felt very keenly, even if somewhat irrationally. The wearer feels more secure and safer knowing they have a diaper on, but not for protection against wetting, as most Little Ones are actually continent. The protection is *emotional*. This sense of protection is often most keenly experienced in bed, where the Little One may be subconsciously reliving their early childhood fears and traumas.

As the parent, you need to be acutely aware that the diaper has a huge range of secondary purposes and you will probably discover them fairly easily. If you expect your Little One to only wear his diaper for nightly bedwetting or to treat the diaper as a functional object, then you will get a lot of argument from him. Understand that the diaper means far more to him than you understand right now and so please be a little tolerant. The time for restricting things a little comes later.

It is a bit hard to argue with a behaviour that gives comfort, security and happiness to your Little One. The danger here is one of exclusivity. If a Little One can *only* feel safe and secure in the diaper, he has totally transferred these needs to an inanimate object and this will create difficulties later on.

The diaper is the single most important object to the Little One. Many would happily wear them 24/7/365 if able to. Many do that and many more wish to do so. Just be aware of the singular importance and the essential nature of the diaper in your Little One's life. Even in the ages of regression, such as Little Girls (ages 5-12), they still involve diapers to a considerable degree, even if they don't really need them as part of the age-specific behavioural profile. They are quite simply, ubiquitous to the Little One.

Baby/Toddler/Little Girl Clothing:

The normal role of adult-sized baby clothing is for role play (Age Play) and for some, costume parties. For Little Ones however, they are far, far more important and form an integral part of the experience. Domestic limitations usually preclude most Little Ones from having much in the way of baby clothing, but that doesn't stop them from getting at least some of it and dreaming of a closet-full of outfits for every day, night and every desire and whim! Just as in the case of biological children, there is a moderate range of lovely little boy's clothing, but when you get to the girls…

Adult Sized *Little Wear* is available in a vast array of styles, ranging from functional day-to-day infant/toddler wear to special purpose, over-stylised *sissy wear*. Your Little One could probably choose twenty complete outfits to buy in twenty minutes, if given the chance.

The most obvious attachment here is the **Identification Attachment**. We teach adults to 'dress as they want to be' or to 'power-dress' and a variety of other good, but often oversold, concepts. So then, why should we be so surprised that this current generation is infatuated with dressing as the *inner* self? The baby, toddler or Little Girl outfit very clearly identifies who they feel they are deep within. The sheer quantity and variety of adult-sized children's clothing now available underscores the current generation's infatuation with the inner child. The Japanese have an entire Lolita sub-culture, where dressing young is key and then there is the whole infatuation with Hello Kitty, which is essentially suited to five year olds.

If you are aiming to be a good parent, then this is one area to take particular note of. Your Little One's fashion choices will reveal a great deal about them. For instance, if they buy a lot of overly-frilly and impractical outfits, then your child's primary motivation is to feel special and to be noticed. He is also more focussed on the immediate gratification, rather than the longer baby experience. This is common for the Little One, whose opportunities to dress-up are rare and short-lived. He has to cram as much Little experience as possible into a limited amount of time. If your Little One buys more practical outfits with less frills and easier to wash materials, then he wants the Little *existence,* rather than just short-term encounters. What he chooses to buy and wear really does speak volumes about how he feels and views as the age and gender he wants to experience.

I know of one Little Girl aged about eight years old, who bought many pretty yet practical outfits, in the hope that when his wife finally agreed to be his *mother,* then he was all set up with everything she needed to dress him with. It was a false expectation based on hope alone. He had no plan whatsoever.

The efforts many Little Ones put into their clothing choices reveals their inner needs and expectations. Sometimes it can be sad to see so much effort being put into something that the relationship will not support. Make sure your relationship is not like this. As best you can, ensure that expectations for your Little One match reality.

When you are finally confronted by your Little One's clothing collection, keep your opinions to yourself. They may be mismatched, wrong size, inappropriate and even a bit (or a lot) ugly. But when they wear them, the ugly duckling becomes the Princess they want to be. Your option is to get involved and help out. Select outfits for your Little and then help buy better suited ones in the future, or make them yourself.

If you involve yourself in his clothing to a substantial degree, but without condemnation, you will bring your Little One a huge step closer to yourself.

Little One clothing has a secondary purpose of once again providing emotional security and safety. One baby said this:

"Only when I am in my Pooh dress do I feel really normal. With my nappy and dummy and my dress on top I can look in the mirror and not loathe myself. This is who I am. I am a baby girl!" [from email]

Clothing can help to *normalise* a Little One's view of themselves. An adult man may have close to zero interest in clothes, but when the subject is his Little One's clothing, he may have a huge interest in them and when he wears them he feels 'just right'. An inner need has been met and for a brief moment in time, he looks into a mirror and sees the inner child he has known for so long and finally recognises *her* and experiences *normalisation*. There is nothing intrinsically wrong with that. Our personalities are so complex that when we find a safe activity which helps us to feel truly normal and relaxed, even for only a brief moment, then we should embrace it. Life can be tough. Finding a safe haven where we can relax and feel at peace is not something to be quickly demolished.

In summary: Treat your Little One's clothing as an *opportunity* for you to develop the relationship. It is also a chance to build a better wardrobe!

Shoes and Booties:

Brian* is a typical male. He owns three pairs of shoes and complains about shopping for new ones, but in a classic demonstration of the difference between his Little self and his adult self, he will spend hours browsing the web, looking for new Mary Jane girls shoes or to search for more baby booties!

Footwear isn't as important as some other areas, but once again it is still significant, especially to some. Baby Booties can identify that this is a *very young child* and possible a part-time or full-time crawler. If your Little One has multiple ages (refer later), then the choice of footwear is usually age-driven. Wearing shoes may indicate not only that this child is a walker, but also that she may be a 'big girl'. The 'big girl' tag is a relative one. For some, 'big girl' may mean they are in their oldest age and still be only four years old. The *choice* of shoes is also important. It may be a Mary Jane flat or even a version of first walking shoes. A Little Girl may have much older school-type shoes or even experiment with dressing up in older girl's high heel or fashion shoes, just as regular girls that age do.

Shoes and booties *identify* the wearer as a baby, toddler or Little Girl. They can be of crucial importance in identifying age differences for multiple Little Ones. Do not understate their importance, although if you are a woman, I think you already understand the importance of shoes!

The Baby Crib or Cot and other furniture:

Most Little Ones crave the idea of owning their own baby crib (cot) or toddler bed, especially in the context of a fully equipped adult nursery. The bed is where each of us spends one third of our lives and the identification potential of a crib is very significant. Furniture is obviously problematic for most people and especially couples. Other baby accessories can be easily hidden, but a baby crib cannot, unless you have a secret or locked special 'baby room'.

Furniture is probably the least used Attachment Objects by Little Ones, but only because of practicality and cost. The value of such objects to Little Ones is huge. The Crib is probably the most desired, yet difficult-to-obtain object for Little Ones that are aged five and below.

The baby crib is one of those ultimate identifiers of a Little One. The fact that it cannot be hidden ironically adds to its power. Deep inside every Little One is the almost insatiable need to be known, loved and <u>identified</u> as their inner age. If there is one item that your Little One will desperately want, it is the Crib.

Having a crib means that becoming known as a baby by your family and possibly friends will probably happen. The reason most don't have a crib is just that; the line has been crossed in terms of who knows, but for most, a crib is hugely important and desirable and that is understandable. He might not have one, but it doesn't mean he doesn't want one and want it desperately!

"A crib for most people is simply a place to put a baby to sleep in. But for me, it means MUCH more than that. A crib provides a place to sleep, a place to be safe, a place to cuddle stuffed animals, a place to dream, and a way to forget about the world and be transported back to a simpler time.

My crib allows me to sleep soundly – knowing that all around me is softness and safety. No matter where I turn, it holds me securely. The crib keeps me inside so I don't get up and wander around the house or get into trouble. My various stuffed animals help keep me warm and in company. They give me peace and something to hold.

While in my crib, I can dream about having a different life. A simpler life, free of all the stresses and obligations I have outside of it. I can imagine having a caring mom again. Her hands tucking me into bed.

This is what a crib means to me."

[personal email]

Clearly, a crib is an enormous identifier that 'a baby lives here'. The same thing applies to a toddler bed or even a single bed with all the accessories that a five year old girl would have – princess quilt, fairy lights, dolls, toys etc.

Once again, a crib can provide a secondary purpose aspect of providing emotional security and safety. For some who were abused physically and/or sexually as children, the crib can sometimes be a place of very real refuge. While we don't deal with these issues here, you may see that your child's need for a crib is tied to this safety aspect. This need can be extremely strong. If it is, then keep in mind that there may be deep trauma underlying it. For those with some trauma in the past or who frequently feel 'unsafe', a crib can be a very real place of refuge, even surprisingly, for the top age of twelve years old.

If you cannot get a crib – and most can't – then you may consider some other crib options, such as a single bed made up as a crib and even place pillows around it for safety or place the sides of a play pen around it. Another option is to take a large playpen and put a light mattress inside it and make it up as a crib. It is nowhere near as authentic as a genuine crib, *but you can make it so*. Put bumpers and baby toys inside it and most importantly *refer* to it as his crib. Help him to identify with it as a crib and many of the advantages of one will be gained without the obvious problems associated with a permanent crib.

Other nursery furniture includes a change table and a high chair. An adult-sized play pen is quite common and is highly recommended for putting your baby or toddler in one place and keeping them there for specific activities during an extended Little time. It helps them, as well as you, by having a defined place for play. Most play pens are now modular in design meaning it is quite simple to add panels to the sides to make it more than suitable for a larger baby, such as a Little.

The identification attachment of baby furniture is very high which explains why it is on almost every Little One's wish list and appears in so many bedrooms/nurseries.

The dummy/pacifier:

The pacifier or dummy is ubiquitous among Little Ones. Almost all of them have one and most use them much of the time. Little Girls may not use them during the day, but at night will still revert to one automatically, just as a growing number of young children still use a pacifier beyond what used to be the usual age. It is interesting to note that pacifier manufacturers now make a school-age version of their pacifiers, because there is such a strong demand.

The pacifier has exceptionally strong identification attachment and is second only to the diaper in this regard. The modern NUK 5 pacifier is by far the best for adults, as it fits comfortably in the mouth for extended periods of time. The variety of colours and styles available now makes it common for Little Ones to have many pacifiers, depending on their mood.

Do not assume that a pacifier is unimportant. For many it is absolutely pivotal and to others, just part of the scene and no more than an optional extra. For some, a pacifier is just a pacifier and is not an attachment object. For others however, (and this is the majority), it is the key to sleeping, comfort and even for reduction of night-terrors. The pacifier satisfies the sucking urge, but while that is its primary function, its secondary purpose for Little Ones is to make them feel *right*. For most, not having a pacifier in their mouth when in baby mode, makes them feel uncomfortably incomplete.

A baby without a diaper is just wrong. They *all* wear diapers. A baby without a pacifier is just as wrong. Expect your baby to have a pacifier as one of his *essentials*. Don't even try to completely stop him using one. You can and should have rules regarding them, such as when and where, but they are an immutable part of your Little One's needs.

Bras and Lingerie:

Clearly, these items have nothing to do with being a baby, toddler or even Little Girl. However, many Baby Girls wear them despite having no breasts (for men!) and no genuine physical need. Yet it is a relatively common thing for a Baby Girl to be wearing a bra underneath her two-year old baby dress! Obviously for women the reasoning is a different one!

I mentioned previously that the things your baby wears and his actions and behaviours don't have to match those of a biological child of the same age or even their gender. This is perhaps *the* classic example of that.

This behaviour is all about perception; about how your child perceives themself to be. Reality is what stands in the way of perception.

To some Little Ones, the notion of wearing a bra is ridiculous and hopelessly out of place, while at the same time they prance around wearing a toddler dress with booties, sucking a pacifier and claiming to be five years old! But to other Little Ones, the bra fits them perfectly (metaphorically, not literally).

The multi-age Little One can have some ages that do and some that don't. The four-year old may wear a bra, but the two year old does not. He has bra inserts that he wears to pad them out and give some degree of authenticity. One such baby writes as to why *she* wears a bra when *she* is just four years old and lacks breasts.

"When I was growing up I used to wear my mum's bras and my sister's panties and nighties. I loved them. I didn't know why then and I don't know why now really. I just know that when I put on a bra I feel 'special'. I love the feel and some days when I feel older and especially when the older girls show up [she has three older girl ages but they are relatively rare] I feel totally undressed without one.

Sometimes I wear a bra during the day under my street clothes and I feel just remarkable. I feel energised for work, I smile more and I feel like the world is a bit brighter.

I love my bras."

[personal email]

Little Ones will often have girl's panties as well and for many it is the only underwear they ever wear. One put it this way:

"When I am at work and cannot wear my diaper I know I have pink panties on and it connects me to Lilly [her inner baby]. If I wear panties then Lilly is never far away. I'm never alone." [internet forum post]

While it might not make as much sense as some other attachment objects, panties and bras *identify* the wearer as female. The Little One makes the internal contradictory transition to *infant* female. Often the panties are a substitute for the diaper they cannot wear for practical reasons.

The clue for you, the parent, in all of this, is not to expect it to make sense all of the time. Your two-year old might want a bra. Your five-year old might want suspenders and stockings. It all makes sense to *them* and that is enough. The understanding may come later or not at all. It just doesn't matter that much as long as there is a measure of contentment and it is leading towards that place of balance. And balance is the goal out of all of this. Never forget that.

Dolls and Toys:

There is something very special about age-specific toys for Little Ones. Almost all Littles have at least one toy and many have quite a number, and there are never quite enough toys! Just ask any child or Little One! Toys for Little Ones tend to be quite gender-specific and in fact, more specific than for biological children. A physically male Little One who regresses to a baby girl will almost certainly favour dolls and pink toys such as doll-houses, tea sets and Barbie-style paraphernalia than the more generic fare.

There is a very strong Identification Aspect in toys and play. The choice of toys and the method of play very strongly identifies the Little One as a child, but more than most attachment objects, dolls and toys are *very* specific in both age and gender.

Your Little One's attachment to dolls and toys may be peripheral and not much more than just a prop or it may be a very large part of his experience of regression. Playtimes, in which dolls and toys are pivotal, are a very important element of regression. Regressing to a certain age is one thing, but what do you do when you get there? You play, of course! And to play properly, you need toys – lots of them. Once you begin the Parent/Child relationship, you are likely to be overwhelmed with his requests for toys. This is one area that many little Ones cut back on for fear of discovery, and when the relationship commences, it exerts itself with considerable force. You will need to get a good array of toys, but you will almost certainly need to curtail his requests for more and more.

Transference to an Attachment Object:

I alluded previously to how some Littles can 'transfer' an emotion or feeling to an object. This is not dissimilar to how very young children behave, such as when a child cannot sleep without a particular teddy bear. That child may believe that the teddy bear literally provides safety and companionship. As young children, that is acceptable and they eventually transition to older toys and finally to emotional maturity. Some Little Ones are not as internally mature as to have fully made that transition along the road to adulthood. This is often part of the reason behind emotional immaturity in Little Ones.

I think it is fairly obvious that for regressive Little Ones, somewhere on the path to growing up, some aspects still remain firmly rooted back in childhood. When you have a regressed Little One, you may notice that they *literally* feel safer or more secure when cuddling a specific toy. It is not an act or a role play or even just a habit, but rather where the Little One has *transferred* feelings of safety and security to an object.

This transfer is normally a partial transfer only and while it can be disconcerting to a parent, it is still acceptable. A Little One may be terrified of thunder and lightning, but if a bonnet is put on and a select group of toys given, the fear is countered. These objects have been granted a status by the Little One of 'protector'.

A Little One may experience genuine fear and insecurity which no amount of talking will reduce, yet if you place them in a crib it instantly evaporates. *Safety and security* has been transferred to the crib. Keep in mind however, that as adults we also employ transference to a degree. We may for example, feel safe in a particular place such as our homes and experience low-level anxiety or discomfort when not there and have therefore transferred *safety* to the home.

In most adults, this transference is low-level and generally trivial because we transitioned throughout childhood reasonably effectively and didn't leave any emotions and feelings still attached to objects as we matured. In some Little Ones however, this is not so and causes an otherwise still functional adult to *need* a teddy bear at night or to require a nightlight. These attachments can be broken in time, if the Parent/Child relationship is providing the emotional support and security that allows the Little to transition beyond those childhood attachments.

There are more extreme examples, such as one where a Little One who had been sexually abused as a child sometimes regressed to an age where they re-experienced some of the trauma of the abuse. As a child at the time, they learned that if they soiled their diaper, the abuse was unlikely to happen. Now as a regressed adult, they soil their diaper just to feel safe, even though the original danger and abuse no longer exists. The dirty diaper was a behaviour they still employed as a general safety mechanism. Because this transference still existed, it was not easy to modify the soiling behaviour, but in time, was eventually reduced. Issues such as childhood abuse are not covered in this book and they certainly can be very traumatic and I do not wish to trivialise them.

Transference to some degree or other is part and parcel of the Little One's existence. When we discussed Attachment Objects, I mentioned secondary purpose aspect, and for many of these objects, this is where the Little One has transferred an emotion to the object. Its secondary purpose aspect is comfort or security or protection etcetera.

Transference of emotions and feelings only becomes a real problem when the transference is *total or near-total,* i.e. the feeling and emotion exists almost solely in the object. For example, if a Little One is only ever safe when cuddling a particular toy inside or outside of regression, then there is a problem. For most however, it is just another aspect of a Little's behaviour that can be awkward and sometimes limiting, but is not really dysfunctional.

Summary:

Attachment objects can be found throughout the Little One's lifestyle. It is essential that you come to grips with the concept as well as some of the specifics. Very few items in the Little One's universe are simply what they appear to be. Most of them have significant identification and secondary purpose attachment and it can be enormously helpful to understand that. It just makes some of the Little One's seemingly peculiar needs and wants, just that little bit more tolerable. The more you understand them, the easier they are to deal with. Once you are dealing with them, you can then learn to use these special aspects of these objects to your advantage in developing the Parent/Child relationship. I cover this in the Interaction and Modification sections.

SECTION THREE – IDENTIFICATION

Now that you have a bit more information about the wide and varied world of Adult Babies and Little Ones, the next step is to discover exactly what kind of baby or toddler that *you* have in your relationship. The number of variations available for Little Ones is so large that you need to find out about *your* baby specifically.

You cannot hope to have a good Parent/Child relationship if you don't know who he is or what are his likes and dislikes. You need to identify his needs and wants and how to communicate with him at his particular level.

There are two levels for getting to know your Little One. The first is the adult self, telling you about his Little side. The other is the Little One telling you directly about himself. Experience tells me that the Little One is more honest, but less able to articulate the facts, while the adult is more able to explain, but less likely to do so from the kind of embarrassment that a Little One is less likely to feel.

Things that you need to discover are:

- Your baby's gender: male, female, sissy or indeterminate.

- Your baby's self-identified age: how old they *think* they are.

- Your baby's actual regressive age(s) based on behaviours compared to other children.

- Play preferences: blocks, soft toys, dolls, colouring books etcetera.

- Clothing preferences: modern baby/toddler, traditional baby/toddler, older child.

- Walking or crawling or both (and when).

- Pacifier or thumb (or both).

- Feeding and drinking. Does he use or want a bottle or sippy cup. Does he want baby foods or formula?

- Does he masturbate as an infant/toddler or as an adult and how often. It's embarrassing, but necessary to be informed on this. These actions can affect the rest of the Little's behaviours and experiences.

- State of continence. Does your baby wet his diaper and/or soil it? Yes, you do need to know this, as it is crucial. How continent is he at every regressive level (and age if appropriate). Do not assume that your Little One is toilet trained at all stages and ages.

It is not too hard to find out all these things if you use the following basic skills:

- **Observation**. Keep your eyes open and look at what he does. Monitor his behaviour and simply watch and learn. Little Ones might think that they are sneaky and good at hiding things, but that's only because most people don't understand or recognise what they see, when they see it.

- **Investigation**. Don't just sit around and wait for your child to reveal himself. Take some pre-emptive steps. If you know where your baby keeps his clothes, diapers and accessories, then look through them. It isn't prying when you are seeking to help him and to build the relationship. If you are developing a Parent/Child relationship, then it is reasonable to check out your child's *things*. Find out what he has and refer to the chapter on Attachment Objects to help you understand what you find.

- **Intuition**. You are a clever and intuitive parent. Armed with the information you have just read about Little Ones, you can start to *intuit* some of the things he does. Watch what he does, listen to the things he says and use your intuition and experience to learn more about your child. You will be right far more often than you will be wrong!

Basics of Identification

Discover their Gender:

This might seem like an odd topic, but it isn't and it is perhaps the single most important identifying feature of your Little One. Do not assume that your child's gender is the same as his physical gender. Like so many other things in the Little One's world, it can be very, very different from the adult world.

As you can imagine, gender is the top identifying factor for a child and is for a Little One as well. You will occasionally hear people say boys and girls are identical until they are about five years old. If you have a book that says that, then throw it away, as it is absolute rubbish. Gender is quite obvious very early on in a infant's life.

Gender is normally connected to physiology, but in the case of a Little One far less so. Existence of a penis in no way means your Little One is male. In fact, around half of physically male Adult Babies and Little Ones identify as female infant/toddler, indeterminate or sissy.

The 'sissy' gender is a controversial one. The word seems a bit offensive and perhaps it is, but it has become a very commonly used term. You will see that while some Little Ones regress to a girl using typical girl's things, some however, regress to a far more stylised, over-the-top expression of femininity that is not really quite like a girl, but more the extreme *image* of the girl. There are the rows and rows of lace and frills and the excessively infant or feminine designs. 'Sissy' and 'girl' are quite similar and when determining your Little One's gender, keep in mind the *sissy* option. It is a subset of the female gender, but for simplicity, I have used it as a separate one.

Fortunately, your Little One's gender will be extremely obvious, even if he thinks he is hiding it. If he chooses pink plastic pants and pink pins and secretly (or openly) wears panties and bras then he is a girl baby, but generally, if you watch your baby, you will easily see their gender. I'd be surprised if you don't already know what it is, even if you are in denial. And denial is nothing to be ashamed of, since most of us practise it on a regular basis! The problem only occurs if you *stay* in denial. Your Little's wardrobe will tell you a great deal about them including their gender. You have gone through it by now, haven't you?

This gender confusion is normally just in males, but it is not unknown in females. Just keep an open mind until you are sure. An obvious question is *'is this just cross-dressing'*? Well, the answer is both yes and no!

It is cross-dressing in the classic sense and it is distinctly likely that the adult self enjoys some women's clothes, but cross-dressing isn't true gender confusion. It is little more than role-play or enjoying the crossing of gender boundaries. There may be some wishful thinking about having some female gender experience, but it is rarely more than that. Trans-sexuals however *do* wish to change gender. That is not what is at play here.

The answer to the question is also 'no', in that it is not *just* cross-dressing. It is far more than that. You will quickly see that it is far more than just clothing at issue. He wants girl's books, toys, pacifiers and movies. Yet as an adult, he wants to watch sport, wear jeans and drink beer from a tall glass. It can look confusing for a while until you realise that the Little One can be, and usually is, *very different* from the Big adult. Why should gender be any different?

You may feel rejection watching your husband act as a Baby Girl, even after you begin working together as a Parent/Child. This can be hard one to deal with at first and even more so to try and understand. Your husband can be happily male and heterosexual, yet your Little One is female or sissy. The co-existence of the two seems awkward, except that it actually works. Unfortunately, this problem is yours and yours alone and you have to work on it. To be honest, only time truly resolves this one to any satisfaction, as you see your adult male thrive just as the female infant/toddler thrives. Keep an open and uncritical mind for as long as you can and in time you will see that he is still the man you love, as well as the Toddler Girl you now also need to get to know and love.

Give it time. Don't dwell on the hurt and confusion too much as clarity and assurance *will* come. Remember that the rejection you feel now is the flip-side of the rejection he feels and has felt probably all his life, to some degree. Also, both of you shouldn't blame each other for a situation that neither of you asked for. The rejection comes of its own accord, but it also disappears if you show commitment to the relationship and to understanding the unique dynamic of the Parent and Child. When balance comes – and it will – much of this frustration and embarrassment you currently feel will evaporate.

Your first job is to identify and confirm the gender. Make sure you do it carefully and accurately. One missing option here is 'indeterminate'. Children's clothes and toys can be gender neutral, now more so than ever before. Typically, Little Ones use very obvious gender-specific clothes and toys, as if to clearly shout out who they are. A few however, don't really show a gender preference and seemingly don't really care. These are also the group that are typically totally non-sexual in their Little play. Sexuality and sexual drives will definitely cause a Little One to reveal their gender.

Discover their self-identified age:

The very essence of regression is to move to a lower age. It is therefore absolutely critical that you know your child's self-identified age. Most Little Ones know their age and are almost invariably wrong. Or are they?

Based on typical infant/toddler/child behaviours, most Little Ones guess their inner age wrongly. However, that doesn't really matter. If they think they are three years old yet still crawl, then that is acceptable, even though that is atypical behaviour for that age child. They are three years old by the only measuring stick that really matters – theirs. You need to know what age your baby *self-identifies* as, not what you *think* they are.

Your baby's self-determined age will probably not change much over time, if at all. Some of the behaviours might mature or regress, but his self-image will probably remain fairly constant at the age he chose a long time ago. For the regressive Little One, he probably chose this age as a child himself, so it might not be very accurate. In addition, most Little Ones have a range of behaviours that cover a wide array of ages anyhow. They choose an age that feels right even though it isn't really. A variation on this is 'multiple Little Ones', all of whom have a separate age [*refer the following for more details*].

There are however, a small number of Little Ones that grow up (after a fashion), from one age to another, but do not take hold of this as some kind of lifejacket! It is rare and in any case, the age might change from a diapered three year old, up to a diapered seven year old. Your problem doesn't go away. It only morphs to a different age and then he needs new clothes and toys!

Discover how many Little Ones there are:

This question comes up more often than you think, but don't freak out over this. Your Little One may actually be more than one! Of course, that is not actually true at all, or anything even remotely close. As previously mentioned, Little One's behaviours often span the range from a few years, up to as many as ten years. To cope with this disparity, some Littles pseudo-create separate identities and assign behaviours and objects to each.

NOTE: This is not to be confused with genuine dissociative disorders (or multiple personality). If your baby shows dissociative behaviour then he <u>must</u> be taken to professional help.

For example, a Little might have behaviours ranging from ages twelve months up to eight years old. In this case, they may separate into one, three, five and eight year old identities and have different names for each. They may have separate clothing preferences, toys and other objects. Their behaviours might range from a non-walking, baby-talking one year old, to an eight year old with all the abilities and more of a typical child that age. This is not to be feared, although at first it might sound literally crazy. Instead, this is the way that a highly intelligent and creative adult handles the obvious disparities between behaviours and ages in their regressed state. They create multiple pseudo-identities that can act out the various behaviours they want and need. It is more like trying to create some logic and consistency in a behaviour that has very little.

The problem for you, as the parent, is that you now need to know the differences between them and to learn how to identify them. Depending on the level of regression and the creativity of the adult, these identities can be quite different from each other. For example, one Little One has a one year old that is left-handed, while all other identities and the adult are right-handed! As any parent knows, this is common for very young children who have not yet found their dominant hand.

While we know that there is not a genuinely separate set of personalities, in the mind of a Little One however, several different age children may 'exist'. They are not real personalities however, but represent no more than *stages* in the Little One's regression or development.

I cannot over-emphasise the need to know your different inner children and to identify them uniquely. This is not as hard as it seems, as the Little One himself will behave in an obvious manner to let you know. One typical test is the use of colouring-in sheets. A two year old will colour very differently to a seven year old. Speech is also an excellent indicator as well. For example, a two year old may use baby talk, the four year old stammer and the seven year old be reasonably articulate, yet they all exist within the same Little One.

The different ages might give the impression that the adult you know and love isn't there. He is, but he is putting his adult nature well into the background and allowing the Little behaviours to have the foreground.

Never forget that the adult is never gone!

Discover their name(s):

Of all the failures of Parent/Child relationships, this is one of the worst: failure or refusal to use your Little One's baby name(s).

We all strongly identify with our own name as infants and for the remainder of our lives, we highly respect people who use our name and remember it. If you don't know your Little One's name, then find out! Usually, they are quite willing to tell you, with the only exception being the very young baby of six months or younger. Part of the personality profile of the very young, is limited to no communication. One parent of a baby aged six months *gave* him a name, as his 'parent', because he didn't already have one. Personally, I find the sub-twelve months old age difficult to work with, due to the poor communication and limited abilities. Generally, a Little One should be at least one year old, to enable a functional relationship to work. However, I have also seen that extreme distress can cause a Little One to regress to sub twelve months. Treat this carefully. It should not happen too often or it can be indicative of a serious trauma that may require professional attention. If your Little One does regress to a very young age of six months or so, nurture him carefully and subtly try and raise their age some. If it happens a lot, you will need to investigate why.

If you want to cement a relationship with your baby, then use their name often and pointedly. If you won't use their name, then you will probably torpedo the Parent/Child relationship before it gets started.

Beware the non-speaking child!

Speech is one of the better indicators of mental health and we need to watch over it well. Most six month old Little Ones *cannot* speak, but nor can he do much of anything else either, so that is not overly worrying, as it is part of a normal behavioural profile. (I discuss behavioural profiles later on). But if older Little Ones are or become non-verbal, then it is a sign of inner distress, just as it is with a regular child. This is something that should be taken notice of and not ignored.

The Little One is simply unprepared to speak, not incapable of it.

This phenomenon is not rare. If it happens to your child, then you need to look at the stressors that might be causing it. When you begin your Parent/Child relationship, it might still happen from time to time. The best method to overcoming this is to immediately revert him to the youngest state you can. Then *baby* him for a short period and let the speech return slowly, as the regression eases. You will find your own way. Just don't ignore it.

A bottle or breast feeding is often ideal for helping to calm him down enough to get him back on track and to find his way again. In all of the Parent/Child relationship, this aspect is one of the few that are simply *not* acceptable. Becoming non-verbal outside of an age-appropriate regression is something that needs to be addressed. Usually, the parent can resolve it with an abundance of love, care and acceptance.

DONT GET SCARED! Sometimes ignorance is bliss, but actually it only <u>seems</u> like bliss. It is still just ignorance. Some of the above may seem scary, but it isn't really. Most of the warnings I've given will never be experienced, but I need to be honest, just the same. The reality is that the Parent/Child relationship has much to offer, including an unconditional love that so many adult-adult relationships don't have. You have much to gain, but you also have much to lose if you ignore it. The choice remains essentially yours, the parent.

Pants-wetting:

Another of the major behaviours, pants-wetting is the next step up from bedwetting in the journey of a Little One to where he wishes to go. Genuine medical bedwetting in adults is reasonably common. Pants-wetting however, is not. Deliberate pants-wetting in children is identified as a social and/or mental disorder, whose roots usually lie in an area other than their bladder.

If your Little One is wetting their pants, then you need to take serious notice.

Pants-wetting is a cry to be noticed; to be taken seriously. Wet pants are considered <u>good</u>, not <u>bad</u>. It is an external validation of the inner belief that "I am not toilet trained" and/or "I am a baby".

A Little One will probably not seek treatment, for fear of breaking the illusion or of ending the wet pants. Neither is acceptable to him.

Does your partner do any of the following:

- Wet their pants during the day, but conveniently in *safe* locations, such as the car, home, walks near home or somewhere where *you* can notice, but no one else?

- Hide their wet pants from you?

- Tell you all the details of their pants-wetting, as opposed to simply informing you of an accident, as an adult would do.

- Soil their pants?

- Not wash their wet things, but allow them to air dry?

- Refuse a medical assessment of their condition?

Pants-wetting is obviously dealt with by wearing day diapers or pads, which may be just what your Little One wants, but in many cases, it is a lot more than just that.

Your Little One wants to be noticed.

He wants to be supported, assisted and loved, as a mother would love a child who has had an accident. A diaper hides the evidence of their childishness. Another common feature of diaper-protected pants-wetting is leaving the evidence (wet or even soiled diaper), openly visible at home, so that the partner is not unaware of what has happened. Some Littles will rarely throw their used diapers out without being forced to. They either secretly keep them as *trophies* (note: look for secret stashes of used trophy diapers) or left visible to you or others. Your child is proud of his wet pants and of his wet diapers. He is hoping you will be too and compliment him on it.

The pants-wetting may be deliberate or it may be more a case of the baby being *unwilling* to exercise the control necessary to remain dry. In both cases, it is overly simplistic to call it purely deliberate wetting, as many pressures and needs are at play.

EXPERIMENT: When your baby next wets his pants, make a big deal about it. Fuss over him like you would a child. Tell him it is okay and that you don't mind it and that it is just normal. Watch his reaction and especially see if there is an increase in wet pants. If you are game to try, set up a large bag for his wet disposable diapers and allow him to throw them out when and if, he is ready. See how long he will keep his trophies.

Pants-wetting is a behaviour that occurs frequently for Little Ones who are having major difficulty in keeping their regression under wraps and under control. If your partner is at this stage now, then he will soon be unable to hide his Little nature from you. If he is pants-wetting already, then be developing for the next step: childish behaviour.

Childish behaviours:

Some women would suggest that *all* men act like children! The behaviours I am looking at however, are far more obviously and definitionally *childish*. When the internal pressure builds up, a Little One may find it increasingly hard to maintain their adult facade. This leads to leakage (refer to Behavioural Leakage in the Information Section). Childish behaviours, needs and actions then begin to leak into the adult world. The adult will be increasingly unable to control the leakage or sometimes, to even recognise it. At this stage, the Little One is nearly ready to emerge openly, whether either of you are ready or not! You need to look for some of these behaviours and to identify them early on to be fore-warned.

Most experienced parents can tell the age of their Little just by watching how they sit and lay down. A toddler and young child will often lie in the foetal position. An infant might sleep up on all fours. If your partner does any of this, then it is also a clue to getting into his head.

Does your Little One:

- Sleep in infant or toddler positions?

- Suck his thumb unconsciously?

- Rub himself in a form of infantile masturbation, often while unaware of it. Often this is shown by hands inside the diaper or underwear, even while watching TV or eating or sleeping?

- Crawl on hands and knees when you are not around? Crawling is a purely infant activity and a lot of Little Ones don't crawl unless they view themselves as three years old or younger. Many do crawl however, and it brings its own internal emotional and self-identification rewards for them. It is hard to catch them at it usually, unless you already know about it. Red marks/abrasions on the knees are a clue, as is unusual wear on trousers or jeans just beneath the knees. If your partner is crawling, then you have to deal with it and not ignore it. It is a high-level infant activity and needs to be addressed. I deal with crawling separately later on.

- Look at children's toys with more than passing curiosity, or perhaps even play with some of them, when he doesn't think anyone notices?

An example of leakage comes from one parent whose Little One was at a biological child's birthday party. He began to colour in the children's pages which had been given to most of the pre-schoolers in attendance. He drifted into a child-mode (Level one regression) and began to colour in the entire page, before his wife took it away from him. Both adults were embarrassed by the action, but it occurred because of behavioural leakage due to internal pressure. Because there was no Parent/ Child relationship in place, there were no pre-determined procedures to deal with this kind of action.

Look out for these leaking behaviours. They may *look* a lot like the typical juvenile actions that most adults display at times, but the difference becomes quickly obvious. Be aware and primarily recognise that if your Little One has not yet 'come out', then he certainly will before long.

Boundary issues:

Babies and toddlers don't naturally have boundaries to their behaviours. They are not born with many boundaries at all and instead, learn them as they go along.

Little Ones have a particularly bad habit of not having good and proper boundaries in some areas of their lives, but not all areas. Their behaviour is sometimes inappropriate and worse, they don't always know why it is so, or why they do it in the first place. A Little One may not really understand why you object to him wearing his diapers openly outside the house, or even wearing his baby clothes where he could be seen by others. He might *say* he understands, but deep inside, he doesn't really. He just knows you object to diapers outside and yet will use his pacifier outside without understanding the principle involved. As you can see, it is quite typical childish behaviour.

This problem does not just apply to the Little One. It can also affect the adult, as the infantile thinking patterns from the Little One leaks into and sometimes dominates the normal adult thinking, which would put natural boundaries in place. It is not exhibitionism per se (which is covered next) or even bad behaviour, but rather an inability to fully understand appropriateness, limitations and boundaries.

How does this happen? Well, the answer is simple. **It has probably always been so**. It is as if a part of the learning process on boundaries and behaviours that most of us learn when growing up, just doesn't properly take root in the Little One. If you ask other family or friends (assuming that is possible) about your partner's younger days, you will probably discover that they have *always* had some boundary issues, even as children. This can sometimes lead to serious consequences, if the boundaries are social or legal ones and the Little One breaks them.

Sometimes boundary issues are life-long aspects of your adult partner's behaviour, but in other cases, the boundary issues are a new an evolving problem. This is yet another symptom of behavioural leakage, where the internal pressure on the Little One spills over and affects the adult, by reducing or removing boundaries that would normally be there.

This is a typical behavioural problem for many Little Ones. Be aware that your child may simply *not truly understand* the boundaries and the consequences of some actions. This may be inconceivable to you if you find that your Little One has high intelligence and advanced social skills. It is unfortunate that one significant aspect of regressive behaviour is poor boundaries in *some* behaviours and yet not in others.

A primary role of a care-giver is to help teach and re-establish boundaries and to enforce them, just as you would with a toddler. More on how to do this later.

Exhibitionism:

Seemingly in-bred in the Little One is a good dose of exhibitionism. Or is it really?

Many Little Ones show off their inner infant/toddler nature to a partner or friends, usually in highly inappropriate ways and times. Rather than being classical exhibitionism, which could be considered abnormal or even deviant, it is instead a significant cry for acknowledgment and acceptance, which is the one thing Little Ones lack from almost every partner. It is not just mere intellectual assent to your Little One's existence that he wants. Don't consider that your mere tolerance of Little behaviour as something overly impressive to him. Your child doesn't want just tolerance; he wants acceptance and certainly a degree of interaction with you.

Exhibitionism is driven by the insatiable need within a Little One to be truly accepted, acknowledged and seen for who he is.

Society doesn't acknowledge regressive Littles and won't for some time. Only you and perhaps his family, can ever truly accept a Little One. Let's look at a few exhibitionist-like behaviours. Does your child do any of the following?

- Leave his wet bed or diapers out in plain view, hoping to be seen?

- Leave his baby clothes in easily found places or in plain view?

- Wear unnecessarily thick diapers, so that they can be seen, yet not seen?

- Crawl where he might be caught doing so?

- Watch children's TV or read toddler-age books where he might be seen?

- Masturbate at times and places where you could catch him?

- Other risky behaviour?

Exhibitionism can be a very real problem and plain dangerous when not under control. The best way of dealing with it is to deal with the inner driving need which is quite simply, *acknowledgement*. When you accept your Little One's existence, you start the process of reducing the exhibitionist drive, but it is not enough to do just that alone. You must also interact with him at a significant level and allow him to be seen by you as a Little. As part of a working Parent/Child relationship, you will interact with your child in multiple ways. It is the best defence against exhibitionist behaviour. I discuss this in depth in the Interaction Section.

Poor Self-control:

We all suffer from self-control problems to some degree or other and it is similar to boundary issues. I have however, noticed that self-control can be exceptionally poor in many Little Ones and sometimes to such an extent, that it has a seriously debilitating effect on their lives and outcomes. Let's look at some of these typical self-control behaviours.

Does your child do any of the following?

- Get unnecessarily angry, at times, and yet at other times have no worries?

- Does he swear when it is not his true nature?

- Get overly and inappropriately frustrated, but only at certain times?

- Masturbate to excess?

- Look at pornography? I don't mean like most men, but compulsively and excessively?

- Have impulse control problems: spending, gambling, drinking, extreme behaviours?

- Have spending problems, either as extreme over-spending or refusal to spend on anything, other than his Little items?

Some of the above might just look like a typical adult having a bad day, and on its own that's probably all it is. But when you combine it with the other behaviours that have been listed, it is just more evidence of the existence of the Little One inside your partner.

Secrecy:

We all love our secrets and privacy. The right to our own secrets is a fundamental part of how our society and our relationships work effectively, but secrecy can become a problem, when it becomes excessive.

Many Littles hide their diapers, panties, bras, pacifiers, dolls, dresses and all manner of things from their partner for fear of their reaction. If you are like most partners though, you probably have some idea what is going on, if not the complete details.

If you are serious about being a proper Parent to your Little One, then you need to deal with secrets, as a matter of some priority. Get them out in the open as soon as you can. You can start by looking at your Little One's stash of items – privately. Don't be ignorant of your child's secret life any more than you would with your biological child's drug addiction. Knowledge and openness are important concepts for you *both* to develop.

Use discretion, wisdom and intelligence, but break the cycle of extreme secrecy that you probably both still maintain over this issue. An effective, working and satisfactory Parent/Child relationship will founder, if secrets are allowed to grow and develop and to overwhelm the mutual trust that is essential to making it work.

Continence and your Little One

Since diapers are an integral part of regression, we need to discuss continence and toilet training and how it applies to your partner.

It seems that almost all regressive Little Ones have a degree of continence dysfunction, ranging from occasional wet bed/pants, right through to total loss of bladder and bowel control. This dysfunction can be either physical or psychological or a combination of both.

In children, there is acknowledgment that some wet and soil themselves semi-deliberately for a variety of reasons (enuresis/encopresis). Your Little One may be wetting and soiling for similar reasons. These can be stress, immaturity or social/psychological disorders.

A Little One however, is more likely to deliberately wet and soil their diaper, because it is in keeping with their inner age and the regression they are building on and seeking to enhance. They are seeking to use the wet and soiled diaper as an *identification* of their infancy. The problem then develops that, because the inner child is never really shut down, the Little exerts some influence (behavioural leakage) over the adult's behaviour, which can lead to adult wet beds and pants.

Your adult may be fully continent, but your Little One may not be so.
All you get to see however, is <u>adult</u> wet beds and pants.

There is also 'situational incontinence'(SI), where a normally fully or mostly continent adult becomes *incontinent* in a particular situation, such as when becoming a Little One. It is a common experience for many Adult Babies to experience semi-automatic loss of bladder and even bowel control, but *only* when diapered and without there being any regression involved. This is primarily a conditioned response, where the mere wearing of a diaper triggers incontinence.

Some other conditioned responses can be for an un-diapered Little One to wet the bed in their sleep, but only in a protected bed. For some, simply using a pacifier – even as an adult – can trigger some incontinence or bedwetting. These conditioned responses can get out of hand, if there are too many of them and they interfere with life. I refer later to a related topic of letting some of the Little behaviours, such as diapers and pacifiers, play out in the adult, as well as Little realms. This helps reduce the power of some of these conditioned responses.

Many Little Ones experience something like situational incontinence and often, extensively. This form of incontinence is psychological, but not necessarily a dysfunction. SI will cause a Little (or adult) to become effectively incontinent when wearing a diaper, but usually not when unprotected. This is not necessarily a bad thing. For example, adults who are already struggling with continence issues will typically become much more incontinent when reverting to full-time diaper use, even those where there is no regression anywhere in their personality. It is also a feature of young children who wet their bed at home in their protected safe, accepting environment, but won't wet at camp or sleepovers, yet will wet again when back home.

SI fits within the role a Diaper Lover (DL) is playing and is most certainly a typical regressed infant/toddler behaviour. Because it occurs within the confines of a diaper, and the Little One normally wears one anyhow, it has little adverse effect on behaviour. It is important to understand that your Little One's wet diaper is legitimate, if SI is involved.

Some adults actually never truly wet their bed themselves, but during the night, the emerging Little One comes to the fore and wets, just as any other young child. As absurd as that may sound, it can actually be quite true and if you think about it carefully, it may exactly match the behaviours you are seeing.

It is also true that some adults were never really properly toilet trained. Sure, they managed dry pants and mainly dry beds, but not like most children or adults have. You and I don't have to *try* to stay dry. We just *are*. Some people spend all their lives constantly trying to stay dry. If they don't regularly think about it, wet beds or pants ensue. It simply isn't part of their training to be automatically dry. This is not that dissimilar to a recently toilet-trained child who has frequent failures, as continence is not yet an automatic or autonomic behaviour. There is some conjecture that traumatic toilet training may in fact sow the seeds for regression later on. That is certainly interesting, but not of much practical help to us at this point. We are more fixated here on *solutions,* rather than the reasons behind it.

One male Little One I know is 'functionally incontinent'. He has no significant physical reasons why he cannot be dry, but his inner children are always there making it hard for him to remain so and the pressure to remain dry became intolerable. Moving him to diapers fulltime eliminated the stress of this conflict, as well as the accidents, but effectively put the Littles in charge of his bladder function. He now needs diapers all the time. The trade-off however, was that a far less stressed adult ensued. This may be a question you will also face: the trade-off of an incontinent, fully diapered partner, but a happier one. Don't jump into it, but don't reject it either as part of the future. Sometimes the decision ends up being made for you, anyhow. Later on in the book, I discuss pre-emptive measures you can take to help reduce the worst elements of regression. Diaper wearing is one of those possible measures.

Statistics show that 11% of Adult Babies and Little Ones [Bittergrey] report severe incontinence at around three times the national average. Part of the reason of course, is that some become Adult Babies or Little Ones, as a *result* of their early experiences with bed wetting and childhood incontinence. And for others, simply being Adult Baby or a regressive Little One *causes* the incontinence.

An interesting study by Robert Pretlow MD (USA) determined that infantilism and diaper fetishism were both *common and legitimate causes of incontinence* and bedwetting. He determined that:

> *"...preliminary results... indicate that more than 50% of children and teenagers wet on purpose to justify wearing diapers...*
>
> *In light of our questionnaire results and the fact that emotional attraction to diapers and diaper fetish appear to be quite prevalent on the Internet, it can be argued that these behaviours are a significant cause of enuresis and incontinence. Emotional attraction to diapers and diaper fetish should, therefore, be included in the differential diagnoses of enuresis and incontinence."*
>
> *[http://www.mednet2002.org/abstracts/display.cfm?id=166472151]*

What is being said in effect, is that incontinence can be quite legitimate, yet its cause is not physical, but rather psychological and in this case, that regression or fetishism is the underlying cause. What is important about this medically supported conclusion, is that your Little One could quite easily be incontinent, simply as a result of the extent of his regression. It has already been discovered through surveys, that the rate of *severe* incontinence in Littles is several times that of the adult population.

This is part of the reason why some Littles choose to become incontinent. It is a big decision and is almost always the wrong one. Some Littles think that becoming incontinent is a worthy goal in its own right, whereas it isn't that at all.

Achieving *balance* between the adult and Little One is the ultimate goal. Incontinence may be one of the tools or one of the consequences, but it is never the goal.

Summary:

In short, continence is going to be an issue – a big one. It may not be so at the start of your Parent/Child relationship, but it will no doubt become so later on. Every Little One is very susceptible to becoming incontinent and it may even be a positive experience for them. With the plethora of discreet and effective adult diapers, incontinence is no longer a life-limiting problem. There are literally hundreds of disabilities far worse than incontinence. If it helps bring balance and peace to your Little One, then it may be worth it.

Building a Behavioural Profile of your Little One

I wrote earlier that you probably have a fairly poor understanding of your Little One's actual behaviours, because most of them have remained hidden for so long. As the Parent/Child relationship develops, you will learn much more about them. At this point, it can be very helpful to begin to build a Behavioural Profile of your Little One. This is nothing more complex than a simple a list of the various behaviours and aspects of your Little One in tabular form.

Over time, you will add to it and change it, as some behaviours increase, other decrease and some are eliminated altogether. It may be worth saving the profiles and creating a new one every little while (six months or year), to see how your Little One changes or, just as likely, you get to understand him better. As the Little One is given new room to move and grow in the relationship, some new behaviours may also develop as well. This profile worksheet can be an invaluable form of record keeping on how things are changing or developing. This is a critical activity for multiple ages, and you should have a separate profile for each one to record the differences between them.

I don't recommend that you share this profile with your Little One initially. They may be surprised and even offended by some of your assessments of them. In time, you will both come to a closer understanding of who your child is. The process of researching and writing down the behavioural profile is crucial to helping you develop a more complete understanding of your child.

The things your profile will contain are:

- Child's self-identified age.

- Child's true age, according to behaviours (as you see them).

- Child's gender.

- Child's name(s).

- Speech status: non-verbal, basic baby talk, child speech or adult speech.

- Walking status: non-moving, crawling only, crawling/walking, fully walking.

- Feeding status: bottle, sippy cup, formula, baby foods.

- Regressed continence level: bladder, bowel, only in diapers etcetera.

- Current bedwetting status and attraction to wet beds.

- Extent of masturbation (use your own scale).

- A list of unacceptable behaviours and comments on each.

- A list of acceptable Little behaviours and comments on each.

- A list of behaviours you want to see changed or removed.

- A list of behaviours you want to see added.

- Special atypical Little behaviours (e.g. ability to communicate at adult level via writing).

- Fundamental Objects/Behaviours (see next section).

- Important Objects/Behaviours (see next section).

- Peripheral Objects/Behaviours (see next section).

Other things you should also do, is to catalogue all of his baby/toddler belongings from clothes, diapers, panties, toys books etcetera. You may find it interesting over time to see what items are added to his collection and which are dispensed with.

The Behavioural Profile is primarily about encouraging the parent to understand the child and their behaviour and needs. Writing it down in a formal way encourages you to do this and to understand it better.

Discovering the Fundamentals:

No biological child exists solely in a world of special fun events and play times. Their life is composed of sleep, food and a variety of regular, even mundane, every day activities. Your Little One is about to discover that his new relationship is going to involve some regular, repeated and even predictable Little activities. These things provide the *core* to the new relationship. Let's look at some examples of what that might mean.

Not every behaviour that your Little has is a *fundamental* one. Some are absolute essential building blocks of regression. Others may be *important* while others are simply *peripheral* extras and props, built upon the essential regressive foundation. What we are looking to do now, is to discover what is truly *fundamental* – and therefore non-negotiable – in his Little experience.

I will start with an obvious essential: diapers. There is no point in pretending that diapers aren't a fundamental behaviour and object in your Little One's regression, so don't even try and negotiate diapers out of the equation! That doesn't mean however, that you can't negotiate around the edges of it. For example, dirty diapers are, for most, an optional extra, which can be inappropriate and unpleasant for others and could be negotiated away. Don't assume however, that you know yet what is fundamental to them. For some, a dirty diaper may be a *fundamental* behaviour, without which, the Parent/Child relationship becomes problematic. Fortunately, that isn't true for most, for whom a dirty diaper is just an important or peripheral extra.

I mentioned earlier that the fundamentals of your Little One are non-negotiable. That sounds unfair, but what I mean is that you don't really have the option of eliminating it from regression. For regression to be successful, it has to be there. This may change in the future, but for right now, it is a non-negotiable fundamental component.

One of the secrets to achieving balance is having a regular time of experiencing the Little side. The regularity reduces the internal pressure and makes everything else a lot easier to manage. If you want to get the best out of regular Little Time, then you need to <u>emphasise the fundamentals</u>.

It may be that your Little One can only get half an hour, four times a week because of work, children and other commitments. So what do you do in the small amount of time that you have as a Parent/Child? You don't have the time to try out all the peripheral extras that might be exciting and fun. You go straight to the *fundamentals*. This is why you need to know what they are.

You child probably knows what they are, but Little Ones are notorious for not knowing anywhere as much about themselves as they think they do, so don't take their word for it. Watch and investigate yourself.

Some babies just *love* their pacifiers. Whenever they regress, the pacifier is always there. For some others, it is one of those important, yet optional things. If he always has a pacifier, then it is probably a fundamental to him.

Is your baby a sissy? If so, what about panties? Wearing girl's panties is 'Sissy 101', so perhaps you can see if wearing panties is a fundamental behaviour or need. What about a bra? For some, it is of moderate to no interest, yet to others, wearing a bra has huge identifying value as a girl and no regressive experience is complete without one.

Baby Clothes? Bottles? Playing with toys? All of these things are part of his behaviour set, but which are fundamental and which are important, but not really an essential? I am not dismissing the value of these important items, rather I am just saying that they are not at the non-negotiable *core* of his needs. The fundamentals are aspects that you really can't change. To expect him to do so is unreasonable, as well as unlikely to be successful.

The list of fundamentals will be quite short. For example, it may be just diapers, panties, pacifier and crawling. The list is short, simple and fundamental. After this, comes the *important* behaviours which may add things like, baby dresses, bonnets, bottles, dolls etcetera and after this again, comes the category of peripheral items and behaviours, which are really in the 'take it or leave it' category.

So why do I want you to categorise these behaviours and objects into Fundamental, Important and Peripheral? Quite simply, to help ease some of the practicalities of the transition to a Parent/Child relationship. Circumstances will always dictate what we can and cannot do. Time will also restrain us, as will family, friends and opportunity.

When you get opportunity to be a parent and child together, then you need to get the most out of it. This means ensuring that the fundamentals are there and as many important aspects as possible as well. If you have the time and inclination, throw in the peripheral as well. As a parent, you don't want to waste time, effort and money on trying to do the right thing and then realise you are focusing on peripherals and not fundamentals. This is why it is important to get these classifications right. Watch and learn and you will eventually get it right.

On your behavioural profile, try and ensure, to the best of your ability, that you categorise them correctly. It will make things smoother for you when we discuss it further in later chapters.

SECTION FOUR – COMMUNICATION

Communication is the key to success in any relationship. This is not exactly news to you I hope, and the Parent/Child relationship is certainly no different. In fact, it lives and dies on the success of communication. Interaction (detailed in the next section), may be the *pivotal* area of the relationship, but without communication, it will never get off the ground. Communication is the key that unlocks the real potential of the relationship and allows the experience to move beyond merely *being tolerated,* into actual mutual *enjoyment.* It can however, get a little complicated at times and I am sure that by now, that does not surprise you!

In this special relationship, we have the added dynamic of *dual-level communication* – adult-to-adult and adult-to-child – in operation, but it is far more complex than even that implies. As you have probably found out, to your immense frustration, communicating with a Little One can be difficult at times. Let's take a look at how it plays out and what to do about it.

Adult – Adult Communication

This book does not presume to be a primer on regular adult relationships. There are a vast number of excellent publications on this topic if you need some advice on that. The Parent/Child relational dynamic, not surprisingly, does impose some new areas that need to be dealt with quite specifically.

A common mistake is to ignore the communication between the two adults on the topic of the Little One. The adult will know most of what you want to find out, but will often be unable to articulate it honestly, as embarrassment still rules and will for quite a while.

This is something to be reminded of: your partner will take quite a while to get over the embarrassment of regression and to be able to communicate to you honestly, openly and completely. It will take time and possibly some years, before he is really able to communicate openly about the deep-seated issues of his regressive life.

Let's take a look at some ways you can communicate adult-to-adult on the difficult topic of his regression and the inner Little One.

Discussing the child with the adult:

If you want to know more about the child, then asking the adult is always a good place to start. Remember that the adult knows what is going on, even if they aren't totally emotionally connected to it. But what exactly do you ask him?

In the Information Section I asked you to seek out the *facts* about your Little One – their age, gender, likes and dislikes etcetera, but have you ever asked your partner how the Little One *feels*? Have you sought out the Little's state of happiness or contentment? Do you know what upsets him or what pleases and excites him?

For many, especially men, it is easier to ask about facts than feelings, when discussing their partner's regression. It probably hasn't occurred to you yet to ask him deep questions about the Little One. He knows what is going on inside. He knows if the child is happy or sad, frustrated or relaxed and so, it is now time to ask more than the usual surface-level questions.

Note the use of the third-person when addressing the adult. This may be helpful or it may be offensive to him. Don't assume that the adult wishes you to refer to his Little in the third-person. Ask.

Try some of these sample questions:

"How is Baby Holly going? Is she enjoying herself still? Was last night's play time fun for her?"

"I haven't seen Jake for a while. Is he okay? Would you like Jake to play with his cars tomorrow evening?"

"Remember that hour Baby Callie spent playing with her toys yesterday? I know she were pretty excited about it. Can you tell me what you liked best? I want to know what she likes!"

"Bill, I know you slept pretty bad last night. Is this something to do with Baby Andrew? I can tell when he is playing up because you toss and turn. Can you tell me anything about it? Are you upset about something?"

You will also need to develop the art of the *pointed question*. The adult will consistently try and hide negative aspects of their Little One's behaviours, feelings and emotions. It is a very adult thing to build ourselves up and to minimise our negatives, but if you want to be the best parent and to enable him to be the best adult partner, then you need to be a bit more pointed and frankly, nosy! This means that you need to *pry* a little. The questions before are fairly general ones. Try these next ones for size.

"I found Holly's dirty nappy this morning. What's happening? We need to talk about it if she is going to keep doing that!"

"I loved watching you play with the blocks yesterday. Did you really enjoy that? Would you like me to join you next time? You never invite me to play with you and I think that could be fun!"

"You are masturbating again, John! What's going on?"

"You seem very distant, Jeff. I know why you go quiet and it's because I've done something wrong. I know I'm your mother now, but that doesn't mean I know what to do all the time. If I've made a mistake you need to tell me about it."

Part of the clue with talking to the adult about the Little One, is being firm and pointed. Your partner knows what is happening, because he is fully capable of remembering and processing everything, but he may be unwilling to disclose everything, for fear of upsetting you, or for saying something he may regret later. He is still unsure of himself and doesn't want to risk the Parent/Child relationship by saying something wrong. At this stage you may have to get a thicker skin. Your adult or child might say something that is upsetting to you, even though it wasn't meant to be so. Remember that it is new for him to talk about it *at all,* never mind in detail and regularly. In time, he will learn to be more open and hopefully less offensive, if you don't get angry at him when he mentions something inappropriately. He is learning to communicate just as much as you are.

A child's emotions welling up inside an adult can often be a very confusing thing for your partner to process. If the child is upset over something real or perceived, he is upset too, but probably highly embarrassed by the silliness of it. You will need to probe to get the answer and don't be surprised if the reason for his upset is *juvenile.*

HINT: If you are to have an effective Parent/Child relationship, then your Little One has to understand that to do your job properly as the parent you will need to pry and ask probing questions of the <u>adult</u>, as well as the child. While an adult is entitled to a private space in the relationship, the Little One is not. The Little One gives themselves to you as a child fully, or not at all. The adult has to accept, that in matters of the Little One, his rights to private space are a bit more limited than other areas. A good biological parent does not grant their child unlimited private space and nor should the parent of a Little One. Some Littles will object to the notion of not having unlimited privacy. However, this is another of those non-negotiables, only this time it is for the Little One.

Non-verbal communication clues from the adult:

Adults think they are clever in hiding their feelings. For most of us though, that is just a delusion. You don't need to be a body-language expert to pick up your partner's clues. If you have been in a relationship for some time, you will have already picked up many of your partner's non-verbal clues. You already know what being silent means or what constantly shifting position in the seat implies.

Especially in the early days of an emerging Parent/Child relationship, some (or most) of the communication in the adult realm regarding the regression will be non-verbal. Many adults are still highly embarrassed by their regression and communicating their wishes verbally will be difficult. For example, an adult might wet their pants a little to let you know they desperately need some regressive time, rather than ask you directly or just regress anyhow. It is an immature act and it certainly should be eliminated, but early on, it could happen that way or in a similar fashion. They might physically hide somewhere from you because they feel the need to regress, but don't want to show it. I know that many Littles actually want to be separate from their partner when they regress and so it is easy to acquiesce to the Little's desire for space. But don't do it!

It is very important that you are totally aware of his regression and if possible, that you are physically there when he does. We discuss this later on.

You alone are the one who can learn the secret meanings of his body language. Yes, he needs to learn to communicate far better and in time, he will, but in the early days of the relationship, you will need to learn to read his *behaviour,* as much as listen to his words.

What can really help is to start a list of clues which you pick up on and write them down. Not so much because you will forget, but rather because writing them down helps to define them and to remind you to look for more. You will get some wrong and some right, but if you continue to look for them, you will get far more right than wrong and you will have helped the communication with the adult regarding his inner Little.

Adult-Child Communication

Discussing the child with the child:

It should be obvious that to find out more about the child, you need to talk with the child. The prerequisites for this are obvious. The child needs to be able to communicate clearly and effectively. This is however, not always the case with Little Ones.

A very young infant of twelve months may have poor language and use mainly baby-talk. This can make communication frustratingly slow. The inner adult will also be frustrated, because he knows what the Little is trying to say, but to use proper words, he will need to come out of regression, which of course is counter-productive. In many cases, non-verbal communication (discussed next) is a better and more effective solution.

You may however, have a child that is able to write in an adult way or type on a computer without breaking regression. It doesn't make a lot of sense, but it is true just the same that some, but not all, can do that. If that is so, then exploit it! It is a very powerful method of communication with the child, but at an adult level and without disturbing regression.

Most regressed Littles will have a level of verbal communication well above their self-identified age. They might *prefer* to use baby-talk, but actually have command of more advanced language. If you cannot easily communicate at their preferred language level, then you can push them to become a little older to make it easier, yet without breaking their regression.

> **HINT: All communication is best done with a child at their physical level. Sit on the floor with them as they play or lie down next to them and speak eye-to-eye. If you want to talk about something important with a child it is always best to do so in their realm. If they are playing with blocks, then play with them. If they are drawing, draw with them.**

Non-verbal communication with the child:

A great deal of communication with any child is non-verbal in nature. Body posture is important, as well as noticing how they move and react to others and also, how they play with their toys. In time, you will recognise the clues as to what they are feeling, simply by reading their body language.

Sometimes, regression is triggered by a stressor or an actual current trauma. By watching their regression, you will be able to see when it is easing. If the trigger was traumatic, they may have tears or anger-like play. Older Little Ones may also display bad attitudes at the beginning and then slowly settle down.

You need to learn to read the non-verbal clues, just as you already have in the adult. This will come in time, if you persevere.

Finding the child 'with all the knowledge':

Your Little One has full access to his adult memories, right? Well, that is perhaps not altogether accurate. Have you ever forgotten an important or traumatic incident that happened a long time ago and then suddenly, something triggered the memory and it came flooding back and it was almost *news* to you? It happens to a lot of us at times and it happens to Little Ones even more. The reason for this could be because Littles were often formed in their very young years and memories from that time seem to get filed in a dusty corner of our brain and forgotten as a matter of course. Then suddenly, there is some spring cleaning and it all comes out, usually when we don't want it to.

Your Little One has as much access to all the adult's memories as the adult himself, right? Well, maybe not – it might be *more*. I don't want this to sound too overwhelming, but it is sometimes true that your regressed Little One might be better able to tell you about things in his past that were traumatic, than the adult. This might not always be a good thing, as some traumas are better left hidden, unless you are ready and able to deal with it. I bring this up though, because it may happen that your Little One dredges up an old memory from his distant past and it may or may not be related to how the regression began, or some other aspect to it.

There is a slight difference when a regressive Little One has multiple ages associated with them. As mentioned earlier, those with multiple ages do so to rationalise their wide age-range of behaviours. They don't really have different Little Ones inside them, as this is *regression*, not dissociation. However, they feel that by associating specific ages to specific groups of behaviours they are being more *authentic* and logical. One thing that tends to happen though, is that sometimes just *one* of the various ages *has the knowledge,* or retains some of the older memories or at least, is far more likely to be able to remember than the others. For some reason, the hidden secrets or memories are occasionally only accessible by one 'personality'. Again, I only mention this because it might happen and if it does, you need to know that it is not really a big deal or problem, but rather just another fascinating facet of deep regression.

Let's take a look at one Little One's experience with a suddenly revealed memory. He is a sissy baby with three different ages in the preschool range, yet mysteriously, also has an uncharacteristic twelve year old girl who occasionally appears.

> *"I was just eating lunch out with my wife when Molly my twelve year old girl suddenly appeared out of nowhere. I usually feel regression coming on, but I didn't feel anything until it was too late. I was still in control, but the pressure was evident in my speech and behaviour and we went home quickly as Molly decided that that day was time to remember a long-forgotten memory of when she was 'born' – as she calls it.*

Over the next 24 hours the details of something that had taken place over 40 years previously came to the fore. An incident of innocent experimentation with who I now realise was a regressive sissy just like me led to Molly being formed. I was 12 at the time. Molly is also 12.

The incident was remarkable and powerful and I had mostly hidden it from myself for four decades. I remembered going into my friend's bedroom and seeing dolls and toys on his bed. I even remembered seeing his wet nappy on the floor but that was all I had remembered, just a static image of the bed and the nappy. Everything else about it was hidden from me.

In retrospect I probably filed it all away because puberty was happening at the same time and suddenly girls took my fancy and a boy who loved dolls and wore nappies was now a bit of an embarrassment to me even though I continued to wet my own bed for many years after and sometimes played with dolls as well.

The experience of the memory returning was very powerful and not really that pleasant. I particularly hated that it returned when I was in public, but I understand that that is often the way it happens. I have no idea of what triggered it.

I don't know why my other girls exist and I don't really want to know. Finding out the circumstances of Molly's creation was awkward enough not the least of which finding out I kissed a boy a year before I kissed my first girl!

I guess I'm glad I found out in a way and perhaps I am better off for it, but now I wonder how the others came to be."

[personal email]

Child – 'child' Communication

One of the more inventive ways of communicating with your Little One is to do so as a *peer*. Now I know that you are not a regressive as such, but you can certainly role-play being a similar age to him. I write in the Interaction section following, that it is sometimes a good idea to become a baby or toddler and to join him in play time or even just in talking, although play is how most toddlers communicate anyhow.

There are some things that toddlers seem to communicate to each other that adults just don't get. One toddler will know what another likes and dislikes and which are his favourite toys or TV shows. A toddler will know when his playmate is unhappy, even if he doesn't know why himself. Your goal is to pick up on some of this.

If you wish to get a fully-fledged communication regime happening with your Little One, you would be well advised to try out being a toddler with him, at least once or twice. You can play at his level, perhaps wear some identifying or similar toddler attire and just be with him, not as his parent or babysitter or the like, but as a peer, similar to a brother or sister. You might want to practice playing with toys first, if you are rusty at it!

Do some colouring-in and perhaps emulate his level of colouring. Remember that you aren't there to teach him to play or to colour better. That is when you join playtime *as a parent,* rather than now when you are doing so as a *child.* You are there to be his friend, playmate and even perhaps confidante? Who knows?

Perhaps do some chalk drawings together. You could read a picture book together or look out a window at what is going on outside. Make sure that you are physically at the same level, so that there is no perception of authority and power, as there can be for biological children. If he is crawling, then crawl with him or at least walk and then quickly sit down again. If he lies down to play because he is still that young, then do so yourself. If he is a toddler that sits up on the floor, then do the same. Maybe he is a Little Girl who likes to sit at the table and colour. Do that with him. Attempt to be as similar in age and behaviour as he is. You don't have to *mirror* his every behaviour, just emulate his general age range. It is in fact, okay to teach him some new games or play skills, as long as it is age-appropriate.

Gender is probably irrelevant, particularly if gender-swapping is too hard for you to do. No toddler expects a playmate to be a specific gender.

Remember that while you are a *role-playing* child, he is essentially a close approximation of a *real* child. But it is in these times that you may pick up a lot of clues that you may not be able to at any other time, and who knows, you may find you enjoy role-playing being a child with him! Now wouldn't that be an awkward surprise for you!

SECTION FIVE – INTERACTION

By now, you have established basic communication with your Little One and have begun to develop a relationship based predominantly on *observation, identification and communication*. Now is time to move it to the next stage – **interaction**.

One of the facts you start to discover when you interact more with your Little One, is that he may actually be *needing* the developmental aspects of the Parent/Child interaction time and will benefit significantly from it. While we are not seeking to eliminate regression in this book, playtimes and other interactions with your child may actually reduce the need for regression. Don't hold on to this is as some kind of law, because it may be a false hope. You can however, be absolutely guaranteed that the regression will *change*.

———————

HINT: Young children respond best to interaction when it is both verbal and tactile. Your Little One will respond most to you if you talk and touch and communicate at their level. Remember to touch them when they are Little. Physical rejection can be devastating to them. Remember their name(s) and their likes and dislikes. A cuddle and kiss can communicate more than a string of words.

———————

Play and other highly interactive activities will show significant improvement in the Parent/Child relationship. Like all people, children gain most from interaction with others. They develop their self-esteem and relational skills through interaction with others and especially during playtimes. Play times are crucial to their development, so try and understand the following.

You are helping your Little One to develop from the hidden, reclusive child he was, into the open and engaging child (and adult) that you want him to become.

It isn't always easy to interact with your Little One. It often takes a lot of time to get your head into the zone. If you are finding it really daunting, then perhaps the easiest way to do it is to treat him *exactly* as you would a biological child, and then simply remove aspects of that interaction that don't quite fit. You will be surprised by just how little you need to remove. A deeply regressed Little One will mirror a real child quite well, with some obvious exceptions.

You will notice a big change in how you interact with him, based on his specific level of regression. A Level two regressed Little One may not need or want much interaction with you, as they still have a solid adult influence in their behaviour, but a level four regressed child may totally need, want or demand your interaction. You need to work out what level requires what degree of interaction. This may sound complex and perhaps overwhelming, but you already have a Behavioural Profile worksheet in place. Now is the time that you add information on interaction and how the various regression levels affect their needs. Don't get too worried about this. You won't be needing to print and laminate this worksheet for frequent reference. You will quickly pick up where your Little One is, without too much thinking. The act of analysing and writing down this profile will cement it in place for you.

These various interactions that I discuss later on, don't have to be a part of your life all of the time and in fact, would be unhealthy if they were. Study them and see how you can integrate *some* of them into your lives as a regular or occasional activity.

All of these following concepts are important types of interactions. They are huge things in many ways, but are some of the basics you will need to do to establish a relationship and conduit to your Little One. Remember that these activities mostly aren't rare special events, but rather activities you will do regularly or as needed.

Discover their needs

When your biological child is born, their needs are basic and easily determined. You don't need a PhD to work it out. As they get older, their needs vary and you have to observe and enquire more to understand them. Then they become teenagers and no one understands anything at all!

If you are to be a good parent to your Little One, then you will need to discover their special needs. The advantage you have, is that your Little One already knows many of them, but be advised that they don't know *all* of them.

Little Ones can be vain, selfish and arrogant, thinking that they know what they want and need. However, that is only partly true. As a parent, *you* also know what they need, even though you probably don't yet know it. If you have been a biological parent then you most certainly *do* know what some of their needs are!

Let me identify the Little One's primary or fundamental needs:

1. **Acknowledgement that he does indeed exist**. At a most fundamental level, the Little One needs assurance that you accept that he exists. Think this over for a moment, because this is solely *your* area to deal with. Ask yourself if you think that this is some kind of game, or if you *really* believe that your Little One exists. Forget the psychological questions and the science. If the Little One is *real* to you, then you can acknowledge his existence. If you think he is a fake or that it is a ploy, then you might as well give up now. A child will forgive his parents many things, but to pretend he doesn't exist, is the harshest thing you can possibly do.

   So how do we acknowledge a Little One's existence? Easy! Treat him as an individual, *not* as an adult. Remember his name and use it – often. Write his name on his toys or embroider it on his dress. Buy a book and write his name in it. Find a date and call it his birthday. Buy him a small gift. It isn't about the gift; it is about the acknowledgement of his existence.

2. **Love**. *'All you need is love'*. It isn't a totally accurate statement by any means, but if you love your Little One as you would a child, then the rest of this book becomes almost redundant. Your love will teach you much of what you need to know, but sometimes you also need information and skills, so keep on reading...

3. **Safety**. Little Ones do not always feel *safe* in the way that their adult self may feel safe. An Adult that sky-dives may have a Little One who is afraid of the dark. A very young Little One may be terrified of being alone or getting lost. As you get to know your child better, you will discover more and more of his fears. They will come out naturally over time and they will also ebb and flow. Be prepared however, for the traditional child fears of darkness, missing parent, lost toy, rejection etcetera. Many still have a night-light handy when needed and some cannot lose sight of their parent in a crowd for fear of getting lost. (I will talk later on about regression outside of Safe Zones). It isn't always possible to dictate where and when regression occurs, but you probably already know that by now!

4. **Diapers**. At the core of all of this behaviour is the inevitable, undeniable and ubiquitous diaper. Almost every Little One wears and uses them. A very large number of them actually need them, either for night and/or daytime. If you think that you can have a Little One without tons of diapers, then you have a new fact coming your way. You can't.

Just as the cartoon character Linus had his security blanket, so Little Ones have their diapers. The need for diapers is based on psychological, as well as physical issues. Many (most actually) Adult Babies were, or remain, long-term bed-wetters. The fact is that long-term bedwetting *does* have a deleterious effect on the impressionable child and can lead to diaper fetishism or regression-by-choice and is part of the cause-basis of infantile regression and Little Ones. You might not find that last statement in the Psychology text-books, but it remains stunningly true. Your Little One may wet by choice or be fully physically and/or emotionally incontinent. At the beginning, it doesn't really matter. He just needs diapers.

Diapers are *the* single biggest support item that Little Ones need and want. This is not something to skimp on or ignore. The correct selection of a diaper that suits your child is important and is something you and he should discuss and decide upon together. Remember that the diaper has enormous Identification Aspect. They are often worn just to identify that he is a baby or toddler.

5. **The pacifier (dummy)** is also hugely important and I highly recommend the new NUK 5 pacifier, because despite what the manufacturers tell you, it was designed for Adult Babies and sells by the millions. It is the only pacifier that stays in an adult's mouth comfortably and securely during sleep. You don't really think a large company like NUK designed an 'orthodontic device' that *accidentally* looks and functions exactly like a infant's pacifier, do you?

6. **Clothing and Toys**. Your baby will naturally begin to collect age-appropriate and gender-appropriate objects, possibly from early teens, as the awareness of their 'specialness' and difference sinks in. For the cross-gender Little One, panties are often up first, as they are easier to obtain and more traditional. With 62% of men admitting to wearing women's underwear a few times at least, it is a pretty safe starting point. From there comes diapers, if they aren't already wearing them. Clothing and toys then follow. The clothes will mostly be what is available, rather than be truly age-appropriate, but the *image* the clothing projects to the Little One is what is important, not the accuracy. Toys are easier to get for the right age. Soft toys are a classic buy and a safe one for any Little One. Because they are more socially acceptable, it is possible your child has been buying them for some time and keeping them hidden.

Basic Interaction with Little Ones

Playtimes:

Your baby loves to play, just like any other child. He will want age and gender appropriate toys and will love to involve you in his play. Early child-raising books will all tell you the incredible value of play in the development of the child and I need to remind you again, that your Little One *is* a child. As he opens up to you more, he is actually developing even more as a child. He will enjoy play as a child very much and will gain a great deal from it. Play meets a number of needs in the child. It enhances:

- Co-ordination.

- Creativity and imagination.

- Interaction with others.

- Enjoyment.

- Independence.

All of these things are valuable to the Little One and enhances their experience and helps lead to balance, which remains our primary goal. Little Ones with good regular playtimes are happier and less stressed. They also find relationships easier with their partner, because the stress of being Little is being mitigated considerably by play.

There are two basic ways to play. One way is to put them in a place, such as a play mat or play pen, give them their toys and then leave them to it. This is good and quite easy to do for longer periods. It also helps the Little One get used to playing on their own. This might sound odd, since Little Ones typically *always* express themselves in a solitary way, because there is usually no involvement from a partner. When you begin the Parent/Child relationship, your child will want to involve you in *everything,* in a sometimes overwhelming fashion. Again, playtime comes to the rescue by showing the child that they *can* have a complete child-like experience without their parent having to be involved. That said, you should still heavily involve yourself in your child's playtimes, just not *every time.*

The very best thing to do is to read him books, very young ones and certainly not higher than his self-identified age. All children love a good book and your Little One will love them just as well. If you work on it, you will see that your Little One will become engrossed in the book and ask for more. Ironically, it can also help adult reading too, if that is a problem!

There is anecdotal evidence to suggest that some otherwise intelligent adults with reading problems, such as comprehension difficulties, inability to follow a plot and even just basic reading skill deficiencies, respond well to reading books from infant picture books, to first readers, young children's books and then into older ages. They are less demanding and often help build confidence. If your Little One is one of those with reading difficulties in the adult realm, then reading to him as a

Little and encouraging him to read with you, may help initiate an improvement in the adult realm. It may not work, but even if it doesn't, you are still giving your Little One the pleasure of a book that he may otherwise struggle with on his own. If this does show promise, then get a variety of books and help your adult develop his skills in a slowly age-progressing method. This problem is outside the Little One zone, but he was probably far too embarrassed to try this before.

Colouring-in can also be an exceptional individual and joint activity. It is one of a child's favourite activities, especially when they are told to be quiet or to play on their own. The value of colouring-in cannot be overstated. It is, along with play-time, the number one activity you should be encouraging your child to do.

Child therapists will tell you that colouring-in and drawing reveals a lot about a child's fears, needs and traumas. In the case of regression, it is the number-one identifier of age. Drawing and colouring tends to bypass our defences and reveal our inner truths and fears. Your Little One might claim to be four years old, but if when they draw, they are very crude attempts and virtually unidentifiable, then they are much younger, perhaps half that age or less. If your child cannot colour inside the lines at all, they are certainly younger than five. If you have a multi-age Little, then colouring-in will identify each age far more than any other activity, except perhaps speech.

However, colouring-in and drawing are not primarily analytical tools in the context of the Parent/Child relationship, even though it can be very interesting to watch. It is primarily about enjoyment and development for the child. Most Little Ones don't want to change and they are often extremely afraid of it. Colouring does change them for the better. It can make them calmer, happier and more in tune with their inner selves. Sometimes during colouring, a little of their inner pain can surface. This is usually a good thing. You should always have several colouring books for your Little One and if you are going on holiday, ensure that there are activity packs, dot-to-dot books and other age-appropriate things for them to do and experience.

Playing with blocks and cars and soft toys will also go down well. There is no such thing as too many soft toys. It is quite likely that your Little One wants to sleep with a soft toy, but is afraid to ask. Offer one to him and see how it plays out. When your child says he wants more plush toys, then he means it. Like any child, they want *lots* of toys and plushies are the top of most very young children's list. If you involve yourself in the selection and purchase of toys for your child, he will just love it! You could take him shopping and see what gets his interest, and then buy some for presents for Christmas or birthdays. Don't forget the idea of a special birthday, just for your Little One!

You don't have to always be intimately involved in play time. You can set up the play area with some toys and direct him to play, while you watch him and do whatever else you need to do. You don't need to always play *with* him, but you do need to be *there* with him. Remember the maxim: "*parenting is about being there*". No matter what your Little One is doing, you need to be there or at least close at hand. A very helpful suggestion is to get a large play-pen or if that is impractical (and it is for most), get a large play mat where he and the toys are and instruct him to remain on the mat for playtime.

Sleep-times:

Your baby loves to sleep and there is a world of difference between *adult sleep* and *baby sleep.* Your Little One needs *both.* Part of the stress and behavioural difficulties of some Little Ones (and their associated adult) stems from not enough time in the baby sleep realm. Some people might reject this notion, but it is quite real nonetheless.

Physically, your Little One isn't tired, but his inner-self may be exhausted and he needs the experience of *his* sleep. It is harder to explain than it is to demonstrate. Give your Little One some serious baby/toddler sleep times and watch his demeanour change. We all need sleep and so do Little Ones!

When he is playing, give him a pillow and allow him to lie down and sleep. Sometimes when he goes to bed at night, dress him as a child and give him a soft toy and perhaps a bottle and of course his pacifier. Try to encourage him to regress and to then go to sleep that way. For some it is scary and for others exceedingly natural. Your Little One should be getting regular Little sleep. It will make quite a difference.

You can also give him day naps in full infant/toddler mode as well. Don't even call it a rest or sleep, but rather a *baby nap.* Let him sleep in a diaper, in a Little outfit if he has them, fill the bed with soft toys and give him a pacifier or even a pre-nap bottle, then watch the sleep transform your child.

Sleep is one area you may have to take charge of, both in and out of the regressed zone. Little Ones need more sleep than the rest of us and you may need to get tough on it. It is not inappropriate to send your Little One to bed before you, to ensure enough sleep, nor is it wrong to make them stay in bed in the morning. A common trait of deeply regressive Little Ones is waking at the crack of dawn, just like a child. It is not unreasonable for you to require him to stay in bed until you say otherwise. If that doesn't work, then you should require a regular nap or earlier bedtime. I discuss this later when I talk about discipline and boundaries.

It is a truly wonderful experience to hold your Little One in your arms as he drifts off to sleep and it is just as wonderful for the child as well! One of the most difficult aspects of being regressive is the inevitable end of Little Time, but if that time ends with going to sleep, then the effect and value of the regression can last for hours. Some deeply regressed Little Ones wake up still in their regressed state. As long as you are aware of it, then that is fine and can be quite therapeutic.

In short, involve yourself in your Little One's sleep and don't be afraid of taking charge in this area. This is one aspect of life that Little Ones are notoriously bad at and it is one of your responsibilities to repair it. If the Little One wants a relationship as a Little, then he needs to respect your authority regarding sleep. It is a pretty good trade-off for him, so he will grumble some and then comply.

Diaper/nappy Changing:

For some, the most dreaded part of caring for a Little One is the diaper change. It is also one of the most important aspects of care, because it takes place when your baby is at his most vulnerable and most trusting. With his diaper unpinned, everything he has done and his essential infancy is open (literally) for display. I don't suggest you change all of his diapers, unless you want to, but you do need to change some and not just a few. It is non-negotiable part of interaction I'm afraid! And there is so much to gain by the intimacy that is implicit in the diaper change. Vulnerability need not be scary. It can also be very intimate and loving.

A few guidelines for diaper changing are:

- If he is incontinent, then you are not responsible for all of his adult changes. This is not to say you cannot or should not help out, but rather that it is primarily an adult matter, not a child one.

- If he is in full control of his bladder and bowels as a Little One, then he should do the majority of the changes, but you need to do some regularly as well, as part of your intimate interaction.

- If your Little is functionally incontinent when regressed, then you should assume responsibility for most of the changes as a Little, if not all, as part of your parenting role.

- If your Little one is too young to change his own diapers adequately, then you are up for them all! The reality is that a lot of Littles under two years old *are* incapable of changing their own diapers, but because they have no one around to change them, they disrupt the regression long enough to change themselves and then return to play. Or they make a mess where they play! It is not an optimal way of regressing. The functional need for a diaper change should not inhibit the regression, so when he is regressed you need to be up for most if not all of them.

- You may have different rules for dirty diapers than wet ones. You will eventually be asked to change a dirty diaper. It may not be pleasant, but the commitment it requires and the bonding that can result can be remarkable, but mostly, make him change his own stinky ones!

- Having a special diaper-change area can add to the experience. It doesn't have to be a proper adult change table, but if you have a place set aside just for changing your child, then it will add to the authenticity and therefore intimacy, of the change.

- The choice of diaper is important. For incontinents, the criteria is quite different, but as a Little One, the diaper should be infantile if possible or certainly without much consideration for discretion.

Adult diaper changing is different to infant changing and personality non-withstanding, you are still changing an adult. Disposable diapers are much larger and have more tapes. Cloth diapers can be huge and folded and pinned quite differently to infant ones. You will need to learn how to change your baby and he may have to teach you how. Also, let me give you a warning. Little Ones are *very particular* about how well they are diapered! Be prepared for complaints until you do it their preferred way, but it really isn't that hard once you learn how.

Feeding Times:

Depending on age, you should allow your Little One to occasionally experience proper age-appropriate feeding. The choices are the usual ones for any baby or toddler. You can bottle-feed your baby or give him a sippy cup or spoon feed him any meal at all. If you bottle feed, use a NUK5 nipple so that it fits better with custom flow. Use juice, milk, water or even formula. A lot of Little Ones use formula for authenticity, certainly not for taste! You might want to try it out for your child, as it is worth experimenting with. The Sippy cup is easy to use and highly recommended. Spoon feeding is also easy. You might want to try some soft foods or even the baby food selections. At this stage, you simply find what your baby likes and just go with that.

Feel free to experiment and watch your baby's reactions. He has probably never had this before, so he may not know what is good or bad or even what he wants or likes. It is a time of experimentation for you both.

Meal time is one of the family's most important times and so it is for a Little One. Don't rush or avoid the Little feeding experience. Obviously it cannot happen very often, but when it does, make it a real feeding *event*. Extend the bottle feeding times, cuddle during feeds. Simulated or real breastfeeding can certainly add interest to a feeding time.

This is the easiest part of being a parent to ignore, but it is one of the most important. When you bottle feed your child, you will see what I mean. If your child is too old for the bottle, then work with spoon feeding and cutting up food so that he eats with his hands. If older still, use children's cutlery.

A high chair adds authenticity, but frankly is more trouble than it is worth, as the child is then way too high to actually feed!

Bath Times:

All children love/hate baths. Your Little One will be just the same. If he is wearing diapers a lot, then bath times will be more common. Use an actual bath, not a clumsy shower, if at all possible. Get bath toys and bubble-bath and make it an experience. Don't forget to actually to do the washing yourself! Being bathed as a vulnerable young child can be a big thing for Little Ones. They might be nervous or even scared. I'm not quite sure why, but I've heard it mentioned several times.

You can get in the bath with him and interact with him in a new way. Bath time can be fun time, so make it so.

How much baby time is enough?

This question comes up all the time. I can assure you that it is difficult, but not impossible, to give your child more Little Time than he can want or handle, unless you go Full Immersion (detailed later on), where that is the very purpose of the exercise. He will probably always want more. On the other hand, *you* may be wanting as little as possible, unless you find that you enjoy it and gain satisfaction from it as well and don't be surprised if you do!

This is the classic case for compromise. In this instance, he gets less than he *wants*, but enough to meet his needs, and you get to do more than *you* want, but less than your breaking point.

For some people, compromise is never easily achieved and for a few, unobtainable, but the effort to find that compromise is a reward in itself. Your marriage or relationship may never find a more complicated and demanding problem than this. If you can compromise on this and learn how to do so with other future problems, you will add significant strength to your relationship.

You will also find that your compromise will morph over time. Initially you will probably be nervous and even reluctant and that will limit what you can put into the compromise. Just be flexible enough so that over time, you can modify your compromise agreement to meet changing needs, abilities and circumstances.

Regression and Behaviour Zones

Regression in Safe Zones:

Up until now, we have assumed that all regression has occurred inside the 'safe zone', usually your own home or even just a few rooms within that home. A Safe Zone is a place where you both feel relaxed and comfortable enough to experience a level of regression for your Little One, without risk of discovery. Usually it isn't just a place, but also a time. Parents with children may only have a room for an hour or two, once a week or even less. Safe Zones are important and you need to identify them and treat them as something special.

A Safe Zone is a time and place where your Little One can be himself and not fear discovery or embarrassment. It is a time for the parent to explore the relationship without external worries and concerns. It is also your place of comfort, as well as his.

Finding Safe Zones often requires some creativity as well. Perhaps when your children are at school you could both take time off to have some good Parent/Child time. Put a lock on the bedroom door and spend quality time there. It goes without saying that you need to keep your young children away from regression times. If it is hard for *you* to understand, imagine the confusion for a young child?

If you want more time to be with your Little One, then you need to *make* the time and space. There are very few real reasons why Safe Zones cannot be created and regularly used. Turn the TV off and go to your room or send the children elsewhere for a while. Some even go to a motel for a few hours. Yes, it costs money, but if that is necessary for your Parent/Child relationship to function, then you may need to do just that. Be creative and inventive. If the driving force is to find time to work this new aspect to your relationship, then you will manage to find opportunities and Safe Zones.

Regression in Unsafe Zones:

Life conspires sometimes to take away our Safe Zones or to limit them so that they are essentially inadequate to the task. However, regression in *Unsafe Zones* is another option for augmenting your relationship.

An Unsafe Zone is a place and time where you do not have absolute safety or privacy to let your Little One out, without tight boundaries in place. It can be a public place or around family or in locations where privacy cannot be guaranteed.

Unsafe Zones can still be used to let the Little One out, as long as appropriate boundaries are in place and obeyed. This obviously requires your relationship to have developed to a stage where your Little One will obey your directions and boundaries without risk and without question.

Some things are clearly *not* suitable for Unsafe Zones:

- Wearing of baby clothes other than under clothes. However, a diaper, panties or even bra can be worn under street clothes quite satisfactorily.

- Unrestricted use of a pacifier (dummy). They can however, be used in some places, but be ready to take it out.

- Crawling.

Some things can be done in Unsafe Zones depending on where and when, they are.

- Baby talk with volume limitations and without being overheard.

- Holding hands in the Parent/Child style: mother's hand on top and leading.

- Carrying a full baby bag with diapers, bottles, pacifiers, change of baby clothes. This adds to the experience, even if they can't be used. It is essentially a prop.

- Looking at children's toys and books, even clothes and allowing the Little One to see them through their regressed eyes.

- Playing on a playground, as long as no other children are there. It is inappropriate to mix any of this behaviour with biological children, even if they are unaware. Today's society is quite intolerant of anything that might be in any way construed as predatory.

The Little One can actually be in the fore-ground, experiencing the wide world as an infant/ toddler would. Clearly, this takes practice and the parent needs to be on their guard, but it can be a great experience for a Little One, whose life has been restricted to just a few rooms and rare opportunities to express their inner nature. It is an exercise in trust that has to be experienced to know what I mean. When your Little One is allowed an incredible opportunity to explore the world through toddler eyes, it can be quite something to behold.

Let's hear one Baby to explain in her own words how it felt. It comes from her Baby Diary, which is something else you could also consider doing and encouraging your own child to do. Journaling your voyage of discovery can reap important lessons.

"I had the bestest day today. Mummy put me in a nappy and told me we were going to a special place. She called me my own name [Julie] over and over and I was so excited. I got to wear my special panties and bra too! I sat in the car and mummy told me to look at the trees and the birds. We stopped a couple times and we looked at some plants and I saw some birds. We went to a shop in the village and mummy held my hand real tight and I had food and mummy wiped my mouth. We went to heaps of shops but the best was a toy shop. Mummy let me buy a little toy and I held it all the way home. I sat on a seat while Mummy bought some toys I wasn't allowed to see. I got a bit scared but mummy looked at me a few times so I wasn't scared. I held my little toy tight."

[internet blog]

Unsafe Zones can be a wealth of opportunity for him to explore the outside world, once your Little One is *trained* for the big outdoors. Remember, the training that makes Unsafe Zones possible, also makes your at-home life easier. A well-trained Little One can be a joy. Use Unsafe Zones as a reward for good behaviour.

The absolute essential ingredients for Unsafe Zone regression are:

1. The Little One's self control and ability to revert to the adult <u>immediately</u>. Events can occur, such as running into a friend or needing to perform an adult function quickly. The Little One simply *must* be able to revert to the adult state almost instantly. This tends to mean that Level Four regression is too deep to take outside, unless it is very private and the risk is quite low. Remember that the deeper the regression, the harder

and longer it is to revert to adult state. Levels one and two are ideal for Unsafe Zone play – easy to manage and easy to control.

2. Your Little One must have total mastery over boundaries and unacceptable behaviours. We have talked before about Little Ones difficulties with behaviours and boundaries. Most struggle with this early on, but it is normally not hard to implement over time. Babies take time to learn and so does your Little One, but once his regression has reached a stage where he has control over his behaviour *and* will obey you without question, then they are ready for Unsafe Zone regression! I discuss how to get boundaries in place later on.

Unsafe Zones are a wide world of discovery for both of you. Use it wisely, use it often. Use it as a reward for good behaviour. Remember that a Safe Zone may eventually come to feel like a prison to your Little One. A safe, happy prison, but a prison nonetheless. The world beckons to your Little One, just as it does to all of us. Prepare him for the great world outside!

Advanced Interaction with Little Ones

Being involved in your Little One's regression:

You need to meet your Little One personally and to interact with him as he regresses. This is one of the essentials of having a Parent/Child relationship – being deeply involved. If you offer the right environment and safety, your Little One will come to the foreground very easily with you around. Remember his name and use it often! You will blunder around and make many mistakes. That's just par for the course! Just go with it and watch for the clues. Your Little One will let you know how you are going and appreciate the effort. You can't really fail if you care enough to try and persevere.

"Parenting is about being there."   *[anonymous]*

Much of your relationship with your Little One will boil down to nothing more than just *being there* with them and for them. Sure, there are things you will be expected to do, but being there for your Little One is the most important one.

Here are a few easy things to do early on in the Parent/Child relationship as they regress:

- Cuddle him as mother/child with him *cuddling into you.*

- Holding hands. Not fingers interlinked as lovers, but full hand grip with your hand on top and leading, indicating that you are in control.

- If he wears a diaper to bed, invite him to cuddle up to you in the morning even though he is wet.

- If he is feeling regressive and is comfortable with you being there, stay with him as he regresses. Early on, he may feel uncomfortable revealing that side to you, so be ready to pick up on the body language cues, but aim to be there and to be involved as he regresses.

Open the flood-gates:

Many Littles will often fight against a strong regressive episode, such as one that is heading for level three or four. They do so because their life's history is one of trying to keep things in check. Levels three and four are very difficult to enjoy when you have to hide everything from a partner or family. They also represent a significant reduction in self-control, or better described as 'adult influence', and a solo regressive may fear this depth of regression.

If your child is heading towards a deep regression, you may notice fear or upset or some other negative emotions. Normally, you wouldn't expect these emotions, since they presumably *want* their regression and in the lower levels, that is almost always true. However, the higher levels of regression may have conflicting feelings of both *wanting* to go there, but being *afraid* of the lack of control implicit in it. If you spot this irrational fear, then you have a responsibility to guide them through it.

Quite simply, they are afraid of the experience of being almost totally regressed because they have fought it for so long and it may be something they have never yet fully experienced.

Talk to him and tell him that it is okay to go all the way down. Hold his hand or feed him his bottle or do whatever relaxes him, tell him that 'Mummy is here' and that there is nothing to fear. Tell him you will look after his every need for the next little while and mean it. He will go to a level he has probably never been before, or at least he will enjoy it this time. It is no big deal for you because you just do what you normally do, but for him, the removal of the fear is something only *you* can do. It is in this moment that your parenting becomes more genuine than it has been before, because he has no alternative, other than to trust you if he wants to experience this new level. You can take away his fear and make him feel much safer. This is not a bad thing. It is a good and healthy opportunity for you to remove yet another fear and worry from your child. You will both be better off for the experience.

Interaction Outside of Safe Zones:

I've already discussed Safe and Unsafe Zones for Little Ones. The reality for Littles in a developing relationship with their parent is that Safe Zones can feel very restrictive after a while. We all want to be free to move about and experience all that the world has to offer. It can be a very powerful experience for a Little when their parent takes them out – as a Little – into the wide world. Clearly, this is something that can *only ever be done* with a parent firmly in charge.

The real world will impose many restrictions that cannot be easily overcome, if at all. Wearing a diaper in public is one thing, but not baby clothes. Actions that the Little might *want* to take are just not possible, but they can *be* there just the same. They can see the world through the eyes of a child and even at times play on the swings, not merely remembering their childhood, but actually living it.

Full Immersion Baby/Toddler Experiences:

'Full immersion' is pretty much exactly what it sounds like. The realities of most of our lives is that our Little Ones have to juggle life and commitments around to get even some small amount of time to be their inner selves and for you the parent to look after them and to guide them. But sometimes it is possible to organise <u>longer periods</u> of total age-specific existence.

This could be an entire day, an overnight or even a week-long period of time, where your Little One is nothing other than who he *really is* on the inside. There are benefits to this that are not immediately obvious.

Little Ones exist predominantly in a fantasy realm, just like most age-players and Adult Babies. They imagine the *joy* of being incontinent and in diapers 24/7 and when they try it out for themselves, give up after only a few days, when reality kicks in. The same thing applies to the idea of living as a Baby or Little Child fulltime.

Destroying the odd fantasy or two is sometimes a very helpful thing to do. It helps ground your Little One in reality as to how they <u>really</u> fit in the world. It isn't always pleasant, but it is always helpful. Don't try and destroy all fantasies though. We all need hope and fantasy to survive and thrive!

A Full Immersion into a baby or toddler experience firstly, releases some of the tension and over-excitement that your Little One lives with and secondly, once that excitement has been sated, they start to learn what it is like to *live* in such an environment. It never matches up to the fantasy and this is where learning takes place. The key is to take your Little One *past* the point of excitement and fun and to take them to the real *lifestyle* stage. The other key is a proper understanding of *full immersion.*

In your normal Parent/Child playtimes and regression, there are beginnings and endings to the experience and the adult comes back and takes over the day. In Full Immersion, the re-emerged adult remains in the Little environment. This means that even when the adult is back in charge of the personality, the Little environment remains in place. This is crucial to the learning process. The adult learns some of the boundaries and understands them *as an adult,* rather than as a Little One. They also learn that the Little One's wish for full-time baby living is impractical and perhaps not even what they really want anyhow.

If you take a few days off and ask your Little One to be Little the entire time for a Full Immersion experience, then there needs to be some real and practical rules such as:

- He will have to follow your parental instructions *all the time*.

- He goes to bed when you say so, naps when you say so, cleans and tidies when you ask and is fed and changed at your whim – all the time.

- His decision-making is limited to which toy he plays with, or which children's TV show he watches.

- There is no adult time at all. Even when the adult re-emerges they are required to dress, act and play as a child. Normally, this means the child will eventually return again, as the adult normally cannot behave as required. It is a way of forcibly returning the adult to the Little stage again.

This scenario cannot be played out with any real value unless it is done for at least twelve hours and preferably 24-48 hours. Anyone can play out a role for a short time. Playing *lifestyles* is something altogether different and the reality of *lifestyle,* is the point of the exercise.

If, as a parent, you want to really alter your Little One's perceptions of who he is, then try out an extended Full Immersion experience over four to seven days. It is a lot of work for you and makes your holiday less of one, but if you plan it well, the holiday can still be yours as well and as a bonus you will be improving the future as your Little One learns.

Here are some clues.

- **Full Immersion means FULL**. This means that ideally, your Little One should not be having (or permitted) adult experiences <u>at all</u>. Even if the Adult comes back to the foreground, he remains in baby clothes and a diaper and lives the life his Little One has been having. This is important for helping both adult and Little One develop proper perspective. Of course, over an extended period of time, like a holiday, you may not be able to make it fulltime in baby clothes. In this case, minimise the out-of-baby-clothes time, but make sure he is still in a diaper and any baby underclothes. Keep him under your control at all times and refer to him by his Child name(s). Adult activities should be minimised or restricted. You could for example, have four hours of the day when your Little One is allowed adult over-clothes and be permitted to be in the world-at-large, but he remains your child at all times. A good idea is to take a full diaper bag with you at all times, including bottles and some baby clothes, even though you won't be using most of them. The existence of them taken with you, will remind him that he is still your child.

- **Extending his baby/toddler experience**. Full Immersion is when you have the chance to extend the limits of his Little experience. The difference is that you are totally in charge and these extensions do not necessarily have to come with his prior permission. For example, your child may like having the occasional baby bottle. In Full Immersion, make it *every* meal and a large part of his feeding. He may not like (or have even tried) formula. Use formula and insist he drinks it as an experiment. Same with baby foods. He can have a morning *and* afternoon nap, whether or not he wants or needs it. You can send him to bed before you without complaint. It might be only 20-30 minutes earlier, but the principle is that he is a child and so obeys without question. Baths might be morning and night as you require. Diaper changing is when *you* want and when is convenient *to you*. One biggie is to deny all toilet privileges meaning dirty diapers. See how your baby feels after a week of daily dirty diapers. Dirty diapers might sound like fun – until there is no option and are only changed at your convenience! Of course, that means you have to change them, so that might be a trade-off you are unwilling to make!

- **Play time**. Little Ones love to play, but sometimes the fantasy can wear off if it is extended for a long time. You could, for example, give your Little One two play periods each day of an hour or more and require him to stay on the play mat, while you do whatever you need to do. He must stay there and play, or at least sit quietly. You could replace his normal holiday reading with children's or toddler's books.

- **Bath time**. Little Ones have a habit of getting smelly. We mostly suffer through this as parents, but you can now require a bath whenever they need one.

- **Crawling time**. If your Little One has crawling as part of their behavioural profile, then you could require that they crawl all of the time, rather than some of the time. Or you could require crawling for certain hours of the day. Crawling is very restrictive to an adult, but making it a part of their day will remind him that he is really an adult. That is a good thing. Enforced crawling has had quite an impact on some whose partners have required it. (I refer to enforced crawling separately later on).

- **Baby talk**. Many Little Ones have baby talk as part of their behavioural profile. In Full Immersion, that can be wearing on the speaker (and parent!). You can require baby talk, even when the Little One is in adult mode. Full Immersion expects the person to come in and out of Little mode. The difference is that their *external world* does not. They may be Little only half of the time, but in the other half, they are an adult who has to dress and act as a child regardless. *This* is where so much of the learning occurs – when the fantasy has been removed and reality is better understood. This can be a massive help to his development of boundaries.

- **Unpleasant Experiences**. The lifestyle of a child includes times that are not fun and unpleasant. Discipline, restriction from activities, limited food choices, early bedtimes, are all part of it. A proper Full Immersion should contain elements that the Little One finds unpleasant. In fact, you need to ensure that there are some things like that. If you are not generally a smacking parent, this is perhaps a safe and appropriate time to introduce it even if only for this period of time.

- **Discipline**. This is going to come up over the few days or weeks, as your Little One gets tired, cranky or chafes at the limits imposed on him. You need to be well prepared for this and to plan in advance. Imagine that you are a real parent and he is a real child. Use time-outs, early bedtimes, taking away toys and television and perhaps, even smacking, if you have already used that (or even if you haven't). There is a wide range of options available for disciplining the Adult Baby. It is quite common for a parent to use a naughty corner, where the misbehaving child has to sit quietly for a while, as punishment. Given the safety and time available, it is viable to extend the range of discipline considerably. Normal life usually constrains a parent from much of the discipline that is probably needed, but in this experience you should feel free to discipline more. I address the vexed question of smacking in a later chapter.

- **Problems being the parent**. More than any other time, Full Immersion tests the ability of the parent to 'parent'. Remaining in control and essentially dominating the Little One in such a manner, is a big challenge for most wives. It doesn't seem as difficult for men, but it is still an issue. Prior to such an experiment as this, the two adults should discuss it in general terms, so that both are *generally* aware of the rules and consequences. Note that this isn't necessarily seeking *permission* for the details of the Full Immersion, but rather for the concept itself. A simple rule should be, that your child follows the rules of the Full Immersion or it is totally over and there will be *zero* Baby time. It is a harsh rule, but Full Immersion can be difficult to enforce without draconian counter-measures.

Full Immersion is the shorter version of *living the lifestyle*, but is designed to teach the limits that the Little One is currently unaware of. Discovering they really *don't* want to be a baby or toddler all the time is a shock and a painful one. It shatters illusions and fantasies and replaces them with the reality of their adult-side's true dominance.

The obvious question is 'what if we find that he just wants a baby life without any adult experience'? Well, you won't. We all need and crave our adult experiences and there is simply no substitute for it. Even with the well-known examples of Little Ones supposedly living a lifestyle of regression, the facts are that they don't really do that at all. Simply wearing baby clothes most of the time isn't living a lifestyle. That is wearing an outfit. Shopping for yourself and earning a living isn't lifestyle. That is just life. There are very, very few Littles that live a genuinely 24/7 totally dependent, regressed lifestyle and to do so in the absence of serious mental impairment is dysfunctional.

**Every Little One needs their significant time in the real adult world
– they just don't always completely understand that. One of the
tasks of the responsible parent is to show their Little One where that
boundary lies.**

Everyone benefits, including the parent, when the Little One learns more about navigating the adult/child boundary. Let's read an example of a couple who tried a form of Full Immersion. [FetLife 2010]

"It's a month now since our big baby adventure! So it's time to say if it worked or not. I guess I'd have to say it did. Baby Sue [husband Mark] is certainly pestering me less for longer baby times. He won't admit it but he seems to have had a reality check and I don't think he liked it much. But I sure did. It was a good idea although I didn't really think it would achieve much."

[original post]

"Baby Sue and I just had the most amazing time! I took her away for four days and kept her as a baby girl the entire time! And I mean all the time and not one minute as a Big!

...

We talked about it before and I told her what was gonna happen and he agreed to it thinking it was some holiday for Baby Sue and it was but it was amazing! Anyhow, we had to drive nearly three hours to get to the farmhouse we rented and I drove coz I made Baby Sue wear her really thick nappies under her clothes and her bra all padded up and her big boy clothes on top but she had to call me mummy and I called her Sue or baby! It was pretty odd but pretty cool too!

...

The farmhouse was kinda isolated and was pretty good and as soon as we got there I changed her nappy and dressed her in her real little baby clothes. She likes to play from 12-36 months old but I said she was going to be 12 months old for the four days. So I put her in this cute short dress and put these bootie-type thing on her and told her she wasn't allowed to walk without asking me. She hadn't seen that coming! For most of the next four days she crawled except when outside in the dirt but she had to hold my hand at all times when walking. I bought an extra dummy for her coz no way she was not having one all the time. Baby Sue got a bit sick of her dummy by day two! And I told her it was baby talk all the time no matter what. She couldn't do it and started using adult talk before a couple hours was up so I smacked her hand slightly every time she did it and it kinda worked except I was still doing it on day four!

I had so much crap in the car for her! Nappies, clothes and toys filled the back seat. I took every toy she had and borrowed a few extras. I set up the big room with BabySue's toys and I set up a play area on a big mat I found in one of the rooms. Her first big surprise was her first feed. He loves beer, soft-drink and wine. Baby Sue was not even getting soft-drink. Her first bottle was juice but her second was S26 formula! She was not very happy with it. She made a fuss about trying formula two months ago and so I got her some and she didn't like it. But I told her she was having four formula bottles a day now plus any drink she needs would be in her bottle. I didn't realise how many bottles you really need! I only had two and two big teats! I wish I had four or five!

Our first meal there was a bit of a shock to her. I had bought a heap of baby foods without much idea of what I was getting so it was a bit of a mess but I heated up some and spoon fed it to her. It's not really very tasty stuff and sorta bland and boring and I made her eat it and topped it off with another formula bottle.

Bedtime rocked her world! Baby Sue gets very tired and she hadn't had a nap all day and was a bit cranky after a playtime so I sent her to bed at 8 pm!! I had told her earlier that she might have to go to bed earlier than usual so she wasn't surprised but she was also really exhausted. I changed her wet nappy and put her in sleepers and sent her to bed. And I reminded her of the rule that there was no getting up at all without my permission. She fell asleep really quick and when I went to bed at 11 I woke her up for the promised night-feed. Another formula bottle which she didn't complain as much about and I changed her yet again.

Next morning she was awake at dawn. Ugh! But she wasn't allowed out of bed until I said so but I had this schedule all written up so our day started with her on the play mat for an hour with Lion King playing while I kept sleeping.

I kept to the schedule pretty well. She had two one-hour playtimes every day with toys on the mat and no TV and a two hour TV time in the evening which was very young children's TV which I downloaded. I also made her have two naps every day for at least an hour. There was a spare bedroom which I used for her naps and she had to stay there until I let her get up. To be honest, the extra nap every day worked wonders! She was less of a grumpy girl with more sleep.

She pushed back at the limits by day two when she was adult but I made her stay as a child. She had some misbehaviour and I put her in the naughty corner twice for ten minutes. Oddly that worked.

...

On the third day she complained and that's when it got hard. She wanted to watch adult TV and a beer but it wasn't possible. I got pizza for lunch and cut it up so she could eat that so it helped but after that it was back on the play mat and then her nap.

By the time we got home, she was ready to be an adult. But the next morning Baby Sue was still there in bed hoping I would change her. But I think it made an improvement. She's less pushy and demanding and she seems to obey the rules better. At least she knows now that she doesn't really want to be a baby all the time."

Full Immersion doesn't have to be as long or as complex as the above example. You can make it shorter and less intense. You may not be able to design an experience that will take your Little One to the edge where his limits are tested, but you can still give him a time that he will remember fondly as your full-time child. Sometimes, the benefits of just satisfying a fantasy is enough. For others, those limits have to be found and pushed. Only experience will tell which one works for you.

If Full Immersion does nothing else, you have given your Little a gift; a time as a child that they can look back on and remember fondly.

Bedwetting Fantasy:

Bedwetting is a major issue for most Little Ones. A majority of Little Ones were bed wetters well past the expected age and many continued well into teens and beyond. Such exposure to wet sheets does bring its own complications, the major one being that these Little Ones can sometimes be *attracted* to wet beds and develop a fantasy expression around it. This attraction is not necessarily *pleasurable,* although some do enjoy it, but rather an attraction to a powerful yet intrinsically unpleasant event. As adults, we can be oddly drawn to an object or activity which we know is unpleasant, but there is a power that draws us in nonetheless. For many, bedwetting holds such a power.

It is quite common for biological parents to take diapers away from children early, in the hope that the discomfort will motivate an end to bedwetting. For most children, it is an effective methodology. For many Little Ones however, it simply does not work. I talk about bedwetting in more detail in the Incontinence chapter, but suffice to repeat it here, that a lot of Little Ones were bed wetters because they either *wanted* to wet the bed, or because they didn't really see any compelling reason to stop.

You don't have to understand it. You do however, need to accept the possibility that bed wetting without diapers may be one of your Little One's deep wants and needs. They are probably deeply embarrassed about it, for reasons that are obvious. It is one of life's little quirks that people will talk about their pants-wetting issues, but avoid their bedwetting problems. Bed wetting is one of those embarrassing issues that we should have gotten over long before we go to school. Such a pity that the facts tell a different story.

One of the common behaviours of Little Ones is bedwetting – deliberate or otherwise – especially if they are a very young Little One. An adult who wets the bed is normally upset and concerned by it and will seek treatment or mitigation of the effects. A Little One however, often thinks that bedwetting is normal and even praise-worthy. They see it as a normal and natural behaviour and don't really understand why you think otherwise. They might *say* that they do, but deep down inside their own life experience, bedwetting never fazed them at all and so, why should it be a problem to you? Remember, that for many Littles, bedwetting is an external *validation* of their internal feelings. Being a bed wetter is fully consistent with how they feel inside. In fact, *not* wetting their bed, at least occasionally, can be a distress and considered a failure.

Some parents have praised their Little One for a wet bed and been rewarded with a beaming smile and a happy attitude that lasted for days. This kind of result is a clue to what your Little One is thinking, regarding his wet bed.

A Little One will often be very proud of his wet bed and sometimes display it and not understand why no one else is impressed by his efforts. To many Little Ones, a wet bed is an <u>accomplishment,</u> not a failure. It is an external validation of an inner belief that "I am a bed-wetter" and/or "I am a Baby".

Usually a Little One will not seek treatment for his bed wetting for fear of breaking the illusion or of ending the wet nights. Even if he wears diapers at night, he is still secretly impressed by his night wetting. There are many hypnotic CDs available on the internet that seek to help Little Ones develop or improve their bedwetting. Not to cure it, but rather to make the Little One *wetter* and more of a bed wetter. This clearly shows that bedwetting is considered to be an admirable skill by many.

Does your child do any of the following?

- Wet the bed often?

- Sometimes take his diaper off at night or go to bed un-diapered, so that the sheets will be wet?

- Deliberately wet the bed? Your partner may be avoiding the toilet before bed and saving it for the sheets.

- Openly display the wet sheets for you or others to see?

- Tell you how wet he is or his night diaper and always looking for a response?

- Deny that the sheets need changing, even though they are soaked and wanting them to stay on the bed?

- Wet the mattress, pillow or quilt without any protection?

- Ask *you* to wet the bed? (some Little Ones seek approval by asking their partner to wet the bed as well).

- Masturbate in the wet sheets?

- Wet the bed before sleep?

TRY THIS: When your baby/toddler next wets the sheets, compliment him on the size of the wet patch. Watch the reaction and see if it gives you any insight into what he is thinking about it. If he makes no move to cover the wet sheet, leave it open and see how often he returns to look at it. Ask him if he thinks the sheets needs to be changed and allow him to choose if they are or not. Watch his reaction. If your baby wears night diapers, then ask him how wet he is in the morning or even offer <u>diaper-less</u> sleeping some nights and see if he takes up the offer.

Some Little Ones have a quite strong need to sleep in a wet bed, as opposed to a dry bed. They believe that if they could do that, they would be happier. In many ways, this is a connection back to their very young days when they wet the bed every night. By having a wet bed now, they make the strong conection back to the time they recall, even though they may not necessarily have enjoyed it at the time. Generally, they get little opportunity to wet their bed, other than their occasional unprotected wetting. Even that is rare, as the rest of the time they have to wear diapers. For some Little Ones, this connection back to the bedwetting years is exceedingly strong and can't be easily ignored.

You can choose to either integrate unprotected bedwetting (occasional or regular), into your Little One's life or to seek to disavow them of this fantasy altogether. You need to be careful that you don't make the wrong choice and so you need to understand more about their bedwetting past before choosing. For example, you don't want to *encourage* them to wet the bed, in an attempt to minimise the behaviour and then find that they are happy to wet the bed every night. This is not like Full Immersion where a 24/7 baby existence is simply not possible. Wetting the bed every night and every nap *is* possible. If you want to push your Little One beyond the level of fantasy, then you must ensure that it is even possible to do so!

Some parents simply can't handle a wet bed at all, while others are so used to regular wet sheets, that formally integrating it into the relationship is relatively easy. Let's hear from a Little One as to what bedwetting means to them.

"I wet the bed every night until I was 15. I saw nothing wrong with it and didn't see any real reason to stop. I told a few friends about it when I was at school and several had wet nearly as long as me. If I'm honest, I still don't really see anything wrong with it!

I learned early on that my mother wasn't proud of my wet bed even though I was. She mostly just ignored it. Most mornings I would lie in my sister's wet bed and enjoy it after getting out of my own. I started wearing her wet nappies in the morning at age five and when her nappies were taken away I started getting in her wet bed instead.

When I was 18 my pee-stained mattress was replaced with a new one and I was devastated as they burnt a mattress I had spent years making the way I wanted it to be. Every stain meant something to me and a lot of them I had made deliberately.

My bed-wetting never really fully stopped and I continued to have them off and on. Sometimes I would wake in the night needing to pee and just did it in the bed. I guess I often felt more comfortable in a wet bed than a dry one. And certainly I felt fantastic seeing the wet patch I had created. I know my Little Girl adored the sight of the wet bed she had created. Even after marriage I couldn't bring myself to totally give up bedwetting. Most was still accidental but sometimes I just <u>had</u> to wet the sheets. Stress made me wet more and I found that a large wet bed often reduced my stress level enormously which of course meant I did it more!

I started to stain our mattress with unprotected wetting and I felt deeply satisfied every time I saw it soaking wet. When I woke up wet my first thoughts were always happy ones. I felt pleased about it and felt it was a good thing. I went through phases of wetting the bed nightly and not changing them – just drying them and they looked great, smelt fabulous, but weren't real spouse-friendly so I didn't get that for very long.

I've slept wet a number of times – gone to sleep in an already wet bed. When the weather is warmish, it's terrific. I feel happy, relaxed and natural. I don't know why a wet bed has such an attraction, but it always has. I had a few occasions when my wife found I was wet in the morning and then she wet on my side of the bed to give me a sort of gift of sorts. It was absolutely awesome!

I am incontinent now which means nappies day and night. There are wet nappies every night, but never a wet bed. I still miss my wet bed a lot."

[personal email]

It is clear that for some, a wet bed holds huge attraction, while for others, it is something they avoid at all costs.

If you wish to integrate it into your lives, then you need to work out your personal limits. Perhaps you can permit one or two wet beds a month or, if you have a separate single bed, then allow nap-time bedwetting. You also obviously need to work on limits for how much you allow him, so as not to affect your own sleep. The question of washing the sheets every night also comes up. For most, that is a given, but some Little Ones will fight you on that. The reason for this is that washing removes all evidence of their *impressive effort.*

Just as with Full Immersion, you can deal with bedwetting in a similar fashion, with the intention being to remove the fantasy of sleeping in soaked sheets. The easiest way to do this, is to give them a separate bed with a plastic under-sheet and deny them diapers at night and to not permit use of the toilet after 8pm or earlier. A very wet bed will ensue and rather than change it, just open the bed up and let it dry as best it can and repeat the next night. The same applies to the pyjamas or baby nightie that are being worn. Just dry them out. This works well as part of a Full Immersion scenario as well. It could be modified to encourage naps in the wet bed as well. However, unless bedwetting is a primary issue for the Little One, you should not encourage them to sleep in wet sheets. That is just an unnecessary and counter-productive behaviour.

The *unreal bedwetting fantasy* is a common one, so you may have to be inventive in dealing with it, but by and large, this means you will need to *encourage* your Little One to sleep in wet sheets at least once. Once he learns that a wet bed isn't really where he wants to sleep for extended periods, then you can hopefully put that difficult behaviour back in the box where it belongs and deal with bedwetting in a more controlled manner.

There is another aspect of the bedwetting fantasy that may result from deliberate bedwetting. Andrew T Austin writes that deliberate bedwetting can be used as a technique to *end* bedwetting itself! This method is called "paradoxical intention".

*"However, there is another method that is very successful, but that so many therapists are reluctant to suggest and enuretic patients reluctant to try. It turns all logic on its head and is termed "paradoxical intention." Developed by psychiatrist and holocaust survivor Viktor Frankl, paradoxical intention has an astonishing success rate. The essence of the technique is that the person makes a mental shift from trying to not have the problem to **actively engaging in doing the problem**.*

So for example, the panic attack sufferer deliberately practices having panic attacks, the nail biter deliberately bites their nails, the insomniac is encouraged to lie still and try and stay awake as long as possible, and so on. What begins to occur is that the unconscious impulses that drive the behaviour begin to move into consciousness and thus under conscious control. As a therapist I have [seen] this especially helpful with problems such as blushing and anxiety.

What this means for the adult bed wetter is that rather than trying to control the problem, they engage in the conscious effort to produce the problem. As unpleasant as it might seem, getting into bed with a full bladder and deliberately urinating into the bed is the first step.

When I work with a client, I listen carefully to the objections they raise regarding this; often-useful information arises regarding the unconscious nature of the problem.

Now, just deliberately wetting the bed isn't enough. What you have ahead of you is the uncomfortable experience of deliberately spending the night in the wet bed.

You must not change the sheets until morning.

As you can imagine, sleep is unlikely to be very easy doing this experiment. You must carry on your day activities, such as work etc as normal. The experiment must be integrated into your normal daily life-routine and not sectioned off as a special event that is unconnected."

[Andrew T Austin]

You can probably already see a bit of a connection between the way I have suggested *enforced or strongly encouraged* regressive behaviour and our ultimate goal: balance. You may sometimes have to force your Little One to do some things for his own good.

Joining your Little One as a Baby or Toddler:

The idea that you can join your Little One and play with them at their own level doesn't naturally occur to many parents. However, it can be very good for your child and can also be a lot of fun, if you open your mind to it! This is not an idea that naturally springs from the biological parent/child relationship, as it doesn't really happen there very often. In many ways, the nearest parallel to this is having a playmate for your child, except that *you* are the playmate!

In this kind of play scenario, you are *role-playing* being a child or toddler while your Little One is *regressed*. This way, your Little One gets good play time with a similar-aged individual. If you already happen to have a safe and reliable Little play partner for your child, then this may be less helpful, although still valuable. And yes, this can mean wearing a diaper and perhaps even using it. Don't worry, you won't be harmed by the experience!

There are a number of significant pluses to this form of interaction. For one, you get to interact with your child at *their* level. There are some aspects of your child that you may only ever see or understand from being at their own level. Playing tea parties or dolls with your child, will be both fun for them and instructive for you. Playing cars with your Little Boy will help develop a stronger awareness of their inner self. Above all, it can actually be quite good fun, if you open your mind to the concept!

Some parents think that they are either mocking their child or demeaning themselves by playing at their child's level. Not so! Playing at their own level is perhaps the single most powerful act imaginable for closely identifying with your child. I would encourage all parents to try it and to persevere with it. It is never demeaning to help someone or to work or play alongside them in a close and pseudo-intimate manner.

It is possible that your Little One may not want you as a playmate and instead, prefer you as the parent only. However, most would regard your involvement in role-playing being their playmate to be an astonishing act of love and commitment to the relationship. Few will reject it and almost all will embrace it.

One common objection to this interaction is the fear that the parent may *really get into it*. On the surface, this appears to be a valid fear, but if you think about it, it isn't really all that rational or reasonable. Regression, of the type we are discussing here, isn't contagious, nor can it be taught. Role-playing however, can be taught if you want to. Regression cannot. If by some chance, you find yourself enjoying role-playing as your Little One's playmate, then exactly where is the problem? You have found something that is good for him and good for your relationship, that you are both totally in control of and thoroughly enjoy. That sounds like the rare win-win scenario to me. If that happens, enjoy it! If you were likely to be regressive, then you would already have experienced it by now.

There is often a very real fear in discovering that something you previously thought to be stupid or abhorrent, is actually okay and fun. We value our judgements and values very highly and we don't easily alter them. However, that doesn't mean we shouldn't occasionally challenge our presumptions and biases. It is amazing how over the period of years, our previously strongly held opinions can evaporate in the light of new information and experience.

So how do you play with your Little One? The most obvious way to start is by getting down to his level both physically and behaviourally. If your child has a good collection of baby/toddler clothes then you should really wear something babyish, including his play clothes, or at least something convincing. And yes, a diaper is probably an essential. A diaper is *the* dominant Attachment Object for Little Ones and you can't easily avoid wearing one, if you are going to be his playmate. Using the diaper (wetting it) is optional, but doing so makes the experience more authentic to your Little One. It can also lead to additional play activities such as mutual diaper changing, which may lead to an intimacy you are unprepared for: where you meet in the act of love as equals, but also as Littles. If that appears scary to you then just forget about it for now and come back to it later on. There is a great deal of other play aspects to explore first.

The enjoyment of playtimes is not restricted just to regressive Little Ones. There is a huge community of people who role-play being a child (Age Players). They do this deliberately, because it can be fun. How often have you wanted to colour-in or play with a child's toy and wish you had a chance? Don't lie now! The answer is at the very least *sometimes* and for many, *often*. Now you can, and you have a legitimate excuse. You are being your Little One's play partner and there is yet another reason to join your baby in playtime – to direct the play experience.

Playtime Direction:

Many Little Ones *want* to play, but perhaps don't know exactly how to do so. The strictures of adulthood can often affect the Little One so that they find it hard to play, despite the fact that they want to and desperately need to. Also, remember that if your Little One has swapped gender then they probably have little to no real-life experience in playing at that age and gender. Here is where the parent can offer so much valuable assistance. You can offer it either as the carer/babysitter/parent role or, as previously hinted at, you can do so as their playmate.

As a parent, you can direct their playtime better by showing them how to play with their dolls, blocks and other toys in the correct gender role. You can also help choose the better children's television shows or DVD movies and watch with them. One of the most popular Little One television shows is 'Dora the Explorer', which seems to entrance little children and Little Ones alike.

As a playmate, you can direct their play and teach them how to do so better. Few women really forget the fun they had with tea parties and dolls or how to play with a doll-house. They may grow out of it, but they don't forget. Nor do men forget the pleasure of building with blocks and Lego or the fun from racing cars around the room and building tracks for them. Look back into your own childhood and remember how you played. Then pass on the information to your Little One.

Early on in the Parent/Child relationship, the Little One may feel quite inhibited in playtime. This can be because they feel that they don't know how to do it properly or because they are afraid of the parent's reaction. And let's be realistic here, that can be a real problem for some. If you aren't fully committed to the Parent/Child relationship, then watching or participating in toddler-age playtime may feel really stupid and idiotic to you and your Little One will quickly realise how you feel. Yes, it seems odd at first, but the value of play cannot be overstated.

Playtime is essential to the balanced development of any biological child. It is no different for the Little One.

As part of the over-arching goal of seeking balance in their lives and in the relationship, playtime has a pivotal place that cannot be overstated.

You will find many things in the Little One's world you are uncomfortable with and unable to accept or permit. That's life in the real world, but don't let it be playtime. It is one of the essential elements of regression and a very large part of a Little One's inner needs.

Colouring-in and Drawing:

Colouring-in and drawing are very natural play behaviours for children and also for Little Ones. Your Little One may be embarrassed at first or even feel inhibited. Perhaps the reason for that inhibition may be because colouring seems to possess a very special aspect to it.

This activity, along with free-drawing, is the classic play used to communicate with young children about difficult topics, including trauma and abuse. With multiple-age Little Ones, you can easily detect which age personality is there, by watching them colour or draw. You can also detect their inner mood by watching their colour choice. It can be extremely therapeutic and it is worth keeping colouring books and pencils wherever you go, just in case! Colouring may tell you more about your Little One than you expect.

If you are looking for a specific activity to do with your Little One, then this is the top one to try. It is easy and fulfilling and better than watching television. A good idea is to keep all of your Little One's colouring books, date them and occasionally make some notes on them. They are a diary of the journey you and your child are on. In time, you will see some remarkable changes just in their drawings.

Toileting:

This is *not* what you think it is! This is not my idea, but has come up from other couples who practice it. It can be a very powerful experience at times, if it suits you. This is essentially an intimacy experience based on urine and/or faeces. Yes, believe it or not, this does actually work for some.

This is an extension of the 'wet your baby's bed' routine and can work as a reward for a Little One, especially if they have boundary or behavioural problems. The principle at play here is that the Little One believes that your pee and/or poo is an expression of love and intimacy and he wants to be part of that intimate experience. Your child may not have considered the idea (until they read it here), but it does seem to come up reasonably often with Littles and their partners.

This behaviour comes in two basic forms: personal and impersonal toileting. In *impersonal toileting,* you will wee and/or poo either into a potty and then immediately pour it into his diaper, or you will wet and/or soil onto a clean diaper and then put it on him. This is considered a special *gift* to the Little One. *Personal toileting* is where the diaper is opened and you wee and/or poo directly onto your Little One and then re-pin or retape the diaper. Obviously this is a very private experience and the issue of diaper rash is also quite important.

Now that I have disgusted you sufficiently, be aware that this is not uncommon as a fantasy and those that do it in real life find it nowhere near as bad as it sounds here! If it is done for reward and as an expression of intimacy, then it can have very positive results. Just don't discount anything just yet!

I include this form of play primarily to underline the notion that interaction with your Little One is not simply restricted to <u>typical</u> child behaviours. You can extend the formula or add new aspects to it, all of your own design. Be inventive and allow your playtime to develop new and exciting facets.

Toileting may not be your scene and it isn't for most, but it shows that a little imagination and risk can possibly bring a new and exciting chapter into your playtime with your child.

Enforced or Parent-initiated Little Time:

Little Time that is at the convenience and behest of your child is one thing. It is an entirely *other* experience for him to be *required* by you to become Little. You already know his regressive triggers and his baby name, so use them and deliberately create a Little Time for him (and you) to enjoy.

Who said that regression is only at the behest of the Little One? There are a number of reasons why you could choose to initiate the regression yourself.

- You could see that he is clearly in need of Little Time, but is afraid or hesitant to do so.

- You could also be wanting some interaction with your Little One yourself. If you are developing a sexual intimacy that includes the Little One, then this is a primary reason to learn how to initiate regression.

- You may wish to role-play being Little with him and need him to be your child partner.

- In previous adult-adult conversation, your Little One has indicated he would like you to feel free to regress him at your whim.

- Any other reasonable reason.

You may find that your Little One responds quite differently if you initiate it yourself, from when he becomes Little on his own. Play with the concept and enjoy taking a bit of pre-emptive control over his regression. Do not assume he is unwilling to regress for you and the change in dynamic might be good fun!

Playing dress-ups (not just for the girls):

Every child likes to play dress-ups – at least the girls do. Your Little One is probably no different. You can dress him in his own baby/toddler clothes of course, and perhaps try out every outfit he has. You could make it like a fashion show. I'm sure you remember those dress-up times as a child yourself? Fun, right?

You could get him to try out different panties or bras and you can try some older dress-ups. If he has older girl's clothes available, then try those as well as shoes, if they fit.

What about make-up? Remember experimenting with it as a little girl? Replicate the experience for him. Little Ones rarely venture into the big-girl world of make-up, so perhaps you could put him in make-up or teach him how to use it. Decorate his nails and don't forget to do those toenails (which he can keep for a while!). You will find that your Little One is fascinated by make-up, but afraid to use it and probably has no idea how to do so. The same thing also applies to jewellery as well. Bracelets, necklaces and rings are all things you could get for your Little One. Trying some of these things will help you find out what your Little One likes and doesn't.

Don't be afraid to experiment with new things and ideas. It would be difficult to truly fail if you are inventive enough. He may not like it, but he will certainly appreciate the effort. You may also be surprised by an activity that you both like and never even considered before.

Erotic Spanking:

Erotic spanking is a part of many couple's sex lives or role-play times. As part of play, spanking certainly fits into the Little One's experience, if you both desire it and are used to it. The BDSM (Bondage, Domination, Sado-Masochism) community has its own sets of rules and guidelines for spanking, but they are for consensual adults during adult sex play. When a Little One gets involved it is more complex (obviously).

Let's start by being clear on terminology. I use the term 'spanking' when talking about consensual erotic play.

When I refer to 'smacking' I mean disciplinary smacking designed to hurt and to give behavioural guidance and impetus to the Little One.

I cover that subject in the Modification Section, later on. If erotic spanking remains purely in the adult zone, then you already know what you are doing and if not, consult the BDSM literature for advice.

It is common-place for Little Ones that erotic or sexual activity triggers a regression to their Little state. Therefore, you need to carefully consider how erotic spanking fits into a Little One's experience. Sexuality per se, is not part of the biological child's experience, but we still permit and even encourage sexual behaviour among Little Ones with their *parent* (refer Sexual Intimacy and the Little One). We recognise that sexuality cannot be just ignored when it is a biological imperative, regression nor not.

So the question is this: do you spank your Little One or not? Experience is your best teacher in this, so use your eyes, your brain and your intuition. Your Little One will easily distinguish between receiving an erotic spanking and a punishment smack. Or, they may not. You need to find out how they are reacting to it and to act accordingly. You may need to either eliminate it for your Little One, or moderate the severity, so that they know quite clearly that this is play, rather than discipline. The reality is that the deeply regressed Little One can think quite differently to the adult side, so you can't make any assumptions until you are sure.

In short, there is nothing that explicitly excludes erotic spanking from your Little One's life, but you need to be very aware that the ground rules can change dramatically when they regress.

Petticoat Punishment:

This idea comes out of the cross-dressing community, but it also has a significant historical aspect in that in centuries past, boys were sometimes dressed in girls clothes, primarily for reasons of behaviour. A classic definition is:

> *"Petticoat discipline can be defined as the time honoured act by dominant females of the dressing of high-spirited and unruly boys in clothing normally considered appropriate for females as a form of degrading and shameful punishment for males, so as to encourage in them a favourable change towards more obedient behaviour and increased respect for the feminine gender."*

> *[source unknown]*

This kind of interaction is somewhat out of character in a Little One, but its prevalence in the Adult Baby community suggests that it is still part and parcel of many Little's experience and perhaps, needs. It is for many, essentially a subset of *dressing up*.

It may be possible to integrate a form of Petticoat Punishment into your interaction with your Little One. Firstly, it isn't really *punishment* at all, but rather a form of play or acting a role, within their regression. If your Little One is a boy, you could introduce him to panties or pink nappies or even add a bra and dress and of course, don't forget the actual petticoat! Even the Little Boys sometimes like to do a bit of cross-gender play acting.

This is one interaction activity that can extend beyond Little Time. You could encourage your Little one to wear some *sissy* clothing when in adult mode. He could start wearing panties at your discretion or even an unpadded bra. Give it a try and see how it works!

Encouraging Crawling or Baby Walking:

Part of many Littles' playtime experience involves crawling. Sometimes, encouraging them to crawl is good, as it gives them impetus to explore a forbidden or hidden part of their regression. Most adults find it hard to crawl on the knees, yet find using their feet to be lacking in authenticity. To the rescue comes skate-boarding protection! If you want your Little One to experiment with some serious levels of crawling, then get them some kneepads to protect the knees. While totally out of character, it makes crawling much, much easier for them to do on hard surfaces and it works spectacularly well.

A key to remember is that if your Little is wearing a dress, it needs to be a very short one, otherwise boy's clothes, romper or onesie are fine.

To add authenticity to the toddler walking experience you can use *waddle pants*, which are very thickly padded diaper pants that keep the legs wide apart and enforce a more baby-like walking style. You can get the same effect by folding up several thick cloth diapers inside their regular diaper, so that they cannot walk comfortably, but waddle instead. If you make it thick enough, they may find crawling *easier* than walking. In effect, you have enforced a baby behaviour upon them. As part of your playtime, this can be exceptionally valuable, because it means that *you* are directing play and are also directing their age experience.

Crawling and baby-style walking adds tremendous amounts of authenticity to the regressed experience. You should at least sometimes enforce some crawling on your Little One to see how they react. Teaching them authentic behaviours will enhance the regression experience and therefore meet the need more effectively. This helps push the child towards balance – our ultimate goal.

Restraints, locks, reins and mittens:

Babies and toddlers get into things they shouldn't. Normally involuntary misbehaviour such as this should be dealt with as part of the Discipline process. It is far easier for all concerned that you have a well-behaved and happy Little One.

Playtimes however, can be a little different. The rules of behaviour are closer to that of role-play than simple regression. After all, children *all* role-play as a large part of their development. Why expect Littles to be any different?

I do not recommend the use of restraints and locks for real-life discipline of the Little One. That is inappropriate and potentially dangerous, but for playtime, that is altogether different. These props can also add that all-important authenticity to your play-times.

Locks: You can buy plastic pants with chain loops and a lock through the waist band to prevent removal without the key. This is fun for when you want to play 'naughty baby'. Some dresses and other toddler clothes likewise come with chains and locks to prevent removal. Most adult cots and playpens have optional locks to prevent a baby or toddler from getting out, so as to replicate the biological infant's total dependence on the parent to allow them to get them up.

Restraints: A baby can have his movements restrained by straps that hold his hands to the side. There can also be basic straps in the cot that stop the baby from getting up and out.

Reins: They are coming back into vogue now; reins for new walking toddlers, so they don't get lost in a crowd. Obviously highly unsuitable for a real crowd, they are nevertheless fun to use at home during playtime. One use is that the reins can be tied to a table leg and the Little one is therefore restricted in their travel distance. This again seeks to replicate the biological toddler's limitations in movement around the house. There are also walking-reins to simply join a parent's hand with her child's hand while out in a group. This could be used indoors or in limited very safe outdoor experiences, where no other people are around.

Mittens: Normally used to keep baby's hands warm, the mitten has several additional uses for Little Ones. They severely restrict the ability to hold things and can even be thick enough to render that impossible. This adds a great deal of authenticity to the playtime by limiting their motor skills closer to that of a toddler. Mittens can also come with locks which prevent removal. They have a genuine behavioural aspect in that if your Little One has a serious (and even unconscious) masturbation problem, then locking mittens can prevent it. It frustrates them so you still need to handle the underlying cause, but it certainly stops the act itself.

Hypnosis CDs and downloadable files:

There are a lot of hypnosis-like CDs and downloadable files of variable effectiveness available to help the Little One wet and/or soil better. Now this might seem absolutely absurd to you when you are trying to help your Little *control* regression. Stick with me here. It isn't necessarily contrary to the goal, rather it is about enhancing the experience. Firstly, let's start with a few caveats:

- Despite the promises, they don't work all that well. Hypnotic suggestion is often a failure, even when done by a one-on-one professional. When using a audio tape, the chances of success are even lower.

- Hypnosis can't make you do something you don't really want to do or is against your moral code.

- Any behavioural changes or experiences are easily wound back if you want to.

Now that I have that out of the way, let me say that many Little Ones crave an authentic experience during regression. Diapers are an essential part of that and wetting and soiling them is usually a crucial element. Being able to use the diapers without conscious effort is for many, a real desire. Generally, the hypnosis CDs aim to help him become a genuine bed wetter, diaper wetter and messer, or even fully incontinent.

The diaper community's view on these is that they can have *some* effect, but rarely have the full advertised result. However, with a parent's guiding, a Little should be able to improve their level of wetting by using these CDs, if that is truly desired.

Menstruation:

One truly surprising aspect of grown-up play with a Little One is *menstruation*. Most ladies are now wondering what on earth a man can possibly find attractive about that!

This topic doesn't really fit into the Interaction Section, but it had to go somewhere! Some Little Ones and especially Adult Little Girls, are truly fascinated by menstruation and the fantasy possibility of their own *period*. Clearly, the major driver behind this is *identification* with being female.

There are some Little Ones that include a menstruation aspect to their regression. While a period is hardly part of a genuine infant/toddler/little girl experience, some Littles do integrate it into their regression at times. So be aware that if you find pads and tampons in your Little One's collection, this may be why.

Meeting Others:

Not every Little One wants to meet other Littles, nor do parents necessarily wish to meet other parents in similar situations. Many single or still-secretive Littles want to meet others as much for affirmation that they are normal and not alone, as for any other reason. Your Little may find that just by becoming your child and having a deep relationship with you, the sometimes desperate need to meet others diminishes or disappears altogether. However, *your* Little One may still want to meet others, so what do you do?

For starters, you need to ask yourself if *you* wish to meet other parents or Littles yourself. Do you want, or need, to meet another parent like yourself and either get some good advice, or just friendship based on a similar situation?

There are a variety of meetings which you can have. The most common is the 'munch', where like-minded people meet in an open place like a restaurant or cafe in normal attire and behaviour and simply enjoy each other's company, as well as meet those in similar situations. It is primarily social, non-threatening and allows friendships to grow or for mentoring relationships to develop. As good as a book like this can be, it can also be exceptionally valuable to have a friend or mentor who has been through this all before, who can guide you through some of the difficulties and swamps in the Parent/Child world. Check out websites for Adult Babies or Age-Players for more details or even large community sites like Fetlife.com or dailydiapers.com.

Sex. This is not really what meeting others is for and I am sure that is what you are perhaps thinking and worrying about. Sure, some Littles do meet and have intimate relations, but essentially, meeting others is about eliminating the isolation that so often affects Parent/Child couples. For many, isolation is a fine and valid choice. They may still be embarrassed by it, or at least feel no desire whatsoever to talk to anyone else about it. It is certainly safer and more anonymous.

There are advantages and disadvantages either way. The choice is essentially one for *both* of you to make. You both need to feel comfortable meeting others in the adult realm, as well as considering meeting others in the Parent/Child realm. Some do have small groups, where their Little Ones play together and while that sounds cute and fun, it is very hard to find well-matched, well-behaved Littles and parents to make it work well. Having a mutual fetish or behaviour in common is no guarantee for compatibility. It is just like the world at large, where friendships work on the basis of commonality over multiple levels and areas, so keep your expectations reasonable and on the low side and hope to be pleasantly surprised.

Whatever you do, be comfortable with your own lifestyle and how you relate to others or not. The most important thing is to be safe and to be true to your own self.

And a word to Littles here: *your parent's wishes on this are paramount. If she doesn't want to meet others, then that is her right and it is your responsibility to both understand it and to obey it!*

Satisfying the Desire vs Meeting the Need

As you work through the process of interacting with your Little One over a period of time, some things can happen that neither of you are expecting or have any experience in. When you give your partner some Little Time, you typically *satisfy the inner desire* to be little. That makes a lot of sense and it is a big part of this book's goal – to help your Little get these desires satisfied. After all, someone whose deep desires are never met, can be a unhappy and grumpy person and certainly not the person you wish to spend your life with! Therefore, *satisfying the need* is important and an essential part of the Little One's experience.

However, over time, it can develop beyond simply satisfying a desire, as if it were nothing more than a mere biological need, like food. Repeated deep satisfaction of the desire to be Little can ironically, lead to the next stage which is 'meeting the need'. Let me explain the difference.

Your Little One will want all the interaction and littleness you can give him. It satisfies a very deep longing and desire in his heart, but at some point your Little will experience a time when they don't actually feel any need to regress at all! Now this is only a temporary experience and may be hours or days or even as long as a few weeks. What has happened, is that you have helped him meet the *inner need* to be Little and not simply satisfied the desire for a few childish activities. For a brief time, your Little One will feel like everyone else does, with no strong desire to regress lurking in the background. How does that sound for an unexpected development?

This is not a cure, rather, this is the first sign of that all-important goal of *balancing the need* to be Little, with the real world requirement to be an adult. This is where he moves from simply satisfying the desires and actions of being a Little, to meeting the deep-seated need itself. Let's hear one Baby Girl describe how it happened to him.

"I've always felt I was a baby girl inside ever since I can remember. All my life I have sought out opportunities to wear a nappy or a girls dress or to play as a girl or just be little. But it was always moments here and there, not large slabs of time. If anything, just spending ten minutes as a baby in secret made the desires stronger as they reminded me of what I really wanted and could never get much of.

Just recently, my wife entered the Parent/Child relationship with me and I became her baby daughter. I wear baby clothes every night to bed and I am in nappies full-time although that started earlier from incontinence. She bought me a few toys and pencils etc and it has been terrific. My inner child has had time to express herself without as much hiding or rushing to get it over and done with.

Yesterday she bought me a Princess Play mat so I have a safe and bounded place to play, but she also bought me a Dora 'blankie' for me to sleep or nap with. And as if to underscore her parenting role she 'sent' me to bed to nap with my new blankie. It was a wonderful, exciting, wide-eyed child time for me.

Today we went to buy me a pencil case for my growing collection. Normally even being in a toy section is exciting for me – never mind buying something with mummy. But today I felt oddly disconnected from those normal Little feelings. I was quite able to choose a pencil case that I knew my Little Baby Girl would love, but I was buying FOR her not AS her! It was a new thing for me. Even when I am an adult I look through children's eyes to buy the baby things I need or even just to browse the toy stores. Today I looked through adult eyes as I bought it. I realised then that the night before I had slept without my dolls or even my dummy for the first time in quite a while.

It is an odd experience to feel fully adult like this. It is also a bit of a sense of loss but I guess I will get used to that. I know it won't last, but it is amazing just the same."

[personal contact]

The writer is correct when he says that it won't last. His deep regressive need hasn't been solved or cured. It has just been fully *met*, probably for the first time ever. This is the place a parent wants their child to reach – a place of balance, where the *need* is met, not just the desires being satisfied. For a brief moment, the desires are actually not even there!

Be warned that Littles may be terrified of the notion of such an experience. It is because few ever really get there and it sounds quite daunting and even unpleasant. Be understanding of their reaction. It may feel like a sense of loss to them at first, but in time they will understand more. Just be wary of it and give them some space to process these new feelings and reactions.

Reacting to your Little One and his self-image

Seeing your Little One in full regression for the first few times can be a disturbing experience for some. Watching your forty year old husband in a thick wet diaper, toddling around in a frilly baby dress, sucking on an oversized pacifier and clutching an old teddy bear he has kept for years, is not an everyday sight. He looks silly, doesn't he? And this is what you've been thinking about all this time, while reading this book. You have been struggling with the seeming *absurdity* of the situation. You are not alone. One of the biggest hurdles a partner faces initially in developing a working Parent/Child relationship, is dealing with the *absurdity* aspect.

From a normal adult's point of view, dressing up as a baby might be okay at a costume party. It might even be acceptable in a role play situation where sex is the goal (sexual desires excuse almost every behaviour!). But when you consider your partner wanting to *live* as a baby with all the peripheries, like wet and soiled diapers, feeding, crawling, clothing and toys, it all just all-too-easily slips over into the *absurd* category. This is something you really are going to have to deal with, if the

Parent/Child relationship is to truly work. But have you thought about what your Little One thinks of how he looks?

Your Little One does *not* look in the mirror and see the middle-aged man with a paunch, wearing a dirty diaper and an over-the-top baby dress. He sees a two year old girl, who needs her mother to change her diaper. He doesn't feel silly at all, which accounts for at least some of the exhibitionism, but rather, he feels quite happy and at peace. Let me quote someone who wrote of this phenomenon.

"When I put on my whole baby girl outfit from bonnet to booties, I feel transformed from the ugly duckling into a beautiful baby princess. It is as if I stepped through the magic mirror into a world where I am pretty and happy and safe! I feel relaxed and I feel like I am finally being the real me."

[Internet blog]

That says it all really. As hard as you might find it, you are going to have to learn to see through *her* eyes (not your own!). Be aware that a gender shift as a Little One, greatly affects their perception of themselves.

You can try this exercise. Visualise a real two year old sitting on the floor, playing with toys and then look at your Little One and put him into that same place in your mind. The clue is that it really *is* a real two year old on the floor! When you reach the place of accepting that, the absurd image you see before you today, will transform into the happy and contented child that he sees and experiences. It will take time and some creativity, but it is certainly worth it.

If you constantly think that your Little One looks foolish and ridiculous, it will affect how you treat him. This mind-set has the potential to destroy everything you work on. You cannot leave this attitude unresolved!

One plus in all of this, is that you can help out your usually fashion-challenged Little One. Some Adult baby clothes are either poorly made or are ill-suited to a *lifestyle* baby/toddler, as most are costume quality, rather than designed for every-day wear. Using your input, you can get your Little One dressed in proper *lifestyle* childish clothes, without all of the frills and lace that adorn some outfits. Your child will wear anything you choose or make. Try it! It will also help with how you view him.

HOMEWORK: *Check out eBay and Google adult baby clothes. Then as an exercise, make a wish list of several outfits you think would look better on him. At some stage, share this with him and talk about the pros and cons of each outfit you choose.*

Let's put a bit of perspective on the self-image question. We've been talking about your Little One's self-image, but what is your *own* self-image like? If you are like most people, your self-image is based predominantly on lies, delusions and wishful thinking. Like the vast majority of people, you believe yourself to be one thing, but others see you as something quite different – the reality. You may think you are attractive, but really you are most likely, just average. You think you are a *little* overweight, but in fact you are actually a *lot* overweight. Most bald men are the last to realise it is happening or has already happened. You may think you are a great conversationalist, but the truth may be that you just talk a lot.

Most of us are like that. We comfort ourselves with inaccurate and often plain delusional views about ourselves. This not necessarily bad and is in fact normally quite healthy, as long as it is not obsessive. Obsession with self-image develops into narcissism, while zero interest in self-image, turns us into slovenly, non-achieving, self-haters.

When you realise that your own self-image is both incorrect *and healthy,* you may start to realise that your Little One's self-image may not be quite as crazy and absurd as you currently consider it. A Little One's self-image *is* absurd, but it is not necessarily unhealthy. If your Little One feels safe, happy, comfortable and relaxed in his baby outfit or playing with his toys, then where is the *true absurdity* in that? When was the last time *you* felt safe, happy, comfortable and relaxed?

Perhaps, in his absurdity, your Little One has been granted an oasis of peace and serenity that eludes most of us, most of the time. Rather than criticise and even silently mock, we should be jealous that he has found a place that most of us find strangely elusive: peace.

Sexual Intimacy and the Little One

This is a difficult topic to talk about, but one that needs to be tackled head-on. Many, even most, Little Ones have some sexual intimacy issues that arise as a direct result of their regressive personalities.

Sexual problems dominates the list of issues and problems that partners have with their Little Ones. Sometimes the problems are quite severe, leading to a total loss of sexual intimacy or an extremely low frequency, with an equally low satisfaction level. Unfortunately, severe sexual dysfunction is a major reason for relationship failure and therefore, we need to address sexuality within the confines of the Parent/Child relationship.

Here is a list of common causes of sexual problems with Little Ones and their partners:

- **Excessive masturbation**. Many Little Ones masturbate to excess and this lowers the libido, consequently making adult sexual intimacy more difficult, due to erectile dysfunction and other problems.

- **Gender identity issues**. Many Little Ones identify as female or sissy, while as adults, being physically male and happily so. This confusion can sometimes slip into adult behaviour, especially during sexual intimacy and disrupt their performance, as they struggle and sometimes alternate, their gender role during the act of making love.

- **Sexual Skill transfer**. Many Little Ones experience the bulk of their sexual fulfilment (orgasm), while dressed or acting as their Little One. After a while, they may feel unable to fully express themselves sexually to their partner when not wearing Little One clothes or diapers or other props, usually attachment objects.

- **Confidence issues**. These are common problems for everyone. Little Ones have more trouble with this, because they tend to be less confident as a rule.

- **Performance issues**. The reality is that some Little Ones are pseudo-asexual and have either limited sexual desire or zero ability to express it. This is quite okay if the adult is fully sexually capable and able to satisfy his partner. But if not, it can lead to sexual frustration from the partner.

- **Selfishness**. This is a surprising problem, but makes sense when you consider that a child – any child – is essentially selfish and seeks their own pleasure in their own way, much of the time.

- **Issues with perceived and behavioural age during sex**. It can be a bit of a head-spin to be engaging in sex with your Little One, if they are a very convincing pre-schooler. This problem is one that some parents struggle with for obvious reasons.

- **Sexual identification with an inanimate object**. Over time, some Little Ones may develop a sexual attraction and pseudo-relationship with an *object,* rather than a person. This is not the same as masturbating *in* a diaper – which is common – but rather having a form of sexual expression *with* the diaper. This is usually as an alternative to human sexual relations and occurs for a variety of reasons.

- **Taking advantage**. Some parents can feel as if initiating or engaging in sexual intimacy with their Little One is *taking advantage* of their regressive/submissive position.

Excessive masturbation:

Of all the problems, this is perhaps the easiest one to deal with. Essentially, reduce masturbation significantly! Well, perhaps that isn't as easy as it sounds, especially for the uncontrolled Little One, but if the parent becomes involved, then it becomes significantly easier. A parent could impose some restrictions on masturbation, including requiring permission or at least admission-after-the-fact. That will most likely not totally work particularly well, but if the Little One wishes to improve sexual intimacy, then he can certainly do this. Even a little reduction in the frequency of masturbation (with orgasm) can bring improved results. It is certainly worth trying as a first step. Part of the Parent/Child relationship is that you, as the parent, have significant control over your child and this is a place to exert some of it. Require that he inform you of masturbating, either before or after and it will slow things down, right from the start.

A major reason for excessive masturbation is because the Little One sometimes lacks the confidence to perform with another person, which in turn leads to more masturbation etcetera. It is a vicious cycle that needs to be broken, probably by the intervention of the parent. Another major reason can be because they only feel comfortable to express their sexuality when Little. In most relationships, this excludes the partner and starts the vicious cycle all over again.

The major intervention required here is actually no more than to discuss this issue openly and truthfully. Often, simply discussing it in this manner, makes an enormous difference. If a reduction in masturbation leads to improved and more enjoyable intercourse, then it will mainly solve itself. Masturbation rarely disappears completely and this is not a problem. It only becomes a problem when it replaces, hinders or reduces normal healthy sexual relations.

Generally, imposing any form of discipline for masturbating will be less effective than hoped for. It is a primal urge and trying to quash it is pointless and doomed to failure. This is all about *moving the focus* of the Little One's sexual expression from himself to the partner, rather than trying to reduce the desire. It will take time to change, as there is usually a long and very intense history of masturbation. Those behaviours are not changed overnight, even if everyone wants it to. Move *most* of the masturbation to sexual intimacy and the remainder is just the normal adult level.

Gender Identity Issues:

This problem rarely affects women, who generally don't identify as male in their Little state. It is not unknown, but is still relatively rare.

Many happily heterosexual men have female Little One(s), or identify as female when Little. As well as female, men also often identify as the sissy subset of female, along with all its lace and trimmings. This does not make them gay, but during sexual intercourse, the gender conflict often crops up and can cause difficulties. It can feel contradictory to be making love in the physical male role, when there is a constant female or sissy feeling or presence in the background, particularly if the Little is trying to push to the *foreground*. Putting that regressive feeling to one side can be distracting and limiting and after all, during sex who wants to be thinking about anything else?

It is true that strong sexual desire will often bring on an episode of regression or at least a strong desire for it. Consequently, when the sexual desire begins to lead towards sexual intimacy, the Little One is almost always present and involved, even if only at Level One Regression. The conflict between a primal male act and a female Little One can put a man completely off their stride.

It can be so debilitating that it makes intercourse difficult and therefore not enjoyable, thus leading to avoidance of intimacy altogether. While it would be nice to be able to train your Little One to stay in the background and out of adult activities when you want, that is quite difficult, and in the area of sexuality, it is *exceedingly* difficult. Finding coping mechanisms is a much better way.

Sometimes you can't fix problems. You just have to find a way around them.

Probably the best way to handle this is to bow to the inevitable and accept the duality of the Little and Adult One during intimacy and work through the resultant issues. One way to help is to tell your Little One that *she* is doing well and that you accept *she* is partly female, even though it isn't really true. Anything that builds up confidence and confirms your acceptance of her, just the way she is, is a good thing and a help. Use female pronouns and her baby name to instil confidence. If he is a little boy, accentuate his boyishness and tell him what a good job he is doing. Your demonstrated acceptance of their duality will help them to accept it as well. The mind has an astonishing ability to work around contradictory and impossible-sounding circumstances and to find a working solution, if we want to.

It is still the adult male making love, but the male or female Little One is there at the same time, participating and often leading. That is the difference between Gender Identity Confusion and the next topic – Sexual Skill Transfer.

Sexual Skill Transfer:

This particular problem is a complex and difficult one to deal with and perhaps even to fully understand. It is however, a common issue for many Little Ones and even more so with those with multiple Little personalities or ages.

After a long time as a regressive child, some aspects of the adult personality can end up being *transferred* to a Little One for *exclusive* (or near-exclusive) use. Note that this is technically not true, however, this *is* how it effectively plays out in day-to-day life, so we will refer to it in this manner.

Sexual Performance is one of the most common skills that *transfers*. In this situation, the adult has a normally low libido, meaning that he is less easily sexually aroused, while in contrast, the Little One is fairly easily aroused. Ability to gain and maintain an erection then often becomes predominantly available to just the Little One, resulting in full or partial erectile dysfunction for the adult. In the multiple age scenario, generally only one of the *ages* has the full use of sexual function, although others may have some of it. Some of the ages can literally have zero capacity for sexual interaction.

So, how do we deal with it? Handling this effectively requires you, as the parent, to understand how the dynamic is operating in *your relationship*. It is often very different for various couples and it is your responsibility to work out how it would best operate for *you*. Your *adult* may initiate or respond to sexual advances, but be unable to complete it, without reverting to a Little One. He will therefore start to avoid advances, simply because of repeated failure or rejection by you. Alternatively, he may only be able to respond or initiate sexually as a Little One. Of course, another problem, is that Little Ones tend to be less likely to initiate than an adult and even more so if the Little One is female. You need to work out how your Little thinks and operates and involve them in the process of intimacy. You may not want your Little One involved in your sex life, but that may not be totally possible for you. You need to find out what is going on and act accordingly.

Don't be afraid of being sexually intimate with your Little One. **He isn't a real child.** Keep that in mind. It can be off-putting, but working through this will give you a fully operating sexual relationship and that is always a prize worth working towards.

Little Ones will often use props (see Attachment Objects) such as clothing, diapers, toys etcetera for their play-times to feel real to them. During sex, you will find that your Little One will be far more amorous and capable if you use these objects judiciously as well. Dress your infant in a *short* baby dress and an easily-lowered diaper. Add a pacifier and maybe even a bra, booties or other props. You will find this works very well if you get into the role with him. Try cuddling his favourite soft toy or doll. Try and keep him in the role throughout by repeated references to his Little name and to his position as your baby, toddler or Little Girl. It might sound counter-intuitive to do so, but put your effort into *confirming* his Little identity and to encouraging and rewarding his performance. The adult may be the one performing, but the Little may be the one *driving* that performance. You need to enhance both Little and adult for the best results for you both.

This will take some practice for most couples, but it is worth persevering with. It also tends to upturn the traditional sexual dynamic of the man as initiator and aggressor. It can be very exciting, because marital sex can sometimes become bland after a while, but when you add this kind of dynamic, it can instead, be very good or at least very different!

Above all, be open-minded and creative. It has been said that the most sexual organ in the body is the *brain* and the imagination. Many sexual problems develop as the result of predictable repetition of formulaic behaviours and responses. The one thing you can be guaranteed with intimacy with a Little One, is that there is always a great deal of scope for variation!

Confidence Issues:

Once the rush of teenage hormones are over, we all become a little self-conscious of our sexual abilities and performance. Talking about this with each other is an obvious short-circuit for much of this, but in general, that is exactly what Little Ones *don't* do with their partners on many issues and on sex in particular. And so the cycle goes around and around. Lack of confidence becomes their normal state and ultimately, yours as well.

The best antidote for failure is success. This is not a very deep statement I grant, but what it says is that if you can have just *one* successful sexual encounter, then the next one will be so much easier. Find out what your Little One's buttons are and push them – all of them! Discover what gets his blood pumping and do it! As part of the Identification Process earlier on, you will have found some of the things that sexually arouse him.

I know some people will read this and say *'What about me? What about my needs?'*

The essence of a superlative relationship is in pleasing the other person first and expecting nothing in return. The exquisite irony is of course, that by pleasing the other first, you usually get what you want and far, far more!

In the early days of working out a balanced Parent/Child relationship the parent will do most of the compromise and change, while the Little One's changes come later. As previously stated, that may not be fair, but it is how things work. Just keep hanging in there for the improvements that are undoubtedly heading your way. The real pay-off to the parent comes from the well-balanced and controlled Little One.

If you give and bend in the sexual domain, then your Little One will generally respond well and often.

Performance Issues:

It is always embarrassing to discuss sexual performance. It is an area where we usually prefer to be ignorant, but when performance drops down to near zero level, then it can no longer be ignored. The previous topic addressed confidence, and that is the most common performance problem. However, there are others related to the Little experience.

Most regressive Little Ones have a sexual side to them. As contradictory as it may appear on the surface, the Little One is usually well-formed before the biological age of seven and sexuality then grafts onto the personality at puberty, just as it does to the adolescent. Therefore, the Little One normally has a sexual aspect to them, which may either be sublimated or may be quite open, but there are some – not many – whose Little Ones are almost totally non-sexual. They have no significant sexual drive or capacity when deeply in Little mode. Quite obviously, sexual interaction with a non-sexual Little is not possible, or at least should not be attempted. As long as the adult is fully sexually capable, then asexuality as a Little is not a problem. The problem occurs if the adult has sexual problems as well, in which case a medical opinion should be sought.

Some Little's favour masturbation over sexual interaction with their partner, for fear of not being able to perform adequately with them. Masturbation occurs at their speed, their perceived age and their comfort level. There is in fact, no performance criteria involved at all and so it can become the preferred sexual outlet, not because it is better than intercourse, but because it has no expectations or demands.

And so here comes our first clue: **performance criteria and expectations**.

We create our own problems throughout our lives by attempting to live to certain performance standards which are usually artificial and often simply unachievable. We are told what incomes we should have, what size house we should live in, what type of car we should drive, what schools our children should attend and what degrees they should earn. None of these are in any way related to happiness and ironically, the pursuit of them is often the cause of deep, unrelenting *unhappiness*.

So remove *all* performance criteria from intimacy with your Little One!

This is obviously easier said than done, but it helps if you state openly and often to your Little that there are *no* expectations of any kind. The media often portrays an inability to achieve and maintain a solid erection as something to be embarrassed about and calls it *failure*. This is a big mistake and you shouldn't accept it. Sexual intimacy is such a crucial endeavour, that to use such demeaning terms is doomed to give adults performance anxiety. Why should Littles be any different?

Give yourself a break! Lower your expectations and paradoxically, reap more and better sex.

Once again, the delicious irony is that by removing performance expectations you will most likely improve... performance!

For all other performance issues you should consult your doctor.

Selfishness:

Children, and especially infants and toddlers, are essentially selfish by nature. They take and take and demand and carry on, if their wishes are not met immediately. Unfortunately, Little Ones can sometimes behave in a very similar manner. In most areas of life, you can just ignore a Little's intrinsic selfishness, but in intimacy, that isn't quite so easy to do.

You need to start by not assuming that your Little One necessarily fully understands that they can be selfish in this area. Masturbation, in preference to intercourse, is often simply a selfish act by a partner and especially by a child. That's a note to all you Little Ones reading this! Don't be so selfish! Stop masturbating so much!

Like so many relationship problems, proper communication is the key to resolving it. You may need to explain to him that his sexual actions can be selfish. Be it masturbation or love-making without much regard for the other partner, the Little One needs to learn that even as a Little, they have to share and work properly with others, just as all children have to learn. You may be greatly surprised when you tell your Little One that they are selfish. It could be news to them! So tell them!

Issues with being 'under-age':

This is a topic that is very sensitive, so please don't misinterpret anything I say here. A deeply regressive Little One can sometimes be very convincing as a young child in behaviour, speech and mannerisms. If you close your eyes you can almost imagine that they are a *real* child. But they are *not* a real child and the pivotal fact is exactly that. Your partner is both physically and legally, an adult, but sometimes that is not enough to overcome some basic fears.

No responsible adult wants any involvement in or support of under-age sex and it is not uncommon for some partners to have some serious issues with this. For most, it is something they consider, deal with and move on, but for some it isn't that simple. Here are a few things to consider:

- Your partner is a legal and consenting adult.

- Regression does not remove ability to consent – legally or practically.

- Open your eyes – literally and emotionally – and view your partner as an adult wearing toddler clothes and role-playing being Little. That is far, far closer to the truth, than that he is a real child.

- There is no evidence to suggest that having sex with a regressed Little promotes paedophilic tendencies in any way.

- The act of sexual intercourse is the *least child-like* act that your Little One will ever engage in.

Above all, we must be true to our consciences and if having sexual intimacy with your regressed Little irrevocably violates your moral principles or emotional boundaries, then don't do it. Find an alternative solution.

You may have to suffer a less adequate sex life, but that is better than a broken conscience.

Sexual identification with an inanimate object:

This problem is quite rare, but should be mentioned just the same, if only so you can exclude it. If this genuinely occurs, then you really should seek professional help. With this dysfunction, the Little One seeks an actual sexual *relationship* of sorts with an inanimate object. It is not the same as using an object for gratification or masturbation, but rather where an object takes the place of an actual person and they seek *two-way* sexual gratification. It is clearly not healthy, but fortunately, not common.

Taking Advantage:

This fear is a common impediment to sexual intimacy with the Little One (as opposed to the adult). Caring parents can feel as if they are taking advantage of their Little One's regression and perceived extreme submission. It is a reasonable concern, as a deeply regressed Little One *will* do things the parent wants, that they don't necessarily wish to do. It is all part of the obedience structure that a Parent/Child relationship normally develops and needs.

In normal adult/adult sexual relationships, one or other partner will sometimes participate, even though they really don't want to. That is part of the mutual responsibility aspect of an equal, functional relationship, but a Parent/Child relationship isn't an equal relationship. The parent clearly has more authority and *power* than the Little. Just as in a biological parent/child relationship, that inequality should never be abused or exploited.

A Little One retains the adult at all times in the background. If sexual intimacy is not wanted, then you the parent, need to see and understand their Little signs that they don't want to continue. The Little One himself also needs to be prepared to use the adult self to express that desire or lack of it, to the parent.

In most relationships this fear is not a real one. A little practice and communication will make it very clear if there is any stepping over the line from either party.

Summary:

Let me give you some general tips on dealing with sexual intimacy in a Parent/Child relationship.

- As the parent, become the initiator, either indirectly or directly. Dress your Little One in baby clothes and a diaper, even if he isn't regressive at the time, and let him *drift* into his Little state. It won't take much and you will find his triggers quite easily! Then he can naturally initiate sexual intimacy, even though it was actually your idea! Or you could be the sexual initiator and start your normal advances, but when it reaches a certain stage, introduce such baby props as needed, to ensure he stays connected to his sexual capacity as a Little One. Experiment to find what works best.

- Be inventive! Little Ones have so many activities and roles that you can co-opt. Why does the book you read with your Little One have to be a child's picture book? It could be an adult picture book.

- Wear a diaper yourself and let him know that you have it on. This is a *huge* invitation to intimacy for most Little Ones. You could probably wet it to further add interest. Little Ones are exceptionally attracted to wet things and if you wore and wet a diaper, you would be arousing him a great deal. This also applies to those Little Ones who are fascinated by a wet bed. Some parents have wet the bed and then invited their Little One to come over! It comes across as a sexual invitation to them.

- Panty-sniffing. Men are drawn to the smell of women. You could use their attraction to your advantage. Your Little One probably already wears panties – even the boy babies at time! Why not make them yours? And if they are already worn and carry your scent, then all the better. Let him sniff them and gain his arousal that way.

- Making the sexual connection to your Little One is not as different as perhaps you think. It has long been known and understood that variety is the spice of life. Most people with a long and vibrant sex life practice variation and some involve a wide range of fetishes etcetera. While regression isn't a fetish, many of the principles still apply.

NOTE: One problem that may occur is known as the 'crash'. Orgasm usually causes the Little One to temporarily disappear and for the adult to re-emerge. In masturbation, this is expected and understood and is normally, relatively gentle. During sexual intercourse however, the feelings and emotions are far more intense and can cause the re-emergence to be powerful, fast and at times, overwhelming. Be aware of it and comfort your adult if this happens. It is also a good reminder for both of you to realise that sex was actually between two adults, but the 'crash' can also sometimes be disturbing. Be prepared for tears at times. It is all worth it, however. The recovery from the crash is usually quick and becomes easier if the Little One is permitted to crash and then recover with you there, as his primary support.

In short, if you want a satisfying sex life with your Little partner, then you are going to have to co-opt your Little One(s) into it. It isn't that hard and usually very rewarding. The first time can be a little scary but after that, simply enjoyable.

Be inventive.
Be imaginative.
Be arousing.
Be accepting of your Little One.

SECTION SIX – MODIFICATION

The very act of entering into a Parent/Child relationship with your Little One changes his behaviours. It cannot help but do so. In this section, we are going to discuss further modifying the behaviour of the Little One. This is probably the section an Adult Baby does *not* want to read!

Little Ones often recoil at the mere notion of changing their behaviour and take the immature stance that nothing they do is ever wrong! But as any biological parent knows, behaviour changes are both natural and expected. Some happen on their own and others need to be taught. The same is equally true of Little Ones. Your Little One might be physically an adult, but that doesn't mean that his behaviour doesn't need modification. It almost certainly does!

Changing the way he behaves is not stepping over the line in the relationship, as long as you are both fair and rational about it. Remember that the guiding principle is that he *really is a child* and as such, modifying his behaviour is not only acceptable, but also expected and valuable.

———————

The reality for many Little Ones is that there are behaviours they exhibit, both in the Little and Adult worlds, that are simply not good enough and don't belong there.

———————

Some of these are Little behaviours that leak into the adult world and are now just bad habits. Some Little Ones have excellent behaviour, but not all. If your Little One has exemplary behaviour, then you may skip this section, but I doubt you have a Little One like that! They all have aspects you can improve!

One thing you learn as you get older is that well disciplined, well behaved children are happier and have better life outcomes than the reverse. If you love your Little One enough to enter into this aspect of the relationship, then you should love him enough to help him become a better child and that naturally flows into becoming a better adult.

Who's in charge?

It's one of the dominant questions you now face – who is in charge? It's quite simply really.

———————

When your Little One is there, <u>you</u> are in charge – unequivocally.

———————

Keep in mind that the question of who is in charge applies solely to the regressed state. However, you may find that your partner is more compliant and easier to deal with in the adult world as well. The concept of total obedience to you in the regressed state, does tend to make the adult more understanding of working with another person.

This can be a real power-exchange issue for some women. Despite decades of feminism, many women are still more used to the convention of submission and therefore, *taking charge* does not come naturally or in some cases, at all. In the Parent/Child relationship however, this is not an option. **You are in charge, like it or not.** The relationship cannot function effectively if there is not a parent <u>fully in control</u>.

You are the parent of the regressed Little One. This means that you dictate how he behaves, what he does and when. It is important that, just like any biological parent, that this position does not make you a tyrant demanding unreasonable things from your Little One. Since he is actually a physical adult, he may just refuse and you could then badly damage the relational dynamic that you are carefully building up. However, in return for an open acceptance of and interaction with his regressive Little Side, he has to obey you – not just generally, but *specifically*. You choose what he wears, what he eats or drinks and the TV shows he watches when he is Little. Where he goes and what he does is your decision. That is not unfair or controlling. It is called *parenting,* and is an absolutely essential component of the relationship. Your control releases him from some of his pressures and enables him to learn and experience more as a child.

If you do not take charge, then you will more than likely fail in your goal of establishing a long-lasting and secure Parent/Child relationship. You certainly will not achieve all you could have. It is important that you take control, as refusal to do so is just as damaging as being a tyrant. Little children need control; they need guidance. One of the most important aspects of a healthy Parent/ Child relationship is that the parent acts as a parent and accepts the basic responsibilities.

Over time, you will both find that being a parent who decides what your Little One does is pretty easy and is actually liberating, as well as therapeutic. Little Ones can have a penchant for bad and/or destructive behaviours. Ending this cycle begins with the parent taking responsibility for the Little One's actions and dealing with them.

Let's take a look at how you can help your Little One become a happier and better behaved child.

Teaching your Little One how to behave

Natural Behaviour Changes:

You will by now, have already noticed a great deal of changes in how your Little One is behaving and reacting to you and to his adult life. Your adult partner should be quite different as well. Just by becoming involved in their baby life, you will change things a great deal.

When you initially commence the relationship, the volcano of bottled-up emotions and behaviours may look more like an explosion than an improvement! Just give it time to settle down and then you should be seeing some of the following positive changes, but don't be upset if you aren't seeing all of them yet. They can take time to develop.

Adult Changes:

- Happier demeanour.

- Less stressed.

- More and deeper communication.

- More intimacy, including improved sexual intimacy.

- More positive outlook on life.

- More future-focussed, rather than solely based in the present.

Little One Changes:

- Not hiding as much of his behaviour.

- Less general secrecy.

- More communication about needs and perhaps some (or more) baby-talk.

- Either wetter beds and diapers or drier beds and diapers (either could be considered an improvement depending on the Little One's nature).

- A greater desire to please you and others.

- Reduction in aberrant behaviours (this can take time, so don't despair).

The above changes are natural and erupt out of a developing relationship, based on mutual understanding and acceptance. You will probably be pleased to see these improvements, but it is only the beginning. There is a great deal more to do.

Teaching Better Behaviour:

Up until now, you the parent, have been doing all the changing and all of the giving. The Little One has been the one receiving everything. This is natural and frankly, an essential component of typical early childhood relationships, which when morphed into the Little One Relationship, work no differently. However, it has to change; it has to improve. The Little One has to do some growing up on the behavioural front.

Now is the time to start expecting your Little One to reciprocate, not as a reward for you – even though you deserve it – but for your child's development and for the relationship to thrive and grow.

Any relationship that doesn't grow, will go stale and start to wither. It is just as true – if not more so – in the Parent/Child relationship. At this point, you are probably putting a great deal of effort into the Parent/Child aspect of your relationship and that shouldn't change. What you are seeking to do now, is to use the position you have as parent, to help your Little One do some positive changing as well. Little Ones tend to be self-absorbed, greedy and lazy, as are most biological children, but a Little One needs to move beyond some of that and to take a bigger role in the relationship.

Is your Little One responsible for his diapers? If not, then now is the time to make him partly or totally responsible for them. That means washing, folding, putting away, bagging and throwing out used disposables. It is not unreasonable to give a small child some chores and your Little One should have them as well. Now quite obviously, the adult is actually going to do most of these chores, but that doesn't matter. Your adult has his chores already, but the Little One should have some additional ones, preferably directly related to his regression. Diaper cleanup, toy cleanup and so on is a good start. It helps teach responsibility which, as you may have noticed already, is *not* a strength for many Little Ones.

Now what about tidying up? Many partners are quite poor at this (I'm talking mainly to men here!), but if you are giving your Little One all this attention and time, then it is not unreasonable for your partner (and Little One) to take on some additional domestic chores. As part of being a parent, you will naturally assume overall responsibility for the care of his baby items, including clothes and diapers, but that doesn't mean you should necessarily do all of it. Your Little One should take a growing role in this, under your supervision and guidance. That is probably a significant change for you. Up until now, the Little One has taken full responsibility for his baby things. Now you need to assume full responsibility and then delegate much of the work back to him. It doesn't mean more work for you, but it does mean you are taking overall charge of this aspect of his Little existence. It will also probably ensure it gets done properly!

Some spouses have commented, that simply relating to their Little Ones in a new way has energised their adult partner to automatically do more around the house, take more care and generally and ironically, take the lead in the household. Often the natural leadership that lives within an adult, is consumed by the essentially submissive and needy infant side and this can cause a lot of domestic conflict. Once the Little One is receiving some emotional gratification, support and acknowledgement, the adult then feels more able to pursue his skills, talents and destiny. Often this is *the* reward that a partner is really looking for – getting the adult back!

Not all regressed behaviours are good. Some need to change and it is not unreasonable for you to seek to modify some of your Little Ones behaviours, that are either destructive or plain embarrassing.

Here are some examples. I am sure you can add many of your own.

- Excessive masturbation.

- Bad language (baby and adult).

- Tantrums.

- Deliberate unprotected bedwetting and pants-wetting.

- Soiling the pants or diaper (when soiling is not part of the baby behavioural profile).

- Faecal play.

- Damaging toys or other property.

- Exhibitionism.

- Inappropriate crawling.

- Breaching behavioural or other boundaries.

- Regression outside of Safe Zones without approval or support.

Deciding what is acceptable behaviour:

The reality of life is that we all have quite differing standards on what we tolerate or what we think is acceptable behaviour. The highly socially-controlled 1950s pretended that we all shared common standards, beliefs and behaviours. The 1960s blew that fantasy away and since then, society has developed widely varying behaviours and social groups. Now you need to work on which behaviours are acceptable to you and which ones are not.

Some behaviours for Little Ones are *core*. They form an immutable and fundamental part of their personality and needs. These can be problematic for a parent, because they aren't really negotiable. Fortunately however, these fundamentals are usually fairly simple and easy to cope with.

In the rest of this section we are going to deal with other regressive behaviours. These are usually negative ones, which you will want to either control or eliminate. Some of these may disgust you and some will surprise you. But remember that this is the MODIFICATION section of the book, where we discuss which behaviours you will accept and those you won't. Some couples find poo-play acceptable, while the majority would find it disgusting and an absolute no-go zone.

It is up to you, as the parent, to decide what you find is good and acceptable or not. For a long-term Parent/Child relationship to flourish, there needs to be standards of behaviour that *both* can live with comfortably. For most new parents, it means they have to help their Little One adjust to less of the negative and more of the positive.

How do we change these behaviours? Let's take a look at some of them.

Excessive Masturbation:

What is excessive? That is a good question and I don't think there is any one simple answer. This problem is complicated because a majority of Little Ones have a degree of sexual dysfunction or difficulty in their adult relationships. In part, the masturbation may be a full, or partial, substitute for a dysfunctional sex life, in which case, the obvious solution is to deal with the root cause and address the sexual problems themselves. I have dealt with this issue earlier, but we also find that excessive masturbation can stem from a lack of self-control, poor self-image and just plain childish bad habit. This needs to be addressed for everyone's benefit and for the improvement of the Parent/Child relationship.

There are two kinds of masturbation to deal with. One is rubbing the outside of the clothing or diaper or even playing with the hand inside the diaper. The other is seeking orgasm though manual manipulation or by humping the diaper. We deal with each one very differently, as they are quite separate behaviours.

Rubbing the outside of the diaper or even putting the hand inside it, is very typical infant/toddler behaviour. All children – even infants – tend to masturbate in this fashion. It feels good, so they do it. It makes perfect sense to them, as it also does to your Little One. A very effective deterrent is a quick hand slap. This behaviour doesn't often move into the adult realm, but it is an integral part of the infant experience.

Both kinds of masturbation can be extremely concerning and problematic if it extends outside of Safe Zones. Masturbation or rubbing *must* be under control before that is attempted. Public groin rubbing can get your child into trouble, even though he might not be fully aware of it.

The second kind, is masturbation with orgasm as the end goal and while it is very common, in Little Ones it can easily become compulsive and excessive. Some Littles masturbate this way as much as two to four times a day, every day. This level of masturbation is unhealthy. I'm not an opponent of masturbation at all, but I see that it is something that a Little One with full sexual capacity can easily lose control of, and for it to become a compulsion.

Let's look at a real-life situation, where a Little One had a severe masturbation problem. Even when at work he would do it frequently, diapered or not and at home, as a Little One, he was often caught, which was mutually embarrassing. Even though the Parent/Child relationship was deepening, the masturbation remained excessive and was a behaviour that was angering the parent and frustrating him. It was also destroying their sex life.

This is the classic example of why modifying your baby's behaviour is a *good* thing to do. He had lost control of the behaviour and it was now adversely affecting his partner and his adult side. Even his Little side was suffering from the effects of over-doing it. The habit was one he had been doing for a very long time, so much so that he didn't even realise any more that it was truly excessive.

The first step to a solution was talking about it adult-to-adult, during which he admitted to the problem and they decided to address it as part of their ongoing Parent/Child relationship.

HINT: Difficult Little One behavioural issues should be mutually discussed and agreed upon as <u>adults</u> first and then treated with the Little One. They must not be unilateral decisions, as you will need the adult to help the Little One behave.

In the above case, the parent initiated a rule that he must ask permission to masturbate. Now, clearly this is unlike any biological parent/child relationship rule, but not everything will fit neatly into a box. I won't bore you with the details, but suffice to say that it remained problematic! There was a great deal of disobedience on this at the beginning and he was caught doing it quite often. She used time-outs and hand smacks which were moderately effective, but on more than one occasion she gave him several sharp smacks on the tops of the legs for it. I'm sure some of you think this is a terrible thing to do and for some it would certainly be a bad idea, but if you want to be a good parent, then you will do the things that need to be done. Note though, that their personal history was that they came from strong disciplining families. It was very natural for them to employ discipline in dealing with this.

The problem eventually reduced in severity and while it remained an issue that still needed to be monitored, the frequency went back down to a more normal level. For them, it was a win that restored their sex life and made many other improvements in their relationship.

Bad Language:

Another example is a Little One with a bad language problem. This is more common than you think. The Little One has had restraints taken off of his life in a very big way and sometimes that can lead to inappropriate behaviour, such as swearing. And it isn't always just the Little One with the problem! Swearing isn't a normal toddler behaviour, but it can be picked up through behavioural leakage from the adult down to the child. If you wish to help the Little One, you will have to help the adult as well!

This means that discipline has to be applied across the board – both for the adult and Little One. Clearly that complicates matters enormously. You *can* discipline your Little One as a parent and probably *should* do so, but you cannot really discipline your partner. That's just not how adult relationships work, unless you have a *disciplining* aspect to your relationship, which is a different topic altogether.

The best way to curb Little One's swearing is to attack both areas at once. You can discipline the Little One with timeouts, naughty corner, removal of certain toys, privileges and hand smacks. The adult area is where you need to continually reaffirm to your partner, that his swearing is affecting his Little One and that he needs to curb or reduce his bad language to help eliminate that.

Tantrums:

Who hasn't seen a child throw a tantrum in public and been angry at the parent's utter failure to address it? And you know they aren't doing the child any favours either. Children who throw uncontrolled tantrums, grow up to throw tantrums as adults. He might not lie on the floor and kick and scream at the office, but it is a tantrum nonetheless.

Tantrums *are* the experience of some Little Ones. Normally, they are the product of frustration and occur prior to the beginning of a Parent/Child relationship, where anger can sometimes be a big problem. Usually, such problems disappear or reduce significantly once the Parent/Child relationship commences. Sometimes however, tantrums remain and need specific attention.

Early on in the Parent/Child relationship many issues are in flux and sometimes behaviour and emotions can be unpredictable and swing wildly. Let it settle down before you assume you have a genuine behavioural problem, such as tantrums. It may be nothing more than the settling-in phase.

Uncontrolled tantrums in the Parent/Child relationship can undermine and even destroy it. The harsh reality is that a tantrum as a Little One, probably stems not just from frustrations as a regressive, but also as an adult. Not many Little Ones have problems with tantrums, but if yours does, then you need to be very firm and deal with it appropriately.

I would like to quote some highly edited and concatenated writings of one frustrated wife and *mother* whose forty year old husband had tantrums when expressing his inner boy toddler (Adrian), of around four years of age.

"Brian has always had anger problems and I could live with that but his inner child [Adrian] had appalling behaviour. Brian had always wet the bed and it embarrassed him but I eventually realised it was Adrian that was the cause of it...

He [Brian] would sometimes get quite angry and go out of the house and kick the tree or something like that but when Adrian got angry we had tantrums instead. When Brian got angry I often saw Adrian come out...

Even when we started trying to get the relationship thing going with the boy the tantrums were ruining everything. The only time I ever saw Brian cry was after he calmed down and realised he had thrown things like his toys and clothes and upset me. Nothing was working and it was after I lost my cool one time that I found an answer.

One day I had put my best effort into giving Adrian some time to play with his toys and put him in some new rompers. All was going well until he accidentally broke a pencil and he started to throw a tantrum. I was tired and I wasn't ready for it. I wasn't feeling very motherly so I dragged him to the bedroom and without thinking, I did what my mom had done to me once when I was a brat. I pulled down his diaper and pushed him face down on the bed and paddled his ass good! I forget how many times I paddled him. I was just so furious! When I stopped I realised he was sobbing into the bed and I of course joined him.

I said I was sorry but he said thank you to me! He explained to me that his parents never disciplined him at all and he felt like he never knew how to handle his anger and I was the first one to do anything for him...

Adrian is still throwing tantrums at times but they are less now. If he does though, I send him to the corner to cool off or to the bedroom. When he is calm I paddle him. We've kinda worked out how many and all that crap but it's working. Adrian is playing up less and Brian himself is being less angry and moody. I truly hate paddling him. It just damned well works!"

There is not normally a huge call or need for **smacking** in the Parent/Child relationship, but this is one example where it has worked and worked very well.

————————

The big question is: Do you have what it takes to deal with a misbehaving child that threatens your relationship?

————————

Deliberate unprotected pants and bed wetting:

By now you will know that this type of behaviour is part of the modus operandi of a Little One who is seeking to be acknowledged and that the wetting is a scream to be seen and heard. In this context, it is understandable and even excusable as a cry for help. Once the Parent/Child relationship is in place and developing however, this is *not* acceptable. For many though, it remains a problem for the same original reasons.

Very young Little Ones often have quite poor verbal communication skills and even if they don't, they often are unable or unwilling to express their inner feelings particularly well. If your Little One starts wetting or soiling again while not wearing protection, yet is capable of being dry and clean, then you have either disobedience or a communication problem.

Obviously a first place to start is to ask why, but it may take some time and effort to get the answer from him. Little Ones in a deeply regressed state can be difficult to communicate with effectively. Some will say nothing at all, while others will inappropriately reveal everything they fear and are frustrated with.

A likely reason for this kind wetting or soiling, is that the Little One wants diapers full-time. This is a quite common theme and a lot of Little Ones are diapered fulltime, as protection against their inner weakness with wetting, but also a large part of the reason is actually *safety and security*.

Many Little Ones feel much *safer* in a diaper and want full-time diapering to experience that reliable *safety*. It isn't just protection against wetness, but also protection against their fears. You need to be prepared to have a fully or partially diapered Little One at least for a while as things get sorted out. It may be part of being his parent, so don't rush to this solution, but keep it in mind as something that may be necessary. It might seem extreme or draconian, but the problem you face is not simple. Simple solutions are for simple problems. This is not one of those kinds of problems. Diapers may also be only temporary, as the fears and safety issues recede.

Uncontrolled wetting and soiling can also be rebellion or part of a tantrum, so you need to deal with it as such. It is more likely to be your Little One trying to tell you something they feel unable to articulate properly.

Some Little Ones also find a wet bed to be a very comforting place, both emotionally and physically, and probably learned this as a young child, often due to family dysfunction. While it seems incomprehensible to a properly toilet-trained adult, some children grew up with soaked sheets every night and many had never experienced a dry bed until mid to late teens. As part of this extensive exposure to bed wetting, they may not have an aversion to it like most have, and the next step – finding comfort in it – is only a small distance away.

It is possible that your Little One wants a partial or full reversion to that *perceived comfort* of a wet bed. One Little One has a brave parent who keeps a single bed available for him to wet when he needs it. The wet bed is where almost all Little Ones have experienced a significant amount of time. There may be some temporary release of tension by allowing them a deliberately wet bed from time to time.

Listen to one parent:

"I started laughing when I read the part about them [Little Ones] being proud of their wet diapers and wet bed. In the morning he loves to come down stairs in just a wet night diaper and t-shirt and will stay that way until I tell him how wet he is and take him up to be changed. He also loves it when his diaper has leaked and there are the two tell-tale wet marks on his jeans. If he wets the bed he never wants the sheets changed. He just says 'they will dry it's ok'."

[personal email related to a case history]

Deliberate Diaper or Pants Soiling:

Diaper soiling is not at all uncommon among the Adult Baby or diaper community and Little Ones often soil their diaper. It is strongly in keeping with the age of many of the babies/toddlers, but not all of them. A lot of parents try to ban soiling, but the reality is that it is part and parcel of many Little One's experience and sometimes the ban simply doesn't work. You will need to work out if you can cope with it at all, even if it is only very rarely.

Just because it is very common, doesn't mean it can't be limited and done with due regard for everyone else. What I am specifically referring to now is soiling that is done deliberately and provocatively by the Little One, even though it is not part of their normal behavioural profile. It may be done in their diaper or underwear or even in the bed. It is *deliberate* and disobedient and has to be dealt with.

As with pants-wetting, deliberate diaper or pants soiling is often an immature attempt at communicating a dissatisfaction or fear. They may feel their needs are not being met or they are afraid of something, but are unable to articulate this fear. Keep in mind that many Little Ones feel a strong compulsion to soil and to remain soiled for some time and that they find it immensely comfortable. It is anti-social, smelly and all of that, but you may need to find some compromise in this one as well. If you push an anti-soiling rule, you may find strong pushback from them. In that case, relent a little and put in place some workable compromise rules instead. Soiling will naturally reduce as balance come into the relationship, so don't push too hard at this stage. Let the development of the relationship control this one and then later on try and limit this as part of a compromise. Using discipline techniques is only advised once the communication issues have been resolved and the soiling still continues. Then it is simply bad behaviour that needs modifying.

Faecal Play:

Of all the unpleasant topics on here, this one rates near the top. Some Little Ones play with their faeces by smearing it on themselves or their clothes or putting some in their mouth. This is obviously not a good thing to do. Some couples do faecal play as part of role playing and while certainly not very common, it does have a legitimate place for a few.

What I am referring to here however, is dysfunctional play, where the Little One behaves badly with his faeces and it is often linked to masturbation. However you look at it, it simply must *not* be allowed to occur without severe limits and controls. Oral poo play is a health hazard and can be very socially disruptive. If your baby needs poo play and you are happy with it, you *must* impose hard limits that protect him and you. Given the extreme nature of this behaviour, I believe you are well within your rights to ban the practice altogether, regardless of his wants or needs for it. There are many other aspects of Little play that can be used to substitute for this anti-social need.

Exhibitionism:

This is another complex and very common problem. If you are in the phase of developing a Parent/Child relationship, you can now look back and see numerous examples of exhibitionism or pseudo-exhibitionism in the past. Most of this develops out of the Little One's desperate need to be seen and heard. Little Ones usually choose the wrong way to go about it, and exhibitionism can be dangerous and embarrassing. Usually when the Parent/Child relationship begins, exhibitionism will disappear or be greatly reduced, but if it continues, then it needs to be addressed through strong boundaries and discipline, such as reduced Little Time or removal of toys.

If it continues, despite the usual methodologies, then you need to reassess your Parent/Child relationship and find what is not being communicated, as that is most likely the problem.

Exhibitionism is almost always a cry to be noticed and appreciated and loved. You hold the keys to this problem by being an intimate and involved parent.

Inappropriate Crawling:

Crawling is a part of many Little Ones experience, but once again, if it becomes excessive or inappropriate, then it needs to be looked at. One problem could be that your Little One reverts to crawling most of the time when regressed and seems reluctant or flatly refuses to walk. This can because he has either regressed deeply and to a very young age, or he may be scared or fearful and finds comfort in crawling.

Some Little Ones strongly identify crawling with regression and so to them, to be a Little One means to crawl, no exceptions. This can be tiresome for him and for you. The only realistic solution is to help your Little One have other objects that identify him as an infant, which would then reduce his dependency on crawling. The use of a pacifier or bottle or a very strongly infantile outfit, are just some ideas. In this case, a Little one needs to not only *be* a baby, but he needs others to *know* he is a baby, as opposed to a toddler or older child. Crawling is a very obvious activity, but if he starts to move to other activities and objects, then he will still be viewed as a baby in his own mind, but won't need to crawl as much. A word of caution though. This won't happen quickly. The identification of crawling as his primary or fundamental infant behaviour didn't happen overnight, but took some considerable time to develop. Helping him change this will take time as well.

A real problem can be when your Little One crawls when it is *not* appropriate, such as around family or guests. This is a boundary that you will need to establish early on: that your Little One will not demonstrate overt infant or toddler behaviour around others or in Unsafe Zones.

Breaching Boundaries:

If there is one thing babies do poorly, it is in obeying boundaries. It is the kind of thing all children have to learn, often the hard way. One behaviour which you will seek to improve is his adherence to both natural boundaries, as well as those that you impose. These boundaries are both physical, behavioural and temporal.

Your Little One may be restricted to certain baby-play times and certain places, e.g. rooms in the house. He may have rules regarding soiling or other behaviours. All these are boundary conditions that the Little One has to learn to not only respect, but to obey. You will need to carefully articulate and write down the boundary conditions for your Little One.

They can be:

- Times and places of baby play.

- Rules on wetting and soiling.

- Masturbation boundaries.

- Walking/crawling rules.

- What to wear and when.

- What they are to view on the internet and who to talk to and what to say.

- Any others your baby seems to need.

Consider writing these boundaries down for your Little One to see and agree on. Writing something down reinforces the value and importance of the boundaries.

Here is an example of a Rules and Boundaries Worksheet for Baby Clare.

Baby Clare's Boundaries:

1. She will not dress as a baby without mummy's permission.

2. She will only wear a diaper when just mummy is around.

3. She can wet her diaper, but never dirty it without mummy's permission.

4. She cannot masturbate more than twice a week. After that, she needs to ask mummy FIRST.

5. Absolutely no crawling outside of the bedroom, regardless.

6. Baby Clare's girl panties can be worn as long as fully covered up.

7. She cannot interact ever with anyone except mummy. She must become adult around other people.

8. Baby Clare must not disobey mummy ever.

9. She will *never* play with her used diaper.

10. She will keep her hands out of her diaper at all times.

11. Baby Clare is fully responsible for washing cloth diapers and bagging of disposables.

Little Needs Outside of Regression

It should not be assumed that all of your Little One's needs are neatly contained within his regression and related experiences. While one of the goals of the Parent/Child relationship is to help the Little contain and control his needs and behaviours, that doesn't necessarily mean that you should totally separate regression from adulthood.

A number of Littles gain great enjoyment out of expressing some of their inner self through the adult world. Examples of this are:

- Sleeping with a stuffed toy.

- Wearing diapers outside of regression, even though not incontinent.

- Wearing panties outside of regression.

- Using a pacifier at night.

- Submitting to their partner in a semi-parental manner, outside of regressive times.

- Dressing up as a baby or toddler, while still being adult.

- Role-playing being a child, rather than regressing to that level.

What this means to a Little is that by being free to express aspects of their regressive nature in a non-regressive situation, they feel a greater degree of acceptance of themselves, not just from you, but also from within.

Obviously this isn't a first step. In the early days, you will be both struggling to just get the Little One under control and stay within proper boundaries. Once you have the Little under better control, then you can experiment with *controlled release* of his regressive elements into his adult world.

It should not be assumed that a Little One is always happy about his behaviours and needs. Many in fact, feel embarrassed and upset by their drives and I speak about this in the chapter on self-image. By encouraging your Little One to express some aspects of his regression in the adult world, you confirm for him that is okay; that being a child is fine by you.

By allowing your Little some elements from his regression, but in a non-regressive environment, you also give him more control and release. It is true that some Littles actively seek regression simply to enjoy the objects associated with it, rather than the emotional connection with childhood. He may want to wear his baby clothes or to cuddle up to a stuffed toy, but since that is Little behaviour, he feels compelled to regress to have that experience. Your goal is to find balance between competing adult and Little needs. Ironically, one of these ways is to have these elements of regression in the adult world. So how do you help?

Start by encouraging – yes, encouraging – your Little to play with some of his toys when he is not regressed. Perhaps suggest he colour-in a page or two or use a child's activity book. The result may be totally adult, but it will still be a child's activity. Put his favourite soft toy or doll in bed with him at night and put it in his arms. If he is sissy, then consider having him wear panties sometimes under his adult trousers. It might seem a little silly to you both, but it is worth experimenting with.

Does this actually trigger regressive episodes? Yes it can, especially early on, but after a while, your partner will begin to identify some of these objects and activities in a more *normalised* light and so not necessarily identify regression with it per se.

Desensitisation and normalisation:

If you are sneaky like me, then you will have realised that there is another subtext to this activity – *desensitisation or normalisation of objects*. While allowing regressive elements into the adult world is a good thing for you both, as it releases a lot of the pressure in an easy and controlled manner, extensive use of these elements in the adult world will affect how he views them.

In the past, your Little One will have strongly identified an object, e.g. a teddy bear, as part of his Little experience *exclusively*. His experience of cuddling and playing with the teddy will therefore be a short and usually intense experience, before the regression ends. By giving him the teddy every night, he will begin to no longer associate it with such intense needs and emotions. The teddy has been *desensitised* to a degree and having a teddy with him is now far less of an aberration, but rather a *normal* part of life. For a strongly sissy Little, wearing panties regularly can have the same effect, by making it normal underwear, instead of special *girly* wear.

Often, the urge to experience gender shifting in regression is an extremely strong one. This can lead to a lot of pressure in the adult world to want to regress, simply for some of that gender-shift experience. Panties are the major attachment object of this behaviour and by giving your adult regular panty wearing in the adult realm, even if it doesn't mean as much to him, may help reduce the drives somewhat. By desensitising and normalising panty-wearing, these items are less likely to be the powerful regressive triggers they currently are. Your partner may see panties and want to wear them. He has always associated regression with them and therefore, seeks to regress to get them. In time, by repeated non-regressive panty-wearing, he will realise that if he wants panties, he just needs to wear them and does not need to regress to get them.

The classic example of this of course is diapers. As the single most powerful attachment object in regression, the diaper can be a huge trigger for moving a person into Little mode. For a Little, whose only experience of diapers is within regression, the diaper is a beacon that calls out to him frequently and seeks his intimate involvement. Desensitisation and normalisation is something that should really be attempted if your child is not incontinent and therefore not already in diapers. A single fleeting desire for a diaper, perhaps triggered by just seeing one, is sometimes enough to send the person into a regressive episode. Since our aim is to try and control this kind of uncontrolled behaviour, then desensitisation is a good place to start.

The single reason that wearing diapers full-time is such a powerful reducing force in regression, is that this element is no longer totally contained solely within the Little behavioural realm. Diapers are now *normal*. They have been normalised and are no longer a purely regressive activity. In time, the diaper becomes significantly desensitised as a trigger for a Little episode. It will probably never become *un*-important, but it will certainly lose some, or even most, of its power to control.

This doesn't mean that your Little One needs to go into diapers 24/7. For many, that is an intolerable and unnecessary burden. But what about night-times? What about weekends or evenings? Encourage your Little to wear diapers at safe, convenient and regular times, but without regression. You will be astonished at how it helps reduce the power of the regressive urge. I will be honest here and say that one risk of extended diaper wearing for a Little is a degree of incontinence. This may not happen to everyone, but it could for some who may be on the border of this already. If your Little already has a bedwetting issue, moving him to regular night diapers might be enough to increase his bedwetting. It is up to you to decide if that is a positive or negative thing.

The secret of desensitisation is repetition. In the early days of trialling this, your Little One will be excited, edgy, aroused and probably a bit of a pain! Just give it time, until the excitement of wearing panties or diapers wears off they become more akin to normal underwear. If your Little loves his dresses, then get him to wear them while watching TV or reading a book – in adult mode.

Desensitising might be erroneously looked upon as a way of eliminating regression. Sorry, it isn't. It is simply a method of reducing the power of the triggers, with the goal of making life easier and more enjoyable. A full-on regressive episode will still be just as potent an experience as it always has been. It just may not occur so often.

Once you have made some headway into your Parent/Child relationship, it is then time to bring out some of the elements and place them squarely in the adult realm. By doing so, you not only desensitise and normalise, you also do something else. You tell him that he isn't a freak and that you love and accept him. Some Littles can be deeply suspicious that a partner doesn't really love and accept the Little, but rather merely tolerates and role-plays with them. However, if you move some of the regressive elements into the adult world, you signal your acceptance in a very powerful way. That alone can make the notion worth experimenting with.

Smacking your Little One

Perhaps one of the most controversial issues in the parenting of a Little One is that of physical discipline. Smacking biological children is now out of favour and unjustly so, since research has shown notably better life outcomes for smacked children.

You may be anti-smacking for children and that is certainly an on-going debate, but I am almost certain that you are anti-smacking of your own Little One. I'd be surprised and perhaps worried, if you weren't initially so, but I ask you to consider it as a viable option, simply because it can be remarkably effective for intractable behavioural and emotional problems with the Little One.

It must be clearly stated at the onset that this is not erotic spanking or role play. **This is discipline**. It is meant to hurt and if it doesn't, then you are wasting your time. If you are unprepared for proper smacking, then feel free to ignore this chapter. I am going to use the older term 'smack', to highlight that this is not 'erotic spanking'.

Erotic spanking etcetera, can have a place in the life of the Little One, but it is a completely different experience. It is not discipline, but rather playtime. I address this aspect in the Interaction Section, as it is something you can do with your Little One and which can be enjoyable for both partners. Smacking however is discipline; something your Little One definitely won't like, but which may be necessary to effect the changes you both want.

Don't assume that your Little One will reject smacking. If he is as concerned about his behaviours as you are and he realises that they are a threat to the Parent/Child relationship, then he may accept that it works and go along with it.

Reasons to smack your Little One:

Smacking your Little One can be effective on several levels. The most obvious one is for punishment for infractions of rules and boundaries and I talk about that later in this chapter. But another reason is one of deep-seated emotional *need*. Some Littles actually feel a *need* to be smacked for their emotional well-being. This sounds exceptionally perverse and yet, there is certainly evidence to support it.

A Little One unfortunately often carries a lot of emotional baggage from the past. In fact, it is almost ubiquitous. Smacking has been used by loving partners to help reduce or eliminate some of that baggage.

Smacking does work within the Parent/Child relationship, as long as you are both up to speed with the essential rules and the concept.

Permission from the adult:

Under no circumstances should you ever smack your Little One above the level of a cursory slap that draws attention, rather than pain, without having a consensual discipline agreement at the adult level to do so. A light smack or tap to tell him to take his thumb out of his mouth or to stop inappropriate rubbing, is consistent with standard discipline and correction that does not require any prior permission. A proper smacking however, is not. It is the next step up and is not automatically part of the parent role for a Little One.

A consensual agreement is when you and your *adult* partner discuss this subject carefully and openly. Be prepared for rejection – at least initially – as it is a big thing to consider and is deeply embarrassing. It is at this time that the emotional baggage he carries may erupt, so be wary, just in case. Remember to clearly state that the smacking will hurt! It is *not* erotic spanking. It is behavioural modification.

The parameters need to be clearly discussed such as:

- What offences merit a smack and how many and at what level. For example, swearing might be a smack on the tops of the legs. Masturbation without permission might mean a diaper-down hand smack on the bottom.

- **NEVER SLAP THE FACE OR HEAD – EVER!**

- What implements may be used. Some who use a Discipline Agreement (see later on) use either the hand for smacking or a wooden spoon or paddle.

- Diapers down or up? (HINT: dry the bottom first if using the wooden spoon or paddle. A wet or damp bottom will sting a lot more and while the hand smack is fine, the others will leave a mark).

- Times and places. Smacking your Little One *must* be done privately and securely. This is non-negotiable. If it is to be discipline, rather than abuse, then privacy and mutual respect are essential.

- A safe word. A common concept in BDSM, the 'safe word' is a single word or phrase that is used to tell the parent that the boundary has been crossed or is about to be crossed. A Discipline Worksheet may naively specify twenty wooden spoon smacks on the un-diapered bottom for a particular offence, but when it is eventually given, the Little One finds it too much to handle. This is a complex question because it is *supposed* to hurt. Only experience will see how this works out for you. Legally however, a safe word prevents you from crossing a line. A safe word can be abused by a Little One trying to back out of a discipline agreement and if that continues, then the agreement is voided and smacking must cease entirely. Smacking can only be effective if it is consistently and effectively applied in a safe, effective and consensual manner *all the time.*

Why will you smack your Little One?

You need to be able to easily answer this question accurately and concisely or you should not use smacking. There needs to be a real and considered reason why you would do this.

A sample situation is this one. A Little One had some frustrating behaviours that he could not control. Sheer force of will wasn't working. After some light smacks were administered for another issue, both realised it was a surprisingly effective tool. After some frank and embarrassing discussion, they agreed to trial smacking for his consistent problem, which had become well and truly out of control. It worked and continues to work. Smacking is now a rare event, but remains an option that is still occasionally given and therefore remains an effective deterrent.

Another Little One's problem was a seemingly intractable addiction to internet pornography. It seemed out of character for a Little One to be accessing any pornography at all and as such, was deemed to be wholly unsuitable for him. His parent had threatened to end the Parent/Child relationship, which had just begun, if the porn searching didn't end.

They set up a discipline worksheet (refer next page) that detailed the level of porn he had accessed and the punishment. It was to be a voluntary admission, but the punishment was tripled if the parent caught him or found out later.

When to smack your Little One:

'Wait until your father gets home', was a silly statement for children and is just as silly for you as well. An effective smack has to be given at the time of the offence or shortly afterwards. If you can't do it *then*, then you can't do it at all.

You must never smack your <u>adult</u> partner – ever.

You can *only* smack your Little One. This is an immutable rule. If your Little One disappears and the adult comes out, then the smack cannot proceed. However, if this becomes a common occurrence, then clearly your discipline agreement is not working. A Little One is subject to the adult personality. The adult should be responsible for ensuring that the Little One doesn't avoid discipline by using this method.

How to smack your Little One:

If you are a biological parent, then you are half-way there already, but you are probably tempted to throw away all your experience. Don't! Smacking your Little One is not that different to smacking a child.

1. The first thing is to make sure you are not angry and that your Little One is able to handle this discipline. The environment must be right. If you are consistently unable to smack due to anger or your Little One's mood making it unsuitable, then you either have to rectify this or abandon smacking altogether.

2. Identify the appropriate punishment. You will have already extensively discussed this with your Little One. The style and amount of smacking has already been decided by you both.

3. Make a Safe Zone for the smacking. It is usually best in the bedroom or an area you will usually use.

4. Administer the smacking. A guiding principle is that your Little One should be hurting afterwards. That might sound terrible, but you know that is how you smacked your own children and you *are* smacking a child now. If it doesn't hurt, then you are wasting your time. Smacking is a difficult thing to give and receive, therefore you must either put in the effort or consistency to make it work or abandon it altogether.

5. Immediately check the response from your Little One. You may need to administer more if necessary, but be careful, as this means your Discipline Worksheet may need revisiting.

6. Cuddle and hug your Little One and re-diaper him. Assure him of your love and then move on with the rest of the day.

The Discipline Worksheet:

You and your adult partner will need to develop a Discipline Worksheet that helps guide you both through this exercise. The purpose is to establish, ahead of time, exactly what discipline is given out for certain offences. It isn't just regarding smacking, but for all discipline, including timeouts, bedtimes etc. It is a helpful and recommended worksheet in these circumstances, but in the case of smacking it is absolutely *essential*. It will be something you revisit time and time again to improve, add to or change completely, but in time it will be more of a reminder of what once was, rather than your current behavioural problem.

A Discipline Worksheet contains:

- The offence in clear concise detail, e.g. 'going outside without permission – second offence in a week' or 'swearing, level two'

- The clear punishment(s), e.g. 'three medium-force hand smacks on the bottom' or 'six hard smacks with the wooden spoon'

- Number of times it has been meted out and preferably some notes written by you.

Initially, you will find there are only two or three things on the worksheet, but it will expand quickly once you see its effectiveness.

Discipline Worksheet for _____

Offence	Punishment	Number of times and comments

Base-line or pre-emptive smacking:

This concept might seem a little odd in the 21ˢᵗ century, but was actually practiced as a discipline method by some parents and schools in the 18ᵗʰ and 19ᵗʰ centuries. A child would be given a single smack every morning, as a reminder to behave, regardless of their actual behaviour. This same methodology has been applied by some parents now with their Little One. It is also a part of Domestic Discipline – a lifestyle practiced by some couples, whereby one partner will smack the other on a regular basis for *maintenance* of behaviour or for helping to deal with deep-seated fears, regrets and emotions. They also use it to help motivate a partner who is struggling in this area. I don't spend any further time in the area of Domestic Discipline, but it is one of those lifestyles that does intersect somewhat with the Parent/Child Lifestyle.

How pre-emptive smacking works is quite simple. The child is given a pre-determined number of smacks every day, perhaps after the morning bath or first diaper change. Some may use it every second day or perhaps once a week.

Also known as 'maintenance smacking', this methodology is very effective for those with problematic behaviour. Typically, the baseline or maintenance smacking is at a low level, being one to five hand smacks. It is hard enough to felt, be unpleasant and to reinforce the message, yet not too hard as to be a harsh punishment without due cause.

Clearly this is a regime of discipline that requires both partners to be very accepting and understanding of it. This may seem over-the-top, but have you ever considered that your child may *want* you to smack him? I don't mean erotic spanking, but rather proper punishment smacking? This leads to my next topic.

What if your child wants to be smacked?

It seems incomprehensible to most adults that anyone would *want* a punishment smacking, yet it happens far more often that you think. Again, let me draw the distinction between a punishment smacking that hurts and an erotic spanking. We are still talking about a smack given for bad behaviour that actually hurts.

We saw in an example earlier, that one child felt his mother didn't love him enough to smack him as a child and that his bad adult behaviour stemmed from that. For him, the smacking given by his wife was a genuine act of love and so, here is our first clue.

Smacking isn't just punishment. It is also love, guidance and commitment to the child.

Many Little Ones feel deep hurt inside them and often this comes from rejection – either real or perceived – from their parents or (you won't like this) from <u>you</u>. It is also a common experience for biological children that they misbehave, simply to get their parent's attention. The discipline, including a smack, is a small price to pay for the attention and love they receive as a result. The smack actually *proves* to them that their parent loves them enough to do it.

Do not assume that your Little One does not want you to show the love and commitment that his parents perhaps didn't show and expect you to smack him. So how do you know if he does?

A child who wants to feel the love of a smack will often be embarrassingly obvious, if you know what to look for. He will flaunt the rules and boundaries openly and dare you to discipline him, but without saying so. He is deeply embarrassed by this want and may also not be fully cognizant of the fact. If you ask him – as you would a child – if he wants to be smacked, he will of course say no. So, how do you find out if your child wants a smack? Simple, trial it!

Your child will typically have a number of behaviours worthy of some scolding or discipline. They all do. Instead of ignoring it or for example, simply telling him to take his hand out of his diaper, smack his hand. What happens next is your first clue. If he doesn't want to be smacked, he will behave himself. The smack was light and just a slight behavioural correction, nothing more, but if the behaviour continues and the hand deliberately goes back into the diaper, then you should smack again, but a *lot* harder. You still don't know for sure what is happening though. This is where the *third strike* principle applies.

This is an aspect of your relationship that the adult probably cannot tell you about, because he doesn't understand it very well himself. He may feel that *you* don't love him enough to smack him, just as his own parents didn't. It is confusing to him and he cannot communicate it to you any other way than by his behaviour. So what happens if he blatantly defies you and misbehaves for the third time in a short period? He already knows what happens for it – a hand smack – so when he defies you for the third time then jump right in and take him to your room and apply a full bottom smacking. Watch for the signals and let them guide you.

As you smack him, you are actually communicating with him at a level you never have before. It might seem like just discipline to you, but to a needy child like him, he is experiencing your love and commitment. This doesn't mean that you don't smack hard and intend to hurt. That is still the point of it. What happens afterwards is even more important than the smack. Talk to him through the tears and reinforce that you love him, the child, just as much as you love the adult. Do you realise that your child may feel as if you love the adult, but not the child, or that you merely *tolerate* the child? The smack tells him that you love him in a deep way that is shown by this level of commitment.

A child who wants to be smacked can be a problem, because their behaviour can be poor when it doesn't need to be. This is the value of pre-emptive/base-line or maintenance smacking. Your child will regularly get the smacks they want and feel they need, without having to misbehave to get them.

Here is an example of one Little One that wanted smacking and what happened.

"For a long time I have wanted to be spanked [SMACKED] by my wife. It was something I kept deep down inside me because it was acutely embarrassing, even more than wearing diapers. It wasn't about sex play nor was it some masochistic weirdness that I wanted pain. I'm the same as everyone else in that I really don't want to be hurt or feel pain but still deep inside me was this chronic need to be spanked. But even as I imagined it I thought of it as a child-like experience not as some sexy adult time.

I imagined having my diaper pulled down as I stood embarrassed and silent as mom used her hand to spank me. Or I thought of going over her knee and the humiliation of that. I often imagined being lent over the edge of the bed, diaper down as my wife paddled me long and hard until I began to cry or at least felt like doing so.

When I imagine being spanked I feel a real sense of relief wash over me. For years now I've not really understood it nor have I sought to be spanked. It was always something I could just never have. But the need continued to burn and frustrate me immensely.

My wife was a little bit involved in my diapers and baby ways until recently when she increased her involvement. Then it came up about 12 months ago about spanking. I was beyond mortified about it because she had just read an article on it. I was hopelessly transparent about this feeling of mine and I'd not felt such shame in a long time even when discussing being an adult baby with her which as you all know is like surgery without painkillers. Somehow that experience was mainstream compared to this.

She understood far more than I did and a few days later when I was just in my diaper and a baby top she took me to the spare room and pulled down my diaper and wordlessly spanked my bottom about 10 times. After it was over I looked at her and nearly cried. The emotion was overwhelming for us both and as if she could read my mind she smacked me again about the same number but a lot harder. This time the tears flowed freely for us both and for a brief moment in time I felt a release I didn't know I was hiding.

One morning a few days later I awoke in a wet diaper since I wore one to bed and made good use of it. My wife feigned anger at my wet diaper and 'ordered' me to bend over the bed. She pulled down my wet diaper and fortunately dried me off and then she used a paddle on my ass for what seemed like a long time but was probably only a minute or two. It hurt a lot and by the end of it I was blubbering and even some real tears. But the tears weren't from the pain but from the emotional release.

Since that time I've come to understand why I want the spankings – at least in part. My mom didn't spank me much which at the time seemed good but as I got older made me wonder if she didn't care quite as much as she should. When I was caught wearing diapers as a young teen there was just discussion, no spanking. When at 16 I stole diapers and women's underwear I was grounded, not spanked. When I've messed up during my life I've been lectured and little more.

I know that like so many of us I think like a child in some of my inner emotions and I can recall as a little boy breaking something precious and I expected a spanking but there was none. I was sent to my room and for the next few days I felt very unloved because they obviously didn't care enough to spank me. I felt like a nobody in that house. When my older sister was spanked for something I thought less serious a week later I knew it. I was unloved. When my wife spanked me that second time all these memories flooded back.

And in my marriage I've screwed up and of course wasn't spanked. It's just not the adult thing to do. But as life goes on I realise I view a great deal of my feelings just as a child does. When I cheated on my wife once some years back she forgave me and we moved on, but I felt guilty about it and remained so. I felt guilty for things I'd said and done all throughout my life and they never really left me in part because I never paid the price for it. It's the thinking of a child, but hey... that's me!

Over the last year we have begun to belatedly accept that I am a child in more ways than either of us realised. Its more than diapers and baby clothes. It is how I think and react and is a big part of my emotions. When my wife spanked me that second time I felt like I genuinely deserved it – because I did.

I am getting spanked from time to time now. As I let more of my inner baby out for her to see she is feeling easier with spanking me for misbehaviour. But we both discovered something about our pasts. One night we were talking and the incident of the one-time cheating came up and it was obvious she still carried hurt from it. We'd both believed it was in the past and buried but it became obvious that it was still there in us both. To make a long story short, she spanked me. It was very, very hard and she let it all out on my ass big-time. We are very close and we trust each other and as I laid there face down on the bed as she continued to spank me I felt loved and I felt as if I could trust her. I'm glad it was bedtime as I would not be able to sit down but even as it throbbed I felt a sense of peace.

She told me later that she also felt a release from punishing me with the paddle. The anger she had felt about the cheating had come out and she said that she finally feels as if it is over.

Since then we have used spanking to help me (and her) over some things in the past. Things I did wrong and still feel shame over.

I don't know if this helps anyone but just in case I am not alone, that is what happened to me and still is.

I feel that I am a much better person for my time on the wrong side of the paddle."

[dailydiapers.com 2012]

Summary: It might seem bizarre to you that anyone would want a smack, but the need for demonstrated love is always strong and even more so, in a long-term isolated child such as yours. While you need to retain a discipline worksheet (smacking or not) for everyday behaviour, there may be a deep-seated need in your Little One to feel the love they were denied, by giving him a proper paddling from time to time. It is not something that you can simply ignore, even if the idea horrifies you. At least give it some consideration. Let's just hear one wife's thoughts on the matter.

"It is just not me to spank my husband! I'd spanked my kids for sure, but that is 'normal', at least to me and they grew up and out of needing it. He is an adult baby and that was hard enough to deal with, but there were always these weights on him and these things that just dragged him down. I guess I'd gotten used to his ways, even though it was a bit of a disappointment.

I loved to chat online and it was a bit of a glimpse into the world outside my conservative little corner and while that was all titillating and everything, one day I was discussing my husband's babyness with a few other wives and mentioned his behaviour with being messy and slothful at home. One of them said that she spanked her partner for such things and I was shocked! But then she said something to me that I'd never forgotten which was that 'he loves it and needs it so I give it to him'.

Suddenly, my husband's flippant remarks about spanking in the past made sense. They weren't flippant at all. I talked to a few people about it and it the internet was just starting to get a bit of info about such things, so I researched and learned what I could.

I came to the conclusion that my husband's babyness had a lot to do with pain in his past and my natural response is to want to talk about things like that and comfort. But the best advice I got from one wife who clearly had gone through a lot with her own husband's history was to stop trying to understand it and just spank! She explained to me that spanking was how she helped him get over pain and to move on.

Based on what I've learned, I now spank him five times every night before bedtime. And he sleeps better! But the hard part is once a week or thereabouts when I spank him very hard. At first it was pretty hard to deal with and I cried a lot, but now I have my head around it and it works very well. I give him 20 or more with the wooden paddle but I also hit a lot harder than my nightly ones. There are usually some tears but I still remember the words of advice I was given.

'When he cries, he heals. When he hurts, he learns. When he submits, he learns to lead.'

I don't regret smacking him in the least. My adult baby is at least now happy."

[spanking website forum, edited with some spelling and grammar changed]

Seeing Progress:

Smacking is designed to help, not hurt, your Little One. Together, you will define behaviours that are unacceptable as a Little One and deal with it in this effective manner. It is very helpful if both of you maintain a discipline journal that deals with what has happened and how it has progressed. It can be embarrassing and feel like a harsh indictment on both of your behaviour at the start, but as time goes on, you will see how it changes for the better.

The whole goal is to make things better for *both* of you. Some of the behaviours that Little Ones have, are clearly detrimental to the Parent/Child relationship and to how a Little One *wishes* to behave. Little ones aren't thrilled by their bad behaviour or stupid actions, but they often don't know how to change. Using discipline, including smacking, can give them guidance and a goal to head towards. Smacking may also help in areas, other than directly related to your Little One's current behaviour, but also to his past and his emotional pain.

Summary:

One of the hardest things you will ever do, smacking can bring huge rewards. It can also bring failure if you are unwise, so be aware of that too. It is something worth trying, if both of you are serious enough to tackle your Little One's personal and emotional development. Remember this: your Little One feeds into your adult's behaviour. The benefits can be truly dramatic, if the discipline your Little One receives and learns, feeds into the adult.

———————

Use wisdom combined with courage to get the best out of your Little One. Do not be afraid to be unconventional or controversial. It is you and your child's decision to smack, no one else's and you two alone bear the responsibility for it.

———————

Navigating the adult/child boundary

The essential skill for any Little One seeking to find balance in the real world is being able to *navigate the adult/child boundary* correctly and appropriately. However, while the Little One is the individual that needs to do this, it is *you*, the parent, who will have to teach, train and guide them in *how* to do it. It is always harder for a child to correct their own behaviour, than to have someone help and guide them through the process.

The reality that we live with, is that while some Little Ones will be able to academically understand this boundary, many will not. Intelligent, able and successful adults in their real lives may find understanding this boundary difficult. Let me explain why.

Many Little Ones have <u>zero</u> experience of life without their Little One with them.

Many have first memories of being two and three years of age, where the Little One is already present and in the formative stages. They grow up physically and intellectually, yet part of them remains little. It might be cute for a ten year old to behave as a baby or toddler at times, but it is not helpful for a biological child with regression, as these behaviours tend to stay with them.

The rest of us grow up learning many of the boundaries and expectations of behaviour relevant to our age. Little ones typically, do not do this spectacularly well. This is why a ten year old doesn't understand why wetting the bed is wrong or a variety of other infantile behaviours. They are already having trouble navigating the infant/child boundary and this morphs later on into trouble with the adult/child boundary.

We've already discussed boundaries and how you will need to teach and enforce them, until they learn. This boundary is one which is inside them: the boundary between the outer adult and the inner child. This is the boundary they alone must navigate, but at least initially, they cannot do so without your guidance.

For the vast majority of Little Ones, their inner child is never really gone. Their non-regressive state is more easily viewed as a time when their inner child is *asleep*, rather than not there. This metaphor works well for understanding their state. They seem fully functional and indeed they are, but the inner child is there asleep and waiting to *wake up*. The regressive inner child is waiting to move from non-involvement, to becoming part of their personality and often, that involvement can be very quick to arise.

You need to understand this well. The inner child may be asleep, and you may be lulled into a false sense of security into thinking that the child is gone. The Little One himself may also get this sense as well, only to be rudely surprised when the child awakes and he is unprepared to deal with it.

Your Little One will never go away. He will always be there, even if he is playing no part in the adult's behaviour or personality.

What was described as Level One regression, is many Little One's very familiar territory. In this level, the child is awake and shares the foreground with the adult, even though the adult is typically easily in control. This is another fact you need to understand. Your partner may be showing no overt regressive tendencies, but at the same time, the child is right there with them. This state of affairs means that *in an instant,* there can be an infantile response or behaviour, without the adult being aware of it. It can be in the eyes, the quick rub of the groin or the seconds of thumb sucking. You can see it in the face and eyes. For a few seconds there, the child was in front.

Knowing that this is the case, is the key to navigating it. As the parent, you need to recognise the signs of a Level One state of regression and to help your partner to recognise it as well.

A well-informed and aware adult in this state, is better able to deal with the risks of bad behaviour, but he has to be taught how to do this.

It is not really possible for the adult partner to do this alone. They may have zero experience of a life without a regressive side, so they don't quite know what to look for. You do, so teach them how. It isn't hard to do. Start by informing them that you believe they are at level one and then tell them *why.* Then watch for the behaviours that you want to control and tell them when they happen. It takes time and practice. Some Little Ones have little difficulty with this, while others can really struggle with it.

Public expectations (levels one and two):

This is a variation on the behavioural discussions earlier on, but it forms a big part of navigating the boundary.

You cannot always control the regression, but you *can* usually control the behaviours that go along with it, especially when in public. Teach your Little One the differences between acceptable and unacceptable behaviour, at levels one and two. At both of these levels, the adult retains more than enough control to be appropriate in public, so don't accept any excuses! Take note however, that it can be hard work on your Little One trying to find the boundary and to maintain it. It gets easier in time, but early on, it can be a real struggle for some.

Again, you need to teach this and enforce it. It can be humiliating for him and for you, to have to teach the fundamentals of behaviour in public, but this is how he learns to take his inner child into the public arena and to not embarrass or debase himself. Ultimately, this is better for him, because his Little One can have a lot more freedom of expression, but this can only happen if the inner child knows the boundaries that apply. These are important skills that you can teach, and will make your life a lot easier when you can trust him, even when you are in public and regression is becoming a problem.

Some call it 'faking being an adult', when the situation demands it. That actually has it around the wrong way, but if this terminology helps bring the boundary under control, then work with it!

The level three and four boundary:

These levels are totally unacceptable for unprepared public times and can present a huge risk to both of you. You need to teach your Little One the boundary between levels two (low regression) and three (deep regression), and what to do about it.

You both need to become aware of triggers which can start a deep regression, rather than just a shallow one. Sometimes, there are triggers to avoid, such as baby shops, children's books or sights and smells that push regression into higher levels. But remember, that these can't always be predicted or avoided. As you know by now, regression sometimes *just happens* and there is nothing you can do to avoid it or even predict it. How do we deal with an unplanned regression episode?

Let's start by understanding that the unplanned regression episode doesn't really start that way. Little Ones will by now, be often quite aware of the inner pressure from their inner child, well in advance. Not always, but as they get on, they will become more skilled at recognising it. They sometimes feel this odd sensation or pressure, which in time, they learn to recognise as the *pressing need to regress*. Eventually, your Little One will need to learn to monitor this and to handle the regressive needs better and in a more planned manner. Even with that skill, there are times when regression pushes its way out and the Little One struggles to control it. What do we do then?

There are some activities or thinking patterns that can lower the regression level or even eliminate it, at least temporarily. Masturbation is one such method. Having your Little One go off privately and masturbate can usually bring a significant and temporary release of the regressive behaviour. Note that this works for some, but is useless for others. It works for most, however. You will need to be on the lookout however, for better activities that have the ability to lower the regression quickly, reliably and preferably in advance of the *point of no return*. Sometimes, it can even be a discussion on a complex or controversial topic that distracts him from the inner turmoil.

It is worth noting that these measures are always just temporary. The regression *will* return to play out its internal needs, but when in public, this is simply not possible or appropriate.

You are learning to navigate the adult/child boundary properly when you both realise that the boundary exists and that handling it, is just another skill to be learned.

The goal is simply to help your Little One keep his Little activities out of the public realm or out of the view of others. It is also to keep him safe from activities that might be harmful and inappropriate. There is also great benefit in teaching your Little One how to handle such a complex and sometimes difficult problem. This skill can leak into the adult realm and help him with boundaries and problem solving there as well.

Much of regression is about pandering to a deep need. There is nothing wrong with that most times, but it is crucial for a well-balanced life, that we also learn to make our drives subject to our will. Some Little Ones are truly dreadful at this and lack the dedication to identify and observe these boundaries. This is where you need to be very tough and uncompromising. Proper observance of the regression boundaries should be a non-negotiable, but for many, they just don't know how to do it. When regressed, they are unable to identify the boundaries correctly. Then is your job to help them find their way through this problem.

The reward you get is a feeling of safety. The reward the Little One gets, is to be trusted more by his partner, as well as himself. Teaching your Little One to navigate the adult/child boundary will take time and probably more than you think. Just remember, **they may have no experience of how to do this**. He may have a PhD in mathematics, but be unable to recognise when he has slipped over a boundary.

This is your job: to teach and train your Little One with boundary navigation and management.

SECTION SEVEN – PUTTING IT ALL TOGETHER

Now the fun begins! Up until now, it was just information and ideas. Now, we have to put it all together and begin to change things in the relationship.

Many relationships that have unresolved tensions with regression, diapers and cross-dressing, have toxic elements that need to be dealt with and released slowly and carefully. This is not a primer on adult relationship difficulties. This book deals with just one item: Little Ones. I will assume you have the intelligence to use discretion and wisdom in applying the following tips. Don't disappoint me!

First Steps/Baby Steps

Setting your Initial Goals:

The first step is to define your goals for the relationship. This can be a huge and quite difficult step for many. Let my first words be one of encouragement to persevere. Your goals right at the start, should be fairly general in scope and as time goes on, *then* you will make them more defined and specific. If you try and get too fancy with your goals now, you will only disappoint or frustrate yourself when you miss many, or even most of them.

If you are the partner of an Adult Baby or Regressive Little One and have read the book this far, then you are clearly serious about trialling a Parent/Child relationship with your partner. Experience indicates that the motivation behind this is probably because:

- You are experiencing your Little's increasing anger or frustration.

- The stress in your relationship over his infantilism and regression is getting out of control.

- You have a strong curiosity about just what it is that he does, feels and thinks.

- Your Little One is pushing for you to interact with him or to be his parent and you had no idea what that really entailed, until now.

If any of the above is true, then your initial goal should perhaps be no more complex than to **'just make things better'**. That's a simple goal, which will meet the initial need and give you a launching platform for more advanced goals later on. If your relationship is in trouble because of your partner's strong regressive or infant needs and behaviours, then accept this as your primary goal: to make life easier. When the pressure comes off a little and the relationship improves some, then you can find your way around the more complex goals and plans of the Parent/Child relationship.

This special form of relationship is different for every couple. For some, it is very intense and involved and is a huge part of their lives. For others, it is a consistent aspect, but far more peripheral. It is about meeting your respective needs and desires in the way it works for *you*. It will turn out differently for everyone in the end, but many of the steps you take along the way are the same. Let's look at some of them.

Getting Started:

Your goal here is to begin the process, nothing more, so keep that in mind. It is about overcoming the relational inertia or the uncomfortable silence, and to make something happen.

Most Little Ones keep themselves quite secretive and withdrawn, as a defence mechanism against rejection and hurt. Even as their partner, you will need to tread carefully in the beginning, until mutual trust is established. Your adult-adult relationship may be good, even excellent, but don't assume that your Parent/Child relationship will necessarily be the same at first. Unless you have already sought out to know your Little One intimately, you *don't* yet actually know him at all well and he probably doesn't know himself all that well either. It can be a recipe for disaster, if you blunder in making assumptions about him that are completely wrong.

Right at the start of the Parent/Child relationship, we are at best, acquaintances who sees someone the way they wish to be seen, not the way they truly are inside.

Initiating a Parent/Child relationship is as easy, as it is complex. There are no hard-and-fast rules beyond genuineness, love and patience. The average child will respond well to love, even if they still carry great hurt. They may take their time, but they *will* respond to you. Remember though, that you have the added advantage of an adult mind in your child, who can process at that level. If you are genuinely seeking to know your Little, he will know and respond accordingly. He may be suspicious, pessimistic and even a little reluctant, but he *will* respond.

There are five possible situations you are both starting from:

1. **Your Little One has no idea that you are aware of his needs**. This is a naive belief on his part. Most Adult Babies and Little Ones desperately want their partner to know, and sometimes subconsciously make it obvious or easier for them to find out. But now that you do know, and have presumably decided to take it further and pursue a Parent/Child relationship, *you* need to take the first step.

   Choosing the very best, most private and safe time you can, mention to him that you know what is going on. Don't mention this book, as that can be a bit provocative and overwhelming. Ensure that the initial conversation remains totally in the adult realm and simply discuss it, slowly and calmly. A good thing for you to do is to tell him you are 'more or less okay with it'. This gives him the assurance that you are not mad at him and about to divorce him, yet at the same time doesn't give him the erroneous idea that you want to be his parent right now and enthusiastically change a dirty diaper!

2. **You have tried something before and it ended as a miserable failure**. In that case, you are both probably less than enthusiastic about trying all over again, yet you know that you don't really have a choice. The person who coined the phrase 'what doesn't kill you, makes you stronger', obviously never took his own advice. Repeated painful failure *doesn't* always make you stronger. It can make you bitter, reluctant, pessimistic and depressed. If this is how you feel, then you will have a lot of company.

   Having said that, you need to try, try again. This time it *will* be different because now you have a plan, whereas before, you were probably going blind and hoping for the best. Talk about it compassionately and enthusiastically, because he probably also feels defeated about previous failures. A Little One who has tried and failed many times before, will be reluctant to put himself through the cycle of dashed hopes and failure yet again. Mention the book and show it to him. It might give him hope, as well as a lot of ideas, but be ready for him to be embarrassed by the book's exposure of so much of his inner thinking and behaviour. Commit yourselves to trying once again.

3. **You are both aware that he is a Little One, but you don't talk about it.** This is a common situation and is mainly caused by lack of knowledge of 'what to do about it'. Many couples, when faced with a overwhelming issue they are totally ill-equipped to deal with, choose denial instead. They hope it will be *okay* or that it will *go away*. We have already discussed how it *won't* go away, nor will it be okay. If you have previously discussed Infantilism or Adult Babies – even just in passing – then you should both read this book. If nothing else, it will lay a foundation for discussion further on. There are certainly enough topics or controversy within, to begin a discussion.

4. **Your partner is openly pushing the boundaries and showing his baby side to you,** in a non-verbal expression of wanting you to be involved. If this book was bought by you in response to this, then congratulations! If he gave it to you and you've made it this far, then I'm still impressed! If you are totally unwilling to be in a Parent/Child relationship, then you would have stopped reading a long time ago. I am going to assume you have at least an *interest* in this kind of relationship with your partner. I know you are unsure and perhaps reluctant. That's fine. Start talking to him and express exactly that fear. Promise him no more than that you will try. That's all you should do, unless you are more sure of yourself now, than you were at the start of this book. Talk, discuss and think a little about how it can work. Use the book as a conversation starter and director. It will be easier than trying to blunder into the great regressive realm all alone!

5. **You both realise that you need to do something along the lines of bringing the Little One out.** The idea of a Parent/Child relationship sounds like a good idea, you think. Presumably, you have both read the book and are coming to this decision with eyes open. The first thing to do now, is to talk about it at length as adults and to be prepared to bend and break your previous boundaries. Take care you don't leap too far, too fast and find yourselves out of your depth. Doing this slowly might frustrate your Little One, but it remains the safest and most effective method. Go too fast, and you risk the same result as driving too fast: disaster.

You may have noticed that in every situation mentioned above, I end up with both of you *talking about it*. I don't say to put on his diaper or to give him a bottle. Instead, I say *talk about it*, adult to adult, because the Parent/Child relationship is built on the strength of your adult-adult relationship. If you can't talk openly and honestly about all of the issues we have discussed up until now, then you will most likely fail. All the way through the Parent/Child relationship, you will be discussing progress, success, failures, mistakes, fun and boredom. You can't do that in baby talk. The respective adults *must* do the talking.

The biggest single mistake any Adult Baby or Little One can commit, is to make their regressive side the <u>pre-eminent</u> aspect to their relationship. Regression and Little Time can only be successfully built on the foundation of a good, stable, <u>adult</u> relationship.

Announcing your intentions:

If your baby still does all of his Little behaviour in secret, then you need to bring it out of the hidden areas and into the light. Presumably, you already know he has baby/toddler things, so let that be a starting point. Start with something innocuous, but obvious. Tell him you like one of his dresses (even if you don't), that you found by accident. Cuddle him in a childish fashion. If he is stressed, suggest a diaper. (I bet you've never done that before!)

The aim here is to do something unexpected and obvious that announces to your Little One that you want to change the relational dynamic. It doesn't make any promises or give any details. It simply announces <u>intent</u>.

What you *do* is less important than that he gets that singular message – change. Actions speak louder than words and to a child, they are often *all* that is heard.

If he wears diapers to bed already, then snuggle up to him in the morning in a semi-intimate way, even when he is wet. I'm sure you don't normally do that, but in fact, quite the opposite! This feels like rejection to your Little One and let's be honest here, that's exactly what it is. Whatever you do, don't make it a sexual advance! That will just confuse the message. I'm sure you get the idea. Find something that will get him to thinking that you are less 'anti' his little-ness.

What happens next, is where we finally start to work on a relationship that brings mutual satisfaction to everyone.

First Contact:

You've already started talking about it together. Well, don't stop! You simply *must* continue to talk about the Parent/Child relationship and assess how it is going all the time, especially early on. This never ends! Communication is the key to ensuring that the relationship works and grows.

Getting started can be a bit of a struggle for some. Like so many other big jobs and tasks, the first few steps are often the hardest. Once momentum has begun, the rest of the process naturally follows. One idea that has worked well for some, is to initiate the Parent/Child relationship with something *significant*. This is really only suitable to couples, where there has already been some attempt at finding a solution, yet has failed.

The following ('using a significant event') is not suitable for first timers to developing a Parent/Child relationship. You should start by talking first.

You can try a few of the following *significant* ideas, to let him know you want to be his parent.

- Take charge and dress him the way you know he would like, including changing his diaper and putting on his Little clothes. Sit down with him and explain that you are now ready to become his parent. It's less than subtle and it is not a promise to do it all the time. It is more of a *statement of intent,* made in actions, rather than words.

- Buy your Little One a small gift – a toy, a bracelet, a bottle or a child's book. Give him something tangible to demonstrate that you seriously want to become a solution to his issue, by becoming his parent, to some degree or other.

- If he is a fetish bed wetter, then actively encourage/permit him a wet bed, but when he is in it, explain that you now wish to develop the Parent/Child relationship. It is a *statement of intent,* made in actions, rather than words.

- Call the new proposed relationship an adoption. Tell him that you wish to adopt him as your child. Of course it isn't real, but it can feel real and is an incredibly powerful signal of your intentions. In the Case History section at the end of the book, you will find an example of an adoption.

- Give him a special age-appropriate meal or particular Little experience. Just remember to be totally in charge and to use his name. Announce that you now wish to become his parent, as best you can.

Remember that a single show of interest won't overturn all the pain of the past. It may even be viewed with suspicion. Just be prepared for whatever the reaction is. What you are looking for, is the first sign that your child recognises that you are serious about dealing with this aspect of your relationship. At first, he may be very hesitant, even refusing to talk. Just persist, using good timing and some wisdom. Your child is probably carrying decades of hurt and rejection. He may be in shock and disbelief, but it is something he truly wants. He will join you, if you take it slowly and sincerely and give him a little time.

First Contact for first-timers:

If you are very new to all of this or nervous, then a good way to start is by speaking to your Little One *peripherally*. By this, I mean talking *around* the topic, rather than head-on. It is a good way to start and in time will lead to deeper things. Discuss innocuous aspects of what is happening to him. Ask him if his diapers are working okay. Perhaps talk about eBay's Adult Baby things for sale or, if he has Little items, ask him if he likes them. Just be soft, slow and non-threatening. Talking *around* a difficult topic initially, is a classic way of discussing more complex issues. Once that commences, it is easier to subtly shift the topic onto the area of concern.

NOTE: While we don't talk about the beginnings of infantile/toddler regression in this book, you need to be fore-warned. Regression is a psychological issue that often has trauma or abuse at its core. Your child may have been abused or traumatised as a very young child and be either unwilling or unable to talk about it, or may even have no memory of it. Just be careful of digging too deep into a past you are unprepared for and untrained to help. You are aiming to establish a Parent/Child relationship, not fix up his past. The present is where you need to be focussing on.

Let's take a look at one mother that initiated contact with her Little Ones and the difficulties and successes that she had.

"While recently on holidays, my husband and I were struggling to communicate, and this is not a normal thing. We can talk about anything. The major, the minor, the inane, and the ridiculous, so not being able to discuss this THING, this BABY THING, in fact, was not normal at all. So, I decided that enough was enough and to do whatever I could to make things right again for us.

My husband, Chris, was sitting at the kitchen table in the holiday unit doing something on the laptop, so now was my chance. I went into the bedroom and laid out on the bed a brightly coloured dress, white bonnet and a white petticoat. Added some soft toys and went out again. Now you might ask why all those things were with us during our holidays, and the short answer is, I'm not sure. Chris, I think as an adult, was trying to get me to see his Little Self, but wasn't sure how to get me involved and his Little, didn't know how to tell me. As you can see, it now became my choice and responsibility to do the next thing and so my laying out of an outfit was my answer.

After about 30 minutes, Chris went to the bedroom for something and stopped at the door. I was sitting nearby and he turned to look at me quite stunned. The first words out of his mouth were not really momentous, "Well, what's this??", is not what you would call earth shattering, but I could see that my meaning was plain to him. I, as his wife, wanted to take up the role as parent to his regressive self. A job, I see now, as joyous, but then I saw as difficult. I felt embarrassed when I saw him dressed in the little girl clothes and playing with soft toys. I felt frustrated because he longed for me to parent him, whereas normally he would lead us. It was a very trying time, but we've both learnt along the way.

From that one choice, I've now had the privilege of meeting Katie, my husband's regressive self. Katie is certainly complex and she sees herself as 3 years old. She also has several other aspects in Charlotte who is 12 months, Catherine is 5 years, Ally is 8 years and Molly is 12 years old. Each of them is well formed and have their own speech patterns, behaviours and likes and dislikes. This journey is very new for us both, but already I can see more security and less stress in my adult husband, and more joy and release in my Little Girl, Katie.

I still make a mess of things when I don't take the initiative, or expect certain behaviours when out the house, but we are both still learning. I'm finding my hard limits in what I will put up with, but I would think that over time, these will change and develop too. We, Chris and Katie, and me as wife and Parent, are happy for that one choice I made a few weeks ago. Our lives are more complete."

[personal contact]

The Child versus The Behaviours:

When you first begin talking to your Little One about this, you will most likely end up mainly discussing behaviours, not feelings. It will feel odd and perhaps a little ridiculous. The reason for this is because you are talking about what your Little One *does,* not who he *is.* Discussing infant behaviours as adults will seem surreal and awkward at first. It will also feel a little clinical and you might think that you are going nowhere. That is normal, you are doing fine. You are in exactly the right place.

Initial communication is primarily about establishing a platform on which to discuss the things that really matter, later on. When addressing complex and difficult topics, it is always best to establish some form of peripheral communication, first to relax each other then, to build upon it, before attacking the core issue. Do not rush it! Your Little One has had years and probably decades of hiding. He isn't going to share too much with you too soon and even if he is, you *really* don't want him to dump his entire baby history and baggage on you the first day. There really is such a thing as 'too much information'!

'Going slow' is the rule for both of you. He may want to rush right into full babying. Don't do it! The only way a proper Parent/Child relationship can work long-term, is if both of you take it slow and steady and deal with problems as they develop, before they become destructive. Take on too much, too quickly and you risk missing the seeds of damage and destruction when they first appear.

The real learning and growth begins when you start dealing with your Little One as a real person – as a *separate identity*, not simply discussing his behaviours. This will be a quantum leap for you both, but it may not come easily. Most Little Ones spend their entire lives being babies on their own and doing so privately. Sharing these things with someone else is one of their deepest wishes, but also their greatest fear. Your Little truly *wants* to share with you his inner feelings and wishes to be with you as your child, but he also needs to trust you, before he will expose himself to you. Even in great marriages and relationships, exposing the true inner identity is tough and when that inner being is a dysfunctional infant/toddler, it is doubly so.

Establishing regular Little Time:

It is of immense value to get some regular Little Time for your child that is pre-planned and requires little preparation from either of you. Why am I asking you to do this?

Your Little One has, up until now, lived a mainly ad-hoc existence as a regressive and this builds confusion, frustration and makes the pressure harder to deal with. By allowing a regular minimalist expression of his Little side, you take a lot of the pressure off, as well as bring some order and discipline into the behaviour. These regular experiences are not meant to be outlandish or large in scope. In fact, that is the point. They are *meant* to be short or minimal expressions of these behaviours! To a large extent, these times should be spent with your partner, both in the adult and Little realms, but giving peace to his inner Little at the same time!

He will still need and want, full-on regressive times with you, but they will be more special, more powerful and not as frequent. By building a layer of regular simple activities, you allow everyone to cope better.

Perhaps for some, it can mean wearing diapers to bed or even some baby clothes as well. Every night or perhaps every other night? That's up to you to work out. It might mean that a few regular times during the week, your Little can regress in a regular pre-determined manner, even if only for thirty minutes.

In the behavioural profile we built up earlier on, we defined objects and behaviours as Fundamental, Important or Peripheral. Here is where we put that information into practice.

The regular, convenient Little Time you give him should have the following aspects:

- It should be regular, predictable and rarely missed.

- It should not require special permission from you every time. The only time your permission should matter, is if for some reason it is not possible *this time*.

- The *fundamentals* should be involved. All of the fundamental behaviours should be covered. This list is short and doesn't necessarily need to be all at the same time, For example, he could have diapers four nights a week and panties three evenings a week, as long as the fundamentals are being met consistently.

- It doesn't require your partner to be regressed. It can be simply the adult enjoying some Little behaviours *or* it can be a time of regression.

- It should be very easy for everyone to do. It should not upset or concern you, nor should it involve too much effort or displacement. Obviously there will be *some* involvement, but it should be easy enough for you to handle, so that you can keep doing it long-term without becoming onerous.

- It should be effective. If your Little is not happier and more balanced and feeling more in control, then you are perhaps missing a fundamental or not doing it often enough. 'Regular' doesn't mean once a month; it means at least once a week and probably more.

The principle behind this, is that by meeting his *fundamental needs* regularly, in a way that doesn't really upset you, it gives you a better chance of handling the *important* and even the *peripheral* areas more easily.

So now that you have a regular baseline set of Little behaviours that are not impacting on you too much, what comes next? Planning a *longer* Little Time, of course!

Because you are now regularly meeting the fundamental needs, when you and your Little One are ready to have some extended time together, as time and circumstances dictate, you should take the fundamentals and then add the *important* activities and objects to your time together. If you also have the rare opportunity and time, then throw in those *peripheral* items as well, just for fun!

Getting time to be an effective biological parent in the real world, is all about planning. You need to work out what is essential and make sure that that is done, no matter what – feed, wash, dress etcetera. And when you have the time on weekends for example, you will go out with the children and do something a bit more special, playground, school sports and the like. Then on those unique times like birthdays, Christmas or other important days, you bring out the peripheral things that they don't really *need* and perhaps aren't really all that important, but that they appreciate and enjoy anyhow.

It is no different when relating to the Little One as your child. Here are the three levels of need that he has:

1. **Fundamentals**

2. **Important aspects**

3. **Peripherals**

Finding Balance between the Little and the Adult

At the beginning of this book, I wrote that *finding balance* is the primary goal of the Parent/ Child relationship. Hopefully by now, you have some clues as to how to do that, or at least, that it is a possibility for you and your partner.

Rather than seeking a cure for the regression, you should by now realise that a far better option is to seek a way to live comfortably and happily with your Little One's infantile behaviour. I hope you also now understand that you hold the power to bring peace and stability to your Little One, by virtue of your acceptance and interaction with his *entire being*, including the inner child. The unfortunate truth is, that just as all children need a parent to thrive, so does your Little One. You can be that parent to him.

Finding a stability and balance in the Parent/Child relationship takes some work, but once established, can make the relationship wonderful, enriching and safe. Let's look at how we achieve that.

What is stability?

Typically, a Little One without some form of parenting, lives on an emotional roller coaster. The ups and downs might take place over hours, days or even months. This wild ride leads to anger, resentment and binge/purge cycles. The wilder the ride, the more risk of damage to the relationship, and for destructive behaviours to occur.

Stability isn't the end of the ups and downs. That is a worthy goal, but is probably unachievable, as we all have ups and downs in our functional emotional lives. Stability is more about taking the edge off the extremes and bringing them back within normal boundaries. Within these boundaries, your Little One can cope and handle his drives and feelings, just like normal emotions and needs. Stability is essentially about restoring behavioural and emotional control to the child.

Uncontrolled Regression:

One of the worst aspects of an unstable or over-stressed Little One, is where the regression becomes either *uncontrolled* or *uncontrollable*. For some Little Ones, this is the destination to which they are inevitably headed, if there isn't some kind of intervention. If there is no effective outlet, the regressive/infantile need gets bigger, stronger and harder to control, as time goes on. Eventually, it can reach a place where it spills out uncontrollably into the adult world and that's where trouble occurs.

When it is *uncontrolled*, the Little One *permits or initiates* regression, regardless of the circumstances or the appropriateness. This can be exceptionally dangerous, as well as potentially embarrassing. A Little One in this state, may exhibit bedwetting, pants wetting and even crawling and other infantile behaviours, when it is highly inappropriate. This is because the internal pressure has reached a breaking point and some release is demanded, appropriate or not. This is the state that you need to ensure never happens. Even a minimal Parent/Child relationship can achieve a degree of stability.

Uncontrollable regression is even worse. This is where the regression occurs spontaneously or for very long periods, and appears to be beyond the adult's control. If this is true, then professional mental health intervention may be required, but in the vast majority of cases, it isn't really ever needed. It is more about the *deep-seated unwillingness* of the adult to exert control. It only *appears* uncontrollable, because the adult has given up on trying anymore.

Some regression can be hard to control, but for the vast majority of Little Ones, it remains nothing more than a conscious choice – not necessarily an *easy* choice, but a choice nonetheless.

DO NOT let your Little One say he cannot control it. He can! But he needs to feel emotional fulfilment and trust to do so. He also needs to hear that you, the parent, will let him back to a regressed state later on, when it is more convenient or appropriate. The trustworthy promise of a Little Time to come soon, is usually enough to rein in the current pressure to regress. But remember to deliver! A broken promise will only make it harder to keep the regression under control next time.

Defining the need: How much is required?

The key to finding balance is in discovering how much regression is actually needed to meet your Little One's inner needs and then helping him to achieve it. The regression to childhood or infancy meets a very deep and very powerful emotional, and sometimes physical, need. Finding out how much is needed takes time and usually lots of it. If you asked your Little One how much he needs, he will either say he doesn't know or present a figure that is excessive and often wildly so. The question however, is a complicated one because 'how much' has different responses, depending on your *goal*.

Basically there are three goals available for you to pursue in the Parent/Child relationship.

1. **Just enough regression to ease the pain and to avoid a breakdown.** This is the minimal goal and seeks just enough regression time to ensure that your Little One won't explode, or even end the relationship. It isn't really an exceptional goal, because its parsimonious attitude reflects what you truly feel about your Little One and it certainly doesn't come across as total acceptance. It is a perfunctory action, designed to minimise damage. In essence, it is emotional *damage control*. That said, there are thousands of Little Ones who would give their right arm to have even this minimal level of parental relationship. It is certainly vastly better than no involvement at all.

   You may feel deeply intimidated by the notion of the Parent/Child relationship, which is fair enough! It is 'out there' enough to intimidate most people. At first, you may feel only willing and able to perform at this level – the minimal one – where you give what you can and your Little One gets the minimum of what he needs. If this is a *starting point* for you to consider taking it further in the future, then congratulations on your courage and determination. If this is all you are prepared to give, then that is fine, but be warned, that at this goal level, you are highly unlikely to get any significant positives yourself out of the Parent/Child relationship. If you want to get something positive for yourself, then look to the next level.

2. **The right amount of regression so that the Little One is relaxed**. This goal level is an excellent one for most Parent/Child relationships. This goal has you seeking to allow your Little One significant expression of his inner self and needs, but not driven purely by need alone. You will have recognised that he enjoys being Little, so you will give him Little Time, *just for fun*. You may also find some enjoyment out of his Littleness as well. You will find that changing his diaper sometimes or feeding him, is less of a chore and more of an intimate experience that you can both enjoy. You are probably also enjoying a better sex life, either as adult/adult, Parent/Child or both, as the drive-destroying pressure of being a Little, lessens.

   This is a good goal level for you both to live at, as it is highly functional and deep needs are also being met. You, the parent, are also getting some satisfaction out of the experience, beyond the satisfaction of simply meeting your partner's needs.

   A simple test to see if you are giving him the right amount of regression is this rather rough measurement. If he asks for Little Time and you say 'not now' and he is quite happy with it, or if you offer Little Time and he declines, because he has something else to do, then you have now reached the goal level you are after! Congratulations!

3. **More regression than he needs, but not so much that it overwhelms the adult experience.** Here is something you may not expect. You may not only find the Little experience satisfying, you may really, really enjoy it. You may even seek out extended opportunities to indulge in the practical expression of his regression. You may deeply enjoy parenting or you may realise that your Little One truly loves being Little, and you decide that your goal level is to give him *substantial time* as a Little. This is not simply to meet a need or to give him a bit of fun, but rather to allow him a large amount of time in the Little world, simply to enjoy himself. The only caveat in this level is to ensure that the Little doesn't take up too much of the essential adult time and responsibilities. We all have real world obligations to fulfil.

   At this level of balance, needs are obviously being met on both sides and there is now room for a significant degree of enjoyment of the Parent/Child relationship. It is an exciting level to be at, but it only works properly and long term, if both partners are getting a significant emotional return from it. If only the Little One is really enjoying it, then it is unsustainable for the long term and you are better to drop back to goal level two, which is still extraordinarily exciting and fulfilling for you both.

Preventative techniques:

No matter what level of balance you attain in the Little experience, there will always be times and places when the Little One exerts pressure to come out or the amount of regression wanted, exceeds the opportunities that are available. No matter what our best intentions are, sometimes you just can't get or do what you want. For regressive Little Ones, we sometimes need a few techniques to keep things more easily under control.

Here are some ideas and activities that can be done that help minimise or prevent excessive regression, when it isn't appropriate or possible. These ideas will become apparent to you, if you look closely enough over time. These techniques and suggestions may also be things *external* to the behaviour like:

- Better sleep patterns.

- Traditional stress reduction techniques (massage, yoga etcetera).

- Better health and fitness.

- Improved relational communications – essentially talking more with your partner and spending more quality time with them.

- Increased and varied social life – get out more!

- Better and more frequent sexual intimacy.

Pre-emptive Regression:

There are a lot of regression-like behaviours that can ironically be used to help prevent regression.

The risk of wildfires is reduced by controlled burn-offs. The same concept can apply to regression. A period of controlled, predictable regression, can reduce or eliminate the risk of uncontrolled Little Times. It can give back some of the balance that regression typically takes away.

One good example of the concept at work is this one:

"My baby inner was getting out of control and since I lived alone I decided to try living as a baby all the time. That was a fiasco. It was way too much and it just made it worse. Then I tried something a bit different.

Now when I get home from work every day I put on a nappy and a baby dress and have a bottle I had prepared in the morning. I empty my bladder into the nappy and spend the next two hours as a baby. Nothing really special except I do this every day no matter what. Half the time I don't really want to. I'm tired or just not in the mood.

But I still do it. Some days as soon as the two hours is over I'm out of baby mode like a shot! Other days I stay that way for a lot longer.

But the real difference for me is that now I can go out on weekends with friends and not feel anxious about the baby need coming up out of nowhere and distracting me and stopping me from having fun. I used to be with people and just feel like I disappeared when my inner baby wanted to be out.

I went away with some friends for a weekend and not once did my baby bug me. Mind you as soon as I got home I was into a nappy and dress double-quick! It works for me."

[internet blog]

Non-regressive diaper use:

Let's talk about diapers again. They are the central prop or Attachment Object for the Little One and as such, may be part of the key to finding balance. An integral part of regression involves wearing and using diapers. Outside of regression, diapers are only really used for bedwetting and/or incontinence. Or are they? Do they have other uses that we can consider?

In their most basic form, a diaper handles the wearer's elimination needs and compensates for their lack of bladder and/or bowel control. In a regression situation however, they are almost always worn as a part of the child's outfit and as an integral part of the scenario. But another truth, is that a lot of regressive Little Ones actually *need* their diapers during regression (situational incontinence). As they regress, they lose bladder and sometimes bowel control and they are literally unable – and possibly unwilling – to have control. For many, they are continent during the day and mainly continent at night, but from the moment they put on a diaper, they instantly lose that control.

Using the *burn-off* metaphor, it was suggested to one couple that the regressive partner trial wearing diapers fulltime for a few weeks, to see what the results were. This is what the wife had to say (edited):

"At first I thought the idea that Jim wear diapers all the time was idiotic! Here we are struggling with his baby behaviour and his bedwetting and you suggested I give in to it? But we were in such a bad place I thought I had to give it a try before throwing away everything, including Jim!

I wasn't ready for the results and they dumbfounded me. Jim was calmer, happier and I felt there was hope again. I still felt ridiculous when I saw him in diapers but it got easier after a while.

It's now six months to the day and he hasn't been out of diapers since. I expected one of us to crack and dump the whole idea but no one did. He was happier and his baby moods were still there but seemed easier in a way. None of us wanted to change something that seemed to be working.

Jim is afraid of becoming incontinent but he is afraid of the uncontrollable baby that lives inside him much more.

We are still working on balancing everything. It's hard but next week Jim is having a two year old 'birthday party'. I hope it is as effective as the diaper idea."

[personal email]

One of the more effective preventative ideas, is to revert to significant or fulltime diaper use or even just night diapers. The point is that by *burning-off* some of the desires and needs in a regular and controlled way, the worst of the excesses are curbed, at least in part. You may need to experiment with your Little One wearing diapers regularly, regardless of regression or not. It might work and it might not, but experience indicates that it might very well help. Of all the preventative ideas, this one should be trialled first. One possible problem, is that it might initially trigger stronger regression. However, give it a few weeks before you dump the idea. Often with major changes like this, the initial experience is an uncontrolled release of pent-up feelings and behaviours. After a while, it all settles down, and it is then that you can tell if it is going to work or not. The true value appears once diapers become *functional* (normalised and desensitised) items to your Little One, rather than purely infantile objects.

Other preventative ideas:

Other props and activities that can be used regularly, regression or not, are:

- If he is a baby girl, then wearing panties more often or all the time.

- Using a pacifier at night on a regular basis.

- Using a baby bottle.

- The Little One reading a child's book or you reading to him.

- Wearing children's/toddler clothes at fixed pre-defined intervals, such as to bed or in the evenings.

- Other regressive behaviours that you find are easy to do, yet bring a reduction in internal pressure.

As the parent, your role is to help find some of the burn-off activities that help your Little One find balance. It may mean you have to *demand* he do some of these things, even when he doesn't want to. I mean it! Little Ones are very much driven by their need at the moment, rather than looking to the future. If you have established some regular burn-off activities, such as wearing diapers in the evening, then you need to insist that he follows through, even when he doesn't want to. Taking the Little One beyond simply responding to inner needs is crucial. It is in these times where so much of the balance is learned.

Special Events:

If you truly understand that your Little One is a child, then you can draw on your wealth of experience as either a biological parent or as a child yourself. Remember how the promise of something special helped your biological child behave? Remember also how after that exciting time or gift, the child felt special and was less demanding for a period of time? Your Little One is no different.

There are some special events you can plan for your Little One that he will look forward to and enjoy. The amazing thing about it, is that a few of these events can sate or satisfy the Little One's deep needs for quite some time. You could plan a half day Little Time with all the trimmings. This is not primarily about finding balance. It is about nothing more than your Little One having a deep and enjoyable time as a child. The irony is that balance can sometimes be the result!

You could bathe him, change him into his prettiest outfits, do his nails, do his hair or wig and make a fuss over him. For a boy toddler, get out his baby overalls and all his toy cars and trucks. You could also feed him by hand or use a bottle. Read him stories, play games, change his diaper and give him a nap – the whole nine yards. Then sit back and watch him feel happy and satisfied. Sometimes that satisfaction can take the edge of his ongoing needs for days or even weeks.

You can try other things too:

- Birthday Party.

- Themed day.

- 'Baby's Day Out' into Unsafe Zones.

- Meeting with another Little or Parent/Child.

- Joining him as a Little One yourself.

Find some event or activity that is special and rare, but something that *can* be repeated, if needs be. These can be used as rewards, or just something to help your Little feel the satisfaction that so often eludes him. There is nothing wrong with offering rewards to your Little One for good behaviour. While it would be wrong to do this with your adult partner, the promise and reward cycle is quite appropriate and productive for a biological child and also for a Little Child.

Balance comes to happy and satisfied Little Ones, not angry and upset ones.

Summary of Finding Balance:

In essence, balance is the midpoint between fantasy and harsh reality. You need to be clever, inventive and observant. Some things will work, while others won't. For some, being put back into diapers will have no effect, or even make it worse, while for others, it will take the edge off the pressure and make regression much easier to live with. You have to experiment to find out which is true for you. Look to your own childhood for things you loved doing and consider emulating some of that. Feel free to experiment and don't feel intimidated by failure or mistakes. The mere act of attempting to help, is far better than most Little Ones ever get to experience. Your successes will always outweigh your mistakes and your Little One will always appreciate your efforts, including the failures.

A clue to finding balance is this:

Fantasy thrives when it is not allowed to be expressed in the real world. There is nothing more devastating to a fantasy than reality. Believing in the fantasy that you are a baby girl loses a lot of its power when you are required to actually live as one.

Fantasy is your enemy.
Reality is your friend.
Balance sits somewhere between them.

Developing a Parent/Child Relationship Plan

Where do we go now? We've gotten the Parent/Child relationship off to a flying start and begun some regular Little Time, but what comes next? Well, that's up to you *both* to work out together!

At this point in time, you are starting to successfully meet the *fundamental needs* of your Little One's regression and you have averted the problems that leaving them unresolved, inevitably brings. You may want to take a breather at this stage! It doesn't hurt to just stop and smell the roses for a bit. Take a break and let things settle down, until you are ready to move forward again. The next stage is about bringing in some of the *important* and *peripheral* aspects into the relationship. Now that you have met the immediate and fundamental need, that doesn't need to be rushed.

It is now time to formulate a plan for how the Parent/Child relationship needs to develop. I'm going to suggest something now that your Little One probably won't like. I believe that the best way to develop a relationship plan, is to discuss the needs and wants of your Little One with him and then *on your own,* develop what you see as a road-map to the future. The reason I say this, is that your Little One will want everything – today, if possible! That kind of childish rush is not helpful and can actually damage things. If the parent takes their Little's desires into account, as well as considers their own personal limits, then there is a better chance that a Parent/Child Relationship Plan can work.

Now, we all know that every plan gets substantially modified along the way. No project ever gets finished on time or within budget and often looks very different in the end. That may not sound like much of a goal, but it certainly better than no plan at all.

Two year Goal:

Let's start with the end goal first, in about two-five year's time. Now that you have some experience in parenting, where do you see:

A. Your desired end result? In a few year's times, when you have found a Parent/Child situation that you find comfortable and rewarding, what does it look like? For example: *"I expect to have a baby boy that is calm and relaxed and that I am just taking it in my stride and neither of us is bugging each other about it. I really hope I am able to enjoy it as well, if that's possible."*

B. Your parental limits? As part of any long-term plan, you need to list your no-go zones or aspects of regression that you will only visit very occasionally, if at all, no matter how long it goes on. For example: *"I can't abide dirty diapers all the time. Occasionally is okay, I guess. No way I will smack him either – ever. And I won't get involved with another baby or couple."*

C. What level of Adult/Little balance do you expect to have finally achieved? Example: *"I really don't expect this uncontrolled nonsense anymore and I expect to find him adult most of the time and especially when I need it."*

    D.   What negative elements do you expect to still be facing in the relationship? Example: *"I don't think I will ever stop him wetting our bed, but I can hope!"*

    E.   What level of intimacy – including sexual – do you expect to have achieved that is different from today, in both the adult-adult and adult-child realms? Example: *"I expect to be able to talk to him at any time on any subject and get an adult answer. And I expect our sex life to be awesome. I accept that will mean sex with the Little One and I expect that to be great as well."*

You will be reviewing your Relationship Plan regularly and the above will change. For example, bottle-feeding may be something you refuse to do at the moment, yet in a year's time it may move to the *acceptable* category. There will always be development and change in your relationship plan. Any relationship that isn't developing, is dying.

Three month Goals:

Now, let's look at the three month plan. Where do you expect to be in three month's time?

    A.   What new Little activities do you see yourself able to integrate in this time frame? Example*:"I might start doing more diaper changes and I might see if I can dress him. That's probably all I can manage right now."*

    B.   What concepts are you willing to trial, that you haven't yet tried? Example: *"I might see if I can handle him being a baby for a full day and see how I handle it, but not with me doing everything, perhaps just helping out."*

    C.   Where do you see your level of Parent/Child intimacy – including sexual – reaching? Example: *"More sex! And perhaps getting a little better at talking when he's a girl baby."*

    D.   What negative elements do you expect to still be facing in the relationship? Example: *"Somehow I doubt I will be happy with dirty nappies and I'm just as sure that talking about his inner feelings will still be pretty ordinary."*

    E.   Do you have any expectations for getting close to balance for your Adult/Little? Example: *"Anything is better, but in three month's time I'd like to see the end of the grumpy child, at least."*

All of these questions are important and reflect on your capacity and willingness to move the Parent/Child relationship along. That sounds like an onerous obligation, but it isn't meant to be so. As a parent, you are being asked to take on a lot more than you ever expected, and while the payoff is in a happier and more relaxed and relational adult, it is still sometimes 'a little too much'.

It is okay to include in your Relationship Plan some limits, breaks and halts.

To a large degree, you are the one who will largely define where the relationship goes, at least in its scope. Once you have met the fundamental needs and survived the inevitable blow-ups, the rest is about communicating with your child, finding out what he wants, seeing what is good and what you can actually do for him. In this regard, it is not unlike a normal parent trying to handle the competing obligations of raising a biological child in the middle of a busy lifestyle. You do your best, based on your love for the child, but you can't do everything and nor should you. You are not meant to be super-mum! You are meant to be a good and loving parent, not struggling to meet some impossible standard and feeling guilty as a result.

One Year Goal:

Let's look a year down the track. After a year of this relationship, you would expect to have a pretty good idea of who your child is and what they want and need. While every relationship continues to grow and change, after a year, you should have most of the principal pieces in place.

A.   Which parts of the *important* and *peripheral* aspects do you plan to implement by this time? List those aspects you think you can put in place.

B.   How do you think the relationship will look at this time. Do you think you will have found your feet and be handling it well, or still struggling? What level of intimacy, including sexual, do you expect to have reached?

C.   What significant problems do you expect will still be around?

D.   What negative elements do you expect to still be facing in the relationship?

E.   What level of Adult/Little balance do you expect to have achieved by now?

I hope you can see what I am trying to get you to do. This is essentially goal-setting and done by writing down basic goals and expectations for three months, twelve months and two-to-five years. By writing your expectations down, you can start to work out what you need to do, as well as see how you are moving forward.

Take the time now to put in place a Relationship Plan. It will never be any easier than right now!

SECTION EIGHT – PROBLEMS AND SOLUTIONS

Developing and improving your Parent/Child relationship is never easy. It is fraught with problems and challenges, just like anything else worth having. We discuss here some of the typical problems you will face, along with some suggestions and solutions.

Relational Conflict and Refusal

Instituting something as dramatically different as a Parent/Child relationship can often bring its own sets of unique problems when trying to initiate and implement it. The first area of conflict is always the primary relationship and family. Sometimes, the problems are obvious ones, but others are a bit surprising. Let's take a look at some of the conflicts that may occur and what to do about them.

Why should I do all of this for my Little partner?

"It is a lot of work and I don't get much back from it."

This is an unfortunately a common question, but a disturbing one. Marriage, and any other long-term relationship, is a commitment based on a lot more than 'what I get out of it'. That attitude tends to doom a lot of otherwise potentially great relationships. A good working relationship is not 50/50 and probably never will be. That is the stuff of magazines and romantic movies and it is total nonsense. At any point in time, one partner is contributing more than the other and then it turns around.

'From each according to his ability, to each according to his need.'

[Karl Marx 1875]

You could do worse than to take the above quotation to heart. If your partner was injured in a car accident and confined to a wheelchair, would you refuse to care for him because you don't get as much back as you put in? Of course not! And so it is here as well. In some ways, regression *is* a form of disability, when it starts to consume the adult. The difference here though, is that by putting in the effort to help your partner, you *will* reap rewards that you probably just don't recognise right now.

Infantilism and regression can be incomprehensible to many, but assuming you have read the rest of this book, you already know a great deal more than most and the most important thing, is that your partner is *normal*. He is not an axe-murdering psychopath. He is the man you love and live with, but part of him is regressive and needs your touch. You are the only one who can do it. He isn't looking for others to fill this need; he is looking to *you*.

Partner's refusal to be involved (for the Little One):

I am aware that despite this book being targeted primarily to *partners* of Little Ones, it will still be read largely by Little Ones themselves, probably in the hope that their partner will end up reading it, and so this section is written to you, the Little One.

The Parent/Child relationship sounds like heaven to you, but it probably sounds more like a version of hell to some partners. You need to understand, that in the main, this is not what they signed up for. Adult relationships are very important and despite the regular failure of many of them, most people do at least know what they are and how they are supposed to look and function. The Parent/ Child relationship is known about by very few, understood by almost no one and implemented safely by even less. Sorry to burst your bubble, but are you really surprised?

Implementing a Parent/Child relationship is, for most couples, extraordinarily difficult, which is why I wrote this book. The major reason for this, is a total lack of understanding, not a lack of compassion. You simply *have* to realise that the vast majority of people have close to zero knowledge regarding regressive lifestyles, and even less understanding and empathy. It might seem unfair and it probably is, but it *is* how things are. So first thing to do is this: REALITY CHECK. From the start, you are pushing uphill on this one.

How do you deal with your partner's refusal to become involved? First thing is to never give up, never assume that 'never' is the absolute last word. People change, people evolve and mature and events sometimes alter their reactions, but don't push it every two weeks either. All that will do is strengthen her resolve and risk the relationship as a whole.

The next thing to do is to assess your true priorities. Is having a Parent/Child relationship more important to you than the entire adult-adult relationship you currently have? If so, I have bad news for you. You are doomed. Your adult relationship has to be at all times, more important than your regressive needs or you will end up having neither.

I cringe when I read of Littles who will *only* have a relationship with a mummy or daddy, and then you read on to find this is their fifth attempt and every preceding try lasted a few weeks at most. Why is anyone surprised?

The Parent/Child relationship has to be built on the foundation of a functioning, growing and effective, <u>adult</u> relationship. If it isn't, it will most likely fail. Just like a relationship built entirely on sexual enjoyment, what happens to it when the sex fades? What do you do with your partner when you are not being a child, if all they are to you is a parent?

First and foremost, you should be seeking to bolster and improve your adult relationship. If she is refusing to be your parent, then work even *harder* on the adult relationship, not to curry favour, but to benefit you both.

Do not assume that the reason she refuses to parent you is obvious to either of you, or is the one she states. She may think it is paedophilic role-play. She may find it disgusting or she may think she couldn't possibly cope with any of it. Whether any of these reasons are true or not, they are valid, if she *thinks* they are. You will gain far more by being a better husband or partner, than you ever will by being a petulant child.

You may have young children and she is totally unwilling to risk affecting them by any exposure to this. That is a valid reaction and I will address it further on. Perhaps you could alleviate her concerns by demonstrating a rock-solid respect for boundaries by *never* breaching them. I know that Littles are often terrible at handling boundaries, but if your partner is concerned that you will affect your children by not hiding it from them, then prove otherwise to her. You could negotiate a one-time diaper wearing and ensure that absolutely none of it is even remotely close to the children. Afterwards, you can dispose of it so that not even the dog can find it. Show her you have the capacity and desire to be ultra-discreet and safe. And remember that kids grow up – and out. This problem doesn't last forever, it just seems like it when they are teenagers!

Next step. Don't throw a tantrum! Don't deny it, you have thrown one or two, or at least a long, bad, sulky mood. Little Ones are notorious for such behaviour, but if you want to impress your partner, it is the very worst thing you could possibly do. Remember how effective sulking was when you were a real child? The same applies here, except that sometimes you may get contempt in return as well. In other words, grow up when you don't get your own way. It's not over. It may just be delayed.

If your partner cares strongly for you, they won't simply dismiss it out of hand. Initially, it may be rejected because it overwhelms her and sounds creepy. Then as she understands more, it will sound less creepy, but still overwhelming. You may then get to the stage where you have a stated (or unstated) understanding that you can 'do it', but that she doesn't want to know anything about it, or be involved in any way. So make sure she *doesn't* know! Be ultra discreet and remember that she may not mean *doesn't want to know* literally, but rather, she doesn't want to have to see it. Secrets, especially ones that are of a sexual nature, are a toxic influence on any relationship, so in as discreet a way as you can do it, let her know that you are wearing diapers or dressing up, but in such a way that she *doesn't have to know*. Be intelligent and mature. You can do it!

Your first stage is when a partner is willing for you to regress and even to see it, as long as their involvement is nil and not expected. You may never get there or it make take a very long time. The real secret is one of contentment and unfortunately, this is never easy for a regressive with deep and sometimes consuming desires. That doesn't mean you shouldn't try and try hard.

After she has seen you as a child from a distance, seen you behave responsibly within boundaries, cleaning up after yourself and being discreet and not having a tantrum… *then* she might get involved a little. Or not.

And then she can read this book!

In short, your options in the case of total spouse rejection are limited to taking what you can, and giving all you have, to the relationship.

In the end, you will still be far better off living with a loving partner and frustrated by your inner child, than to leave and live openly as a baby in a home where you are the only inhabitant.

Choose wisely.

I find it all just 'too hard':

This is a common problem right at the start of trying to implement a Parent/Child relationship. The very size of this book indicates that this is not a small or trivial matter. Don't reject it out of hand. Instead, give it some time and experiment with minor things to see how it feels. He will love even the smallest thing you do. You may be surprised to find that it isn't quite as hard as you think. Take small steps that you can always retrace, if you feel uncomfortable. Take a look at what he wants to wear. Just glimpse at the lifestyle for a few moments, think about it some, and then step back again.

There is no rush. Your Little One always wants to rush, as it is the nature of a child. Don't let him rush you, but go into it at your own pace. Just make sure that the pace isn't glacial. If progress is so slow that it is not apparent, then he will grow frustrated and assume you no longer want to pursue *any* of it.

I don't want my kids to find out:

Of course you don't! That is both understandable and laudable. In an ideal world, children would not be aware of their parent's sex lives, relational problems or in this case, regression issues, but it isn't an ideal world. You can be perfect in keeping your Little One's regression from your children, until the day you make just one mistake and then you have some explaining to do.

A better approach is to be open about some aspects, such as diapers and bedwetting. Most children will be able to handle it, if you say he is a bed wetter and/or incontinent. The regression and baby dressing should be kept separate of course, but you need to be ready for discovery and have a plan/explanation/lie ready to deliver. Unfortunately, you cannot be a parent to your Little One and avoid risk. If you try to do that, you will ruin the relationship before it begins. No risk means no reward – always.

Don't assume that your children don't already know something about it. If they are twelve years old or over, they are already picking up on the nuances of adult behaviour and they are also sneaky. There is a very good chance they already know about mummy and daddy's 'games' – at least in broad strokes.

Adult children in the 21st century know a lot about Adult Babies, as it is all over the internet and even on television. If they know your partner wears diapers, they may suspect it or conversely, it may not have even entered their heads to consider it. However, if they find baby clothes or other items, they will almost certainly know it.

Discovery to some degree is almost unavoidable. Keep it discreet, keep it safe, but don't assume that you aren't already *busted*. At the same time, remember that while they might already know, they don't *want* to know, and that is your key to moving on. Maintain your normal family relationships and make sure they are healthy. If you do that, the fact that 'daddy is a baby' will be of little to no concern to them.

What about letting the older children know?

There are some couples that have let their older children – usually adult children – know that one or other of them is a regressive. I'm not convinced that there is ever a particularly good reason to do so. As mentioned before, they probably already know some of it and giving them confirmation or additional information seems to me to be unwise, as well as unnecessary. Unless you wish for your partner to live openly as a Little with clothing and accessories, such as cot/crib etcetera, it is usually unnecessary to do so. Perhaps some families could cope with an open Parent/Child relationship, but I think it is ill-advised and even dangerous. If the children are young, an outsider could easily assume evil intent by mistake.

They will end up knowing something, no matter what you do, but that does not mean you should fill in the gaps in their knowledge or flaunt it.

I can't cope with dirty diapers!

As much as it is disgusting, it is part of the experience for almost all Little Ones. If you give in on other cleaner and less smelly aspects of behaviour, then it is not unreasonable to expect your child to limit these to rare occasions and in circumstances where you don't have to suffer! Compromise will normally do it.

There are some things about this I just can't handle:

Don't be surprised if you find yourself coming up against a certain behaviour or attachment object that you just can't cope with. It isn't because it is too weird or too 'out there', but rather just something you *don't like* and can't handle easily. It isn't an uncommon reaction.

One new parent really struggled with baby bottles, for a reason she couldn't really identify. Her child had a full suite of baby clothes and other accessories, but the baby bottle 'bugged her'. On an unrelated shopping trip with her child, she came across a bottle similar to a sports drink bottle with a nozzle you suck from. But this one was smaller, baby pink, adorned with Disney princesses and shaped to fit in little hands. The child fell in love with it and it is like a baby bottle to her. Both were happy and, except for the 6-12 month old age girl, (she is a multi-age Little), this is a more than adequate substitute for a traditional baby bottle.

Don't worry about the odd thing that bugs you. It will probably go away in time and if not, there is almost always, a near-suitable replacement that wont offend you or him.

I can't smack him like you suggest:

"I tried, but I couldn't do it."

To be honest, many partners can't do it either, so don't feel too bad about it as there are plenty of other discipline tools available to you, such as timeouts, restrictions on further play etcetera. Smacking with the intention to *genuinely* modify behaviour isn't easy and only a few can do it effectively for the long-term. It requires the total agreement of your Little One to be successful and that isn't always easy to get or maintain. After all, it hurts and is meant to. Work on the alternatives and you will still have great success. Just don't give up on the first try of this, or anything else for that matter.

Getting stuck in regression:

One of the fears you may have, is that if you enter a Parent/Child relationship with your Little One, he might enter regression and never return. Well, quite simply, that isn't true. Rest assured, you aren't going to get a literal fulltime baby or toddler on your hands. Unless there is a serious mental issue going on – and you would already be well aware of that – the drive behind regression recedes on its own, as the need is met.

This doesn't necessarily mean that your Little One will automatically leave regression once his need is met. He is enjoying himself and so he will probably stay Little a while longer. The point is that he is regressing voluntarily and coming out of it voluntarily. As wrote earlier, regression remains essentially a voluntary act. Having said that, I do need to clearly state, that if the regressive need is left undealt with, it may explode into involuntary regression, just as a pressure cooker will eventually require the release of the steam. Assuming that you give your Little One even a token amount of regression, he will not reach that stage.

Coming Out:

One of the big questions that couples sometimes face is the idea of 'Coming Out' as a Little to others. For some, the reasoning is about being honest to themselves and others around them. I'd caution anyone thinking about this to be very, very careful.

The world at large does not tolerate, understand or accept Adult Babies or the like. The media mercilessly attacks any public figure that is outed as even a Diaper Lover, never mind a regressive Little. It is assumed that you are a paedophile or at the very least, a deviant. Television shows might talk about it on occasion, but it is never flattering and usually highly antagonistic. The world is not yet ready for openly declared Adult Babies.

So, who is it safe to *come out* to? Apart from each other, the obvious first choices are family and friends, but how likely are they to accept it, and what are you aiming to get out of it?

Little Ones can be notorious about wanting to be seen and accepted by others and are sometimes exhibitionist about it. This is often dangerous and incredibly stupid. The first question you should ask if you are considering coming out is 'why?'. What do you think you will gain from coming out? Normally, the only advantage in telling anyone, is the freedom to regress or dress as a Little around others. I doubt very much that your friends will want or understand that!

What about coming out to family? I strongly believe that underage children should be insulated from all aspects of regression since it remains, at least in part, a sexual activity or at the very least, it will *look* like it. *Coming out* to a child has to be restricted to 'daddy is a bed wetter' or 'mummy and daddy play dress up games' and no more, and usually only in response to being caught out.

Adult children are a different matter of course, but again I'd counsel against coming out, unless there is a very real reason for it. That reason shouldn't include 'freedom to regress', since it remains inappropriate to regress around anyone that is not directly involved and who hasn't given express permission. The only real reason to come out among family, is if you are caught and the childish excuses you gave years before no long cut it. In this case, explaining that you are a Little One has some justification in terms of being honest. The same might apply to your friends, if you are caught in a similar fashion. However, that does not necessarily translate into permission to regress around them. Knowledge does not imply acceptance or permission.

In short, *coming out* is not generally a wise decision to make voluntarily. It could so easily end up badly and usually does. Until such time as Littles get as much community acceptance and understanding as gays now do, telling the world you are an Adult Baby is a foolish thing to do and an action you will almost certainly regret.

Sleep Dysfunction

Many Little Ones have poor sleep patterns and usually from a lack of discipline or for other reasons. They are:

- Continence concerns – genuine fear of bed wetting or soiling.

- General night fears – afraid of the dark or being alone.

- Poor sleep practices – going to bed too late or getting up too early or too late on a regular basis.

- Denying the adult and/or child sleep needs as separate requirements.

- Nightmares.

- Night-time crying.

Your responsibility as a new parent, is to help rectify the above, as they present themselves. The first thing any mental health professional will do is to establish good healthy sleep patterns. We have a large capacity to cure ourselves of many ills, but only if we get regular and solid sleep. The aim is to get that Little One of yours sleeping… like a baby!

Denying the adult and/or child sleep needs:

Your Little One has two aspects that need sleep – the adult and the child. The body gets sleep in both realms, but the personality does not. Technically, a personality/ego does not need physical sleep, but it does need time to go on idle and to dream. The inner child also needs this. Many Little Ones will regress unknowingly in their sleep to achieve this, but some are so uptight about it, that their Little One does not get to experience sleep.

As an experiment, dress your Little One in babyish clothes, read him a young book before bed and give him a bottle and try to send him off to sleep as a child. Do this a few times and see if you pick up on any improvements in manner and behaviour from a well-rested child. If so, you may need to schedule regular *child sleeps* for him, either as a nap in full baby/toddler wear or regular night sleeping.

Continence Fears:

Your Little One probably already has some bedwetting or is a high-risk to do so. For most, this is something that disturbs sleep, with repeated wakeups or wet sheets. Unless your Little One is one of those babies that actually finds a wet bed comforting, he could be suffering from poor sleep.

Despite the consequences of bed wetting, some Little Ones are hesitant to use diapers for a multitude of reasons: shame and embarrassment, fear of regression, fear of losing all night-time control and other reasons. Some can sleep soundly in a wet bed, if there is proper mattress protection and they have spousal permission. However, most cannot do so. In this case, you need to put your Little One in night diapers. Deal with the fears, but insist on night diapers to ensure a good night's sleep. You can counter most of these fears by simply declaring that 'it doesn't matter' if they regress, get wetter or enjoy it. Most of these fears never eventuate anyhow and even if they do, they truly *don't* really matter.

General Night Fears:

It is disturbingly common for Little Ones to have regular night fears/terrors. These can be simple fear of the dark, fear of sounds in the night and especially storms. You need to treat this the same way you would with any other biological child. Night Lights, favourite soft toys, pre-sleep reading of a favourite book or cuddling until he drops off to sleep. These fears tend to reduce as the Parent/Child relationship improves, but it doesn't always. Sometimes the fear is that their parent will not stay with them because they are a child. You will need to give repeated assurances in this regard. The fear of the dark and storms may just be part of the behavioural profile of your child. Try and remember, that unlike a biological child who grows up and out of night fears, your Little One may not.

Poor Sleep Practices:

Your task is to ensure eight hours a night sleep for your Little One, or more as needed. The sleep variation that adults often have is not good for Little Ones. You should develop a good routine of *reasonable, regular and consistent* bedtimes and proper waking times. In the early days, you may need to use more draconian measures to get this working well. One couple is in their third year of Parent/Child and the child still has to ask permission to get up in the morning. This ensures that he gets the sleep he needs. Now, it is just part of the ritual that they follow, but it began to stop him getting up early and being tired. We all know what a tired little child is like – a cranky pain!

Nightmares:

Nightmares have many causes, but most are responses to insecurity and real-life disturbances. The best cure is to give your child a safe and secure bedtime through love and attention and any props, such as soft toys, that are needed. If it continues though, medical advice should be sought. Medication, foods and other physical factors can also be the cause.

Some of the best props to ease nightmares are your child's favourite toys, preferably soft toys that he can cuddle or sleep against. Sometimes, it may mean a lot of toys in bed with him. Some other objects may also help reduce nightmares. His pacifier may help, as may bonnets or a baby bottle.

Night-time Crying:

Fortunately, this is relatively uncommon and it really isn't healthy at all. A Little One really shouldn't be crying at night. Occasionally a *very* Little One (under twelve months), may cry for discomfort and hunger, but even that is still dysfunctional. The child should be matured into an older age or taught alternative communication techniques beyond crying.

Dealing with Fear

Many Little Ones are afraid and it can sometimes be a large part of their behavioural profile. It is one of your jobs as a new parent, to seek to reduce the level of fear they experience. Fear can range from a minor area of their psyche to a debilitating experience which makes them almost totally dysfunctional.

Typical fears are:

- **Fear of the dark**. Usually, just the Little One fears the dark, but the adult may do so as well and try to hide it. A night-light is not only cheap and effective, but is also age-appropriate.

- **Fear of discovery**. This is an adult fear and is only really helped by you confirming your love and commitment to the relationship and to your Little One. Remind him that you accept him unconditionally, as both an adult and as a child.

- **Stranger-danger**. This disturbing fear can occur as a reference to an original trauma in childhood. Be aware and if overly troublesome, seek professional help.

- **Fear of being lost.** This can be a big problem in regression outside of Safe Zones. Often your Little One will experience fear if he cannot see you for a length of time, or is unaware of where you went, while he is regressed outside of a Safe Zone. I recommend that you hold hands most of the time or if you need to be away, that you give *explicit* instructions to remain in the one place and then tell him how long you intend to be gone.

- **Fear of losing the parent**. This reflects either a fear of death or a fear of you, the parent, abandoning him. Little Ones are horribly insecure. You will need to often remind him that you are his parent and that you are not going anywhere! This reduces over time, but rarely completely disappears. By your actions and your words, you will need to regularly make him feel safe and secure in the knowledge that you will not abandon him.

- **Fear of losing themselves**. The more intuitive Little Ones sometimes worry that they will become a child and never return. After all, they are happier, more relaxed and feel more like themselves when Little, than at any other time. This fear ebbs away once they find their limit in baby experiences, something the Full Immersion technique delivers. Once they realise that they don't *really* want to be Little all the time, this fear loses much of its power. It is probably a good idea if you trial a Full Immersion at some stage, to help reinforce this fact. It can help eliminate this fear completely.

Summary: What is the Promised Land like?

Well, here we are at the end of the book. By now, you are well into your desert experience and having both tough and enjoyable times, as well as learning a great deal about the Little One you live with along the way. The journey has been tough and perhaps longer than you expected, but now you are here. So what does it look like?

Your Promised Land is whatever you choose it to be. What happens on the journey you take with your Little One through the desert will very much define what the Promised Land will be like, when you finally get there. It is the sum and product of all your efforts to build an effective and durable Parent/Child Relationship.

If you place your relationship above all of the hurts and pains and difficulties, then your Promised Land will be a pleasant and rewarding place. The work never ends, of course. Even the Promised Land had to be cultivated and worked to produce its goods. Your Promised Land will still have some giants to conquer. Regression can sometimes come up with some unexpected and unpleasant surprises. This is just a part of life.

Thank you for coming on the journey with me and your Little One. I trust you have been able to find a working Parent/Child Relationship that suits you both and resolves the tensions.

Life can be so very good when you are both intimate and involved with each other on *all* levels. Perhaps *that* is the true Promised Land we are all seeking.

APPENDIX ONE – CASE STUDIES

Jill (via CompuServe)

I arrived at my apartment one evening after work. When I opened the screen door, I found a poorly wrapped package. I picked it up, and went inside. Tom, my future husband was already in the apartment waiting for me, and watched as I opened the package. It contained a dozen, 21 X 40 cloth baby diapers, and three pair of rubber pants. I asked him if he had any idea what this was all about, and he said "no". I just figured that someone was trying to play a joke on us, and let the subject drop.

Tom was acting somewhat nervous, and shortly afterward said that he had something very embarrassing to tell me. He was sure that his ex-wife had left the package there in order to force him to tell me about his problem.

It seemed that he sometimes had a urinary incontinence problem, and wet the bed at night, and for this reason, he sometimes wore diapers and rubber pants to bed. He was so very nervous about telling me, that my first reaction was; how could she be so cruel as to force him to tell me before he was ready. All I wanted to do at that moment was to hold him in my arms and tell him that it didn't affect my feelings for him in any way.

Perhaps the fact that my younger sister had had a bed wetting problem when she was young, made me more acceptable to his problem. We were talking for an hour or so, and Tom asked me if I would please diaper him. I told him that I would, but that he would have to help me because I wasn't sure how to diaper an adult. After pinning on his diaper, I put a pair of rubber panties on him. After the panties were in place, he held me so tight, and told me that wearing diapers wasn't all that bad. Then he had me pat and rub his bottom, and I could feel that his diaper was already wet. It just seemed that he was trying to test me, to see how I would react to his wearing a wet diaper. I told him as honestly as I could that my feelings on the subject were, that wearing diapers may be a little strange, but it was really no big deal.

Our relationship continued, and we both felt that we were growing closer each day. Then one night, out of the blue, he asked me to diaper him for no reason that I could see. I did, and after he was diapered, we had a talk. He told me that he really didn't have an incontinence problem, and just used that as an excuse to wear diapers and rubber pants. He had wanted to wear them for as long as he could remember. After a long discussion, I learned that it wasn't just that he had the desire to wear these items, but wanted with all his heart to be an infant again.

At work the following day, I thought about it quite often, and came to the conclusion that I could handle it. After all, he was going to be the father of our children. When children would come into our lives, what would it be like for him, to watch me change, bottle feed, and rock the baby to sleep. Would it make him jealous of his own children, and would I be willing to do less for the man I loved, than I would do for our children? Besides that, I was able to rationalize in my own mind that having a big baby around the house might turn out to be fun for both of us.

That night when I got home, I told Tom that I had to go to the store, and asked him to go with me. When we arrived at the store, I went straight for the baby section, and started looking at all the baby things they had. At first, I think Tom thought I was pregnant, but I soon let him know that we were there to shop for him. As I started picking up things like baby bottles, pacifiers, and bibs, I found that I was getting excited about the having a baby in the house. I thought that it was just my maternal instincts kicking in, and didn't give it much more thought.

After we got home, I put Tom in diapers, and while we were watching TV, I put a bib on him, had him lay his head on my lap, and fed him a baby bottle. I kept telling myself that this was very strange, but I was enjoying being his mommy. From that night on, Tom was my baby boy and I treated him as such when we were alone together.

I loved to see his bottom on a diaper while I would powder or put baby oil on him. When I started the whole process I noticed that he wasn't hard, but by the time the diaper was pinned in place, he would be very turned-on, and after I had pulled his rubber pants up over his diaper, I too was ready for him. He always started by sucking my nipples, just as if he were nursing. It wouldn't take long, and both of us would be ready for intercourse. I loved patting his bottom while we made love, and hearing the sound of his plastic pants against his diaper as he moved up and down.

While we were making love, I always got the sensation that I was going to wet myself. I kept telling him this, and one night he told me that if I did, then he would have to diaper me like I diapered him. The first time he told me that, it scared me, but as time went on, and he would tell me that, I would become excited. So excited in fact, that I started trying to wet myself while we were making love. A few times I did let a small amount trickled out, just enough to let him feel it, but he didn't make good on his threat, so I just let the subject drop.

Then about a month later we were getting ready for bed. I had put Tom's diapers and rubber pants on him, and got ready for him to nurse me as he usually did. All of a sudden, he got up, went to the dresser drawer, and took out a diaper. I asked him what it was for, and he told me that it was time that if I was going to wet myself like a baby, then I too, would have to wear a diaper and rubber pants to bed.

At first I was a little scared, but as the soft birdseye cloth was pulled up between my legs and pinned in place, I felt a warm glow come over me. I remember thinking to myself "Oh heavens, this is how I would like to be for the rest of my life." For some reason I thought that Tom was just testing me, and would not allow myself to tell him how much I really enjoyed being put into diapers. After he had finished, he asked me if I liked the feeling of having a diaper on, and I told him "It's OK, but it's no big deal".

That night, while we were making love, I wet the diaper, and the feeling was more pleasurable than I had hoped for. I wore it all night, and the next day while Tom was at work. Every time I would start to walk to the bathroom to urinate, I would remember that I was wearing a diaper and rubber pants, and would just wet my diaper. The feelings I had are hard to describe, but I every time I wet, I almost had an orgasm, as the warm fluid filled the diaper and spread around my bottom.

When Tom arrived home from work, he could tell that I was still wearing the diaper from the night before. When he commented on it, and I panicked, thinking that I might have upset him somehow. I made up some excuse as to why I still had the diaper on, took it off, and told him that I didn't want to do that anymore. I, however, envied him, every time he would wear diapers.

Before I met Tom, I knew very little about sex, and sexual pleasure. Therefore, when he was nervous about telling me the first time about his diaper wearing, I thought that he felt it was unacceptable behaviour. This is probably why I wouldn't let myself tell him how much I also enjoyed being in diapers.

After Tom would leave for work in the morning, I would rush to our bedroom, take a diaper and rubber pants from the dresser drawer, and diaper myself. I would stay that way the whole day until it was time for him to come home. The only draw-back was the fact that I couldn't wet the diaper for fear of him finding it. There were a few times, when he would come home early, and as I heard the car pulling in the driveway, I would rush to the bedroom, and take off the diapers. I never got caught, however, so many times I secretly hoped that I would.

I was never able to tell Tom about my desires until just before our divorce. When I did tell him, it was too late. I found out that he loved to diaper me, and would often fantasize about putting me in diapers and treating me like his baby girl.

Since our divorce, Tom and I have remained friends, and he calls me often. The subject of diapers always comes up. Usually when he calls, I am already diapered. As we talk, I get more and more turned-on, and always end up wetting my diaper, and peacefully sleeping in it the rest of the night.

I would encourage any other wives who may have a husband who likes being babied, to try it at least once with him. If you don't like it, fine. If you do, please don't hesitate to tell your husband how much you do enjoy it. It may open up some new doors to your sexual life, and maybe even save your marriage."

Joe/Joey – Life with a 6' toddler (from the wife)

Since the best place to start is at the beginning, we met in our teens and hit it off right away. He was always fun and exciting but always somewhat guarded and closed at times. It did seem a bit strange that he was 16 and wasn't in school. He had a full time job and was definitely older than his years. It took more than three years for him to start to let me in. He would open up a bit and then close down for a while. I also noticed early on that he didn't mention his parents much and never saw them to my knowledge. From years three to six of our relationship progressed and the door to his past opened up gradually and also his hidden needs. I slowly found out about the abuse that had occurred and the scars they left both physical and mental.

A year before we got married we got an apartment together near the university that I attended. That is when little Joey started to slowly emerge. When we cuddled on the couch or in bed it was always his head on my shoulder instead of the other way around. He would snuggle in more like a child and be really happy to stay that way for quite a while. He also very carefully and slowly let me know that he had a thing for diapers. This was quite a shock and took a fairly long time for the two of us to deal with. I did understand where it was coming from as I know the extremely long history of abuse that started when he was about 2 years old. The other tell-tale sign that this had a much deeper cause was the frustration fits that were thrown. Joe would get so mad and worked up when he was stressed that he would basically throw a temper tantrum. If I managed to get to hold him he would calm down and snuggle into me. He would put his thumb in his mouth and curl up with me and stay that way for up to an hour some times. This was the start of me understanding his deep need to regress especially after a wet lap a few times.

Some people may not believe in regression, but Joe is two different personalities. It isn't as far as a multiple personality, but a toddler version of him. Knowing it has had more than it's challenges, but also benefits to both of us. His two big conflicts where admitting he had a need to regress and dealing with how deep his need for diapers is. It became obvious to me how much happier and relaxed the adult Joe was when he had a diaper on. It made a huge difference in our relationship and his stress levels. The diapers seem to tie both worlds together. Joe accepts that there is a little inside and Joey feels that he is accepted and has a place in our lives and a tie to the outside world.

There are things that make it difficult at times, but I have never wavered from wanting to be with them. There are times were I want to lean on his shoulder and be held by him. It happens, but it's very rare and Joey wants it the other way around. There was getting used to a spouse in diapers all the time and having to worry about people finding out. When Joe is stressed he tends to not notice when his diaper needs changing, on purpose of course, as Joey wants to be looked after by mommy. It took a while to learn when that is and to take him to get his diaper changed discreetly when we are out. I don't get to many dirty diapers but when they happen I can tell Joey wants me to treat him like a real toddler and make a big deal about it and recognize him as a toddler. He loves it when I discreetly check his diaper when we are out at the mall or in a movie theatre to see if he needs changing.

Some people will say I'm crazy for putting up with this but Joe is very attentive. He doesn't sit and watch sports all day. He doesn't go out drinking with his friends or come home drunk after work. He comes home to be with me and I know he loves me deeply. And Joey is kind of cute when he sees me and his face lights up. I have also been a part of the change in him to a healthier happier adult by letting him regress when it's needed. Of course there are times when I'm not in the mood for baby time and it's frustrating especially when I want to be intimate with Joe and I walk into the bedroom to find him with a pacifier and a teddy bear and Joey wants to cuddle. "

Joe/Joey – Life with a 6' toddler (from the husband)

I grew up an only child with abusive parents. My mother was from a large family and she had pressure to have children. My Father was really abusive and had big anger issues and my mother just let it happen. There was never any bond with them growing up. I remember as a little kid seeing a loving mother looking after a baby and wishing I could go home with them. I longed to be cuddled, fed and changed by someone who actually wanted me. A part of me kept hoping that my situation would change. It became apparent when I was 11 that was not about to be.

My mother and I were fighting as usual and she said "I thought I wanted kids but I was wrong". Gradually my desperate wanting for love turned to anger and shutting the rest of the world out and I wasn't going to let anyone close to hurt me again. I spent the next 4 years getting in some serious trouble with everyone from teachers to the police. At 15 I left home and went to work as a labourer on a construction site. I put everything I had into it which helped me to focus my energy into something constructive and stay out of trouble.

I met my now wife when I was 16 but it took a couple of years before I let her close and trusted her to not hurt me. Little did I know it was the little in me who was so scared of being abused again. Over the next few years I slowly let her know about having a diaper fetish. She know there was an infantile way about me at times and over time accepted my need for diapers. My wife realized before me that I had a little. Some nights I would get really agitated and not be able to calm down. My wife found that when she held me I would calm down and snuggle in to her shortly after I would be asleep. It became more and more apparent that there was two of us. My little just wanted to be held and be out and be accepted as his own person. My little's name is Joey and he is 18 months old.

Thanks to an amazing women in our lives I have a wife and he has a mommy. The diapers became more and more important to my little who was desperate to be recognized and wanted his presence known. At age 30 my wife decided that it was back to diapers 24/7 to see if that helped out the inner struggle and we have been in diapers for the last 14 years. It made a huge difference and so did getting him his own possessions. The first thing my wife bought him was a big soft teddy bear. He now has 8 stuffed animals he has to sleep with as well as jammies and onesies. He is the one who goes to sleep every night and on the weekends after a busy week we both feel better after he is fed his bottle and his mommy puts him down for a nap with his teddy bear, he loves to sleep.

There are two of us in one body and we both found the love we needed from an amazing lady. It hasn't been easy on her being married to me and an 18 month old. I don't think she had imagined having a husband who needs his diaper changed and put to bed but she loves us both and has said she would miss not having Joey around. If you have a little embrace it don't fight it. Chances are your little will win out any way."

A Little Boy finds his way

Let me give you a little bit of background. First of all, I am definitely a Little Boy. In that I mean that my inner child is all boy and no girl. The aspects of my child are essentially, little boy, which means that items such as dresses, mary-jane shoes, and baby bonnets don't have any appeal for me. In fact, I've never had any temptation for women's clothing, which my adult persona would be uncomfortable with, and my child persona would react the same way a four-year-old little boy would react if he was put in a dress. Instead I'm much more at home in a sand box. In fact, I'm sure I would reach the level four regression stage if I was placed in a safe sand box, especially if there was water present. At a beach I'll be perfectly comfortable digging trenches and watching waves come in and destroy my wall. It also makes me a very messy child. In fact one of my previous girlfriend (who was unaware of my child persona), made sure I only bought stain resistant pants because I end up with stains. As to the age of my child, he is somewhere between 4 and 8. I find myself pushing more regressive items at times.

The reader's digest version of my story begins with my toilet training. I'm not exactly sure when I was completely potty trained, but I know I was still in diapers full time until nearly four. I may have even been over four by the time I consistently used the toilet, and I've heard stories of me requesting toileting help when I was well past four. I know that I was diapered for an episode of diarrhea when I was four and half, and that is the last time I remember actually being diapered.

After that my toileting pretty much became normal, and I suffered no childhood accidents beyond that age, nor did I wet the bed. However, the first instance of my inner child coming out occurred when I was five, and suddenly realized it had been a long time since I had an accident. I was outside and purposely pooped in my pants. My mom was unaware that this was on purpose, or at least didn't react like she was aware. She didn't make a very big deal about it. She just helped me clean up, and gave me a new pair of pants.

The 'child' appeared in my play for a while as a real child. By that I mean playing in a way less mature than my actual age, as well as playing baby from time to time (not as easy for a little boy with only boy friends). My fascination with diapers was also present, but never really acted on it. As I began to reach puberty the feelings became stronger, but not anything overwhelming. I never chose to wet my bed, or even considered it through this point.

The point in which the desire for incontinence began was ironically when I was 16. It was triggered by two events that happened simultaneously. One was that I finally reached sexual maturity, in terms of completing puberty and having wet dreams. The second, which likely triggered the other event, was the death of my mother. My mother died when I 16 years old, and five days later I had my first wet dream. I remember waking up with the feeling of uncontrollable ejaculation and believing that it was urine.

That is where I began to examine books about bedwetting and finally realized that kids could wear diapers past a young age. It was then that I began to imagine myself as one of those kids, and wished that I could wear diapers myself. I began to build various forms of diapers myself as I wanted disposable diapers, and obviously couldn't buy them. When Huggies came up with Goodnites I purchased my first pair (I was nearly 23). For the next few years I bought Goodnites on occasion and it was the first time I actually could pee my pants. I did have a few unprotected accidents before then, but they were in safe environments.

I bought my first case of diapers the moment I actually moved out of my dad's house. My brother caught me on my second case, but hasn't ever said anything about it since then. In 1996 I discovered the internet. I knew it existed before then, but never really used it until then. I made my first search for bedwetting and diapers, and saw posts on the topic I then found DPF and realized I wasn't the only one who felt this way. Actually I had known about DPF since the Phil Donohue episode, which I only saw in passing, but it was the first time that I really examined the phenomenon.

In some ways that was freeing, because I realized I was less alone, but in other ways it also allowed me to become more open about my child persona. That child had been repressed for so long, and all of the sudden it wanted to come out completely. Thus began my life as little one/adult, which includes all the binge purge cycles. As I've come to accept my persona, those extremes have subsided (age is a wonderful thing, because it is easier to accept who you're truly are).

Kayley adopts her Little One

It took me a long time to connect with my husband's toddler inner child especially since he is a girl inside! At first it seemed like I would never find her and he would never find me, but eventually we connected and things just started to happen. I'm pretty much a conservative while my sister is the crazy liberal where nothing ever really worries or surprises her. I confided in her about Baby Jenny and in true form she didn't have any issues with it. In her own totally uninformed yet uninhibited manner she gave me ideas about how to treat Jenny. She was pretty right most of the time even though she has no interest whatsoever in any of this herself.

Anyhow, we had been in this sort of mother-daughter bond for about 18months and I felt we were a little stuck and I talked to Jenny about it and she had no idea, but my idiot sister did. Her idea was that I ADOPT HER as my daughter! At first I thought it was crazy and I dismissed the idea, but it stayed with me and about a week later I talked with her again about it. For a sister with no stable partners she has some insights that surprise me. She just said that since I was already effectively Jenny's mommy then why not make it official? Well I quickly found out I couldn't really adopt her but I could make a non-binding adoption and I decided to discuss it with Jenny first.

Wow! What an unexpected reaction!! Jenny bubbled out all this stuff about his own mother who was distant and uninvolved and how he felt cheated out of a mother. Somehow I had stumbled onto this big area of hurt and I must admit I was not all that thrilled by it. He cried for hours as he just dumped all this raw emotion onto me about never feeling properly loved. The idea of adopting him suddenly seemed like a scary idea. In talking with both Jenny and my hubby separately it was clear he wanted me to pretty much assume a genuine step-mother/adoptive mother role with him. That was a bit more than I had in mind but over time I got my conservative head around it along with an ear-bashing from my sister!

I decided to informally adopt Baby Jenny as my daughter and then set about working out how to do it. As only three of us knew of Baby Jenny's true personality my sister decided to officiate at an adoption ceremony for us. It was helped that she was in-between partners yet again so had a lot of time!

There was a lot of preparation for the day and a lot of excitement from Jenny and vomit-inducing nerves from me. I bought an entire new outfit for her from expensive baby shoes to an even more expensive dress, bonnet and petticoat. I even bought a matching pacifier for her. I bought Jenny a love-heart gold necklace and matching bracelet. My sister outdid herself with an official-looking adoption certificate which she had framed and presented to us at the start of the ceremony. She said some nice words and made me cry some (I cry easily) when she said a baby had finally found her mommy. We actually exchanged some rings which we still wear which signify that we are mother and daughter and are engraved with both our names.

We had a lovely afternoon tea and Jenny had a bottle and we both helped feed her some of the food. Jenny was very babyish that day.

Since then the relationship has just blossomed. I think that by adopting her I now feel free to be her mommy in every aspect when she is a Little. And when she is my husband again I still feel this special bond that extends beyond the norm. All the things I felt unable to do for her including spanking her misbehaving butt are now easier.

I think that adopting her was the best thing I could have done. I know it isn't official but as far as we are concerned, Jenny is my REAL daughter and we wouldn't have it any other way. A new complication arrived a year later in the form of twins. But even though I have real children, I still have a child who is every bit as real to me and while the twins will grow up and out, Jenny will not. My daughter is mine for good."

Alan – bedwetting and nappies

I have been plagued in a way with very strong baby desires since I was little older than a baby myself. I always wanted nappies and I had to be dragged kicking and screaming away from my heavy bedwetting habit by my parents. It controlled me to a large degree and even when married and with kids the old baby desires would loom large and often interfere.

Incontinence was a continual problem for me although I didn't view it as a problem really. I wet the bed on regular occasions and had some wet pants from time to time. I wore nappies as part of my secretive life as a sissy baby. I didn't really know what else to do. Going cold turkey just made me an unpleasant person and an unhappy one as well.

My incontinence continued to get worse although for me it was part curse and part blessing. To be a baby I had to be wet – that much seemed obvious, but at the same time wet beds and wet pants without control were practical problems. The inner me exalted in a wet bed as a success, but the adult me knew it was a growing problem. So one day I decided it was all too hard and chose the coward's way and started wearing nappies fulltime. It was the best thing I have ever done!

Suddenly, staying dry was a non-issue. After a few weeks of getting my nappy changing rhythm into place it became just an automatic part of my life. The stress of staying dry was gone, literally overnight. The surprise was in how I felt. I was happier, less moody and the inner baby seemed calmer and more relaxed than ever before. On the flipside, the baby was there seemingly more often, but was easier to handle. I had always drunk far less fluids than I should – mainly to prevent wetting accidents – even as a kid. Now I was free to drink whatever I wanted, whenever I wanted at any capacity. I had been plagued by headaches and neck pain and overnight they all but disappeared now that I was drinking enough. I was very wet, but my nappies contained all that anyhow.

So what do I think of the decision to go back into nappies fulltime? BEST THING I HAVE DONE IN YEARS. I'm getting my life back and my sissy baby side no longer rules nor does my bladder. My bladder control has quickly deteriorated to the point where I am rarely dry longer than an hour and usually only 15 minutes – but it no longer matters."

An Adult Baby Couple – a different experience

Okay, since our relationship is rare, I'll start by describing it in terms most would understand. First of all, neither my wife nor I are rare within the AB/DL community by ourselves. She is a female AB who prefers the role of a 2 year old girl. I am a male DL who enjoys wearing diapers and being accepted for it. Coming together as a couple we had some territory to negotiate. For her, I became her "Daddy" and to the extent where it doesn't seem to be too demanding, I snuggle with her, read to her, put her in her night time diapers and do other occasional Daddy appropriate things. She does not play in this role all the time and there are no adult activities associated with this role. In return, she puts me in my night diapers, bathes me once a week, helps me go to sleep and makes sure there are always diapers in the house for both of us.

Of course we are adults and adults will have desires and to the degree that I can write about it to a general audience, I'll try to fill you in. My wife comes out of her little 2 year old role in half a second and will accept affection as my wife. Since we generally take care of our own diapering, we also take our own diapers off to become intimate. This activity has no age regression associated with and while a cloth diaper might be laid out beneath us, it is not part of the activity or necessary.

The relationship dynamic we have is based on the negotiation I mentioned above as well as give and take. Unless one partner feeds on being the nurturing caregiver to other, it can be an emotional drain on the caregiver. When the giving and taking are switched back and forth, there are questions about the equity and that leads to more negotiating. To keep things on an even keel, we show each other our self-reliance by taking care of our own diaper changes and handle all other practical matters like responsible adults. At home, with our privacy, my wife is able to act the way she wants, drink from a bottle when she wants and play with toys. In order to get enough from the relationship, it's important that we ask each other when we want something from the other. This goes from having a story read to going to the bedroom and being adults. We respect each other's requests and understand that a need is being communicated so the request should be accommodated if possible.

A couple on the journey to Parent/Child

This [his baby side] is something that I've felt has been a part of my life as long as I can remember, I'm not sure how it started or why but there are a few moments that stick out. I've shared this side of me with very few people as many people don't understand or want to. My wife and I have been married for almost 4 years now and I just recently told her. In some ways I suspected she might of known somewhat but she never lead on. When we finally sat down and talked, it caused some tension in our relationship because of hurt feelings and hiding this part of my life from her. She has slowly come around to taking an active role in our parent/child relationship. I wear diapers because I am urinary incontinent and my wife accepts me wearing diapers during the day and at night. She noticed that I would wear her panties and recognized my sissy side, she said she had no problems with me wearing her panties, just to make sure they see the hamper. A month or so later we went shopping and she bought me a pair of panties for myself. I wear panties almost every day over my diapers, sometimes it seems silly because I'm wearing a diaper but it makes me feel feminine and sometimes sexy.

I sleep with a pacifier every night, along with my night diapers and plastic panties to make sure I stay dry at night, otherwise often my diaper would leak. It's exciting to finally have a partner who is accepting of who I am, all of me. She decided that I should call her Mama and she has called me by my baby name a few times, that is by far one of the best feelings ever. We have even had sex as Mama and baby. It was a little weird at first but it was extremely fulfilling and a completely different type of intimacy than we normally would experience. It's exciting because as an adult I am the dominant one in our relationship and in the bedroom, but as a little one I am completely submissive waiting for Mama to tell me what to do.

Although, with all of the exciting parts, it hasn't come without it's struggles. It has been difficult at times, I think firstly the hurt of me not initially telling my wife about my little one definitely still lingers. There are many times it's difficult to initiate parent/child time because my wife doesn't fully accept everything yet. She says she's still working through the entire aspect of it. It's frustrating because for the first time I've been able to share this part of me with someone I care about and yet it still feels like sometimes I'm being rejected. I continue to take it one day at a time. Like any relationship, it doesn't develop overnight and there is still bound to be difficulties to overcome. I do think that Mama has an easier time working with it when we are intimate, I think maybe it seems like role-playing. I get it, it's a big deal to think your adult partner is also a little baby. I think the important aspect I keep reminding her is that I am still me, nothing has changed except that now she knows another aspect of me.

APPENDIX TWO – GLOSSARY OF TERMS:

Age-play: Age-play is simply adults who are role-playing being a different age. During age-play, some people will take on the role of children while others take on the role of adult or caregiver roles. Age-play is simply one variation of erotic role-play. Age play spans a spectrum from as simple as the typical student/teacher role-play that so many people have done, to people acting as babies for extended periods of time. People dabble in age-play and then play on this spectrum to the level at which they feel comfortable. *(From Diapers to Diplomas – Nazca Plains)*

Adult Baby, Adult Infant, Adult Toddler, Adult Pre-schooler: The generic term 'Adult baby' comprises Adult Infants, Adult toddlers and Adult Preschoolers for Littles that identify as ages newborn to five years. Note that these ages are at best approximate. A Little might say they are six years old yet still refer to themselves as an adult baby or adult pre-schooler. These ages and definitions are flexible to meet the rather flexible self-image of the average Little.

Attachment Objects: Attachment Objects are items or objects that the Little One has and uses that have two or three special aspects to them in addition to the object's primary or natural function. These are 'identification aspect', 'secondary purpose(s) aspect' and 'initiation or trigger aspect'. All Attachment Objects have an identification and most have a secondary purpose aspect. Very few have an initiation aspect.

Diaper: Identical to a nappy

Dissociative Identity Disorder (DID): Formerly known as Multiple Personality Disorder (MPD) this involves a fracturing of the personality (ego) into multiple selves who are totally unaware of each other's existence. The person typically suffers regular experiences of 'lost time' when an alter takes over and no memory exists for that period of time. This is *not* regression, but rather a very rare and very serious mental problem.

Dummy: A pacifier

Fetish: Fetishism is a narrower field of paraphilia, in which the source of stimulation or arousal is an inanimate article such as high heeled shoes, or a choker, or material such as fur, leather, or rubber. Fetishism also includes arousal by parts of the body such as feet or hair, and ritualistic elements such as used underpants or stolen rubber. These are similar to the rituals of romantic love, and arousal by means of the genitals or breasts, which are considered normal. As a result of the individuality of human development, there are as many "diseases" as there are individuals, and there are no clear lines between one form of sexual response and another. Fetishism and other paraphilias may arise as the result of direct sexual stimulation by the fetish object as when a small boy lies naked on a fur coat, wears rubber lined pants, or rides "horsy" on aunty's high buttoned shoes. More commonly, a paraphilia is accidental, as in voyeurism, and in the excitement of urine smells on rubber, or in the fact that a rubber coat was stolen.

Incontinence: The inability to control the bladder or bowels. It can be anything from light leakage to total failure. In this context we can also include 'situational incontinence' which is when a Little is incontinent *only* when regressed or in diapers.

Infantilism: Infantilism is best described as a post-pubescent person seeking the emotional experience of returning to childhood or infancy using regression and/or other props – such as diapers – to build an authentic experience. Infantilists don't want to involve children; they want to <u>be</u> a child.

Leakage (Behavioural Leakage): The experience of behaviours that would normally be only in the regressed state manifesting partly or completely in the adult state. It also refers to the manifestation of adult attributes such as speech and walking in the very young Little One.

Nappy/Nappies: Identical to a diaper

Pacifier: A dummy

Regression: In the context of Little Ones, regression is where the adult reverts to the behaviours and emotions of a younger age – usually infant or toddler. Regression, according to psychoanalyst Sigmund Freud, is a defense mechanism leading to the temporary or long-term reversion of the ego to an earlier stage of development rather than handling unacceptable impulses in a more adult way. The defense mechanism of regression, in psychoanalytic theory, occurs when thoughts are pushed back out of our consciousness and into our unconscious.

Role-play: See age play

SI (Situational Incontinence): Situational incontinence is bladder and/or bowel control issues that mainly manifest themselves only when the person is 'protected' i.e. wearing a diaper or sleeping in a waterproofed bed.

Sissy: It is a sometimes derogatory term for an effeminate male but in the context of this book it means a Little One whose gender is not simply female but *overtly* so and manifests as overly-frilly or lacy clothing, pink everything and very strong feminine behaviour specifically excluding anything remotely male. It is essentially a subset of being a regressed girl.

Teen Baby: Exactly the same as an adult baby (see above) but in the teen years. The desires and behaviours are similar yet are typically immature due to age.

SOURCES AND REFERENCES:

http://understanding.infantilism.org [Bittergrey]

www.toddlertime.com

www.dailydiapers.com

www.fetlife.com

Diagnostic and Statistical Manual of Mental Disorders (DSM IV)

Sexual deviance: theory assessment and treatment D. Richard Laws

www.idiaper.me

www.clarewinnicott.net

www.experienceproject.com

How to become a bed wetter [sakura.ne.jp]

www.mednet2002.org/abstracts/

www.adisc.org

www.liljennie.com

www.23nlpeople.com

http://socalab.250x.com/hypno.html

Critique of the Gotha Program: Karl Marx

ABOUT THE AUTHOR

Rosalie Bent is an Australian post-graduate level trainer and communicator who has been happily married for almost 40 years to a regressive Adult Baby. With tertiary training in both Mathematics and Psychology, she has learned over the years to understand the unique inner workings of the Adult Baby mind and has combined her experience and the knowledge of others to produce this book: a primer on making relationships work with the 'adult/child'. The mother of four adult children, both her and her husband work as professional trainers and consultants.

Rosalie is an avid reader and also a writer of children's and adult's novels.

Made in the USA
Columbia, SC
25 October 2017